CHINABERRY SIDEWALKS

CHINABERRY SIDEWALKS

Rodney Crowell

Alfred A. Knopf   New York   2011

For my children and their children

Contents

PART ONE

New Year's Eve, 1955

The four beer-blitzed couples dancing in the cramped living room of my parents' shotgun duplex were wearing on my nerves. In particular, I didn't like the sound of their singing along with my prized Hank Williams 78s. Coon hunting with my grandfather, I'd heard bluetick hounds howl with more intonation than this nasal pack of yahoos. For a while I tried contenting myself with sticking my fingers in my ears and staring squinty-eyed at the scuff-mark patterns forming on the linoleum, hoping a likeness of Jesus or Eisenhower—the only famous images I knew of at the time other than "ole Hank," as my father and I referred to our favorite singer—would stare up at me from beneath the dancers' feet. But when all I could summon up was a swarm of black stubby snakes, I gave up and went back to being in a funk.

The next thing I remember, Cookie Chastain was screeching to be heard above the scratchiness of whichever record she'd just gored with the blunt end of the phonograph needle. "Twenty minutes till midnight. Everybody change partners." And while the rest of the gang bumped around and groped for whom to dance with next, she was making a big deal out of sashaying into the waiting arms of the one man whose lust for oblivion I knew could turn this little shindig into a repeat of my worst nightmare. By then I'd guzzled most of the six-pack of Cokes I'd discovered in the icebox and was no longer ready to pretend that this New Year's Eve nonsense was anything but a recipe for disaster. My mother was mad as a hornet, but too ashamed to make a scene just yet; Mr. Chastain and the others were too wasted to notice or care; and my father, the only real singer in the bunch, had once again lowered his standards to a level that guaranteed trouble.

I'd been privy to the shadowy undercurrents detailed in my mother and father's all-night shouting matches long enough to know that drunk husbands and wives swapping two-steps with other drunk wives and husbands, though a time-honored Texas tradition, was anything but harmless fun. I could never grasp what she accused him of doing with Lila May Strickland or Pauline Odell, but I knew by her disdain for the word "screwing" that nothing good ever came of the deed. And it got more complicated when she started screaming about how he'd even screw a light socket if one could spread its legs for him. Grown-ups were weird.

Unlike my father, I was beginning to understand that all this business about who or what he was supposedly screwing served a darker purpose for my mother: setting up yet another reprise of the brain-scalding accusation that he'd belt-whipped her across the belly when, eight months pregnant with me, she stood naked in the bathtub.

The scene is seared in my mind as if I'd actually been able to witness it. A sliver of July dusk creeps in under the canvas window shade, and the dangling circle on the end of its pull string is tapping against the yellowed wallpaper beneath the sill. On the back of the door, an ancient hot-water bottle gives off traces of vinegar douche, mementos from a time before I entered the picture. There's the buck-stitched cowboy belt and fake trophy buckle; for years I imagined a silver-headed rattlesnake in the grip of an escaped convict, though I've yet to conjure how he managed, in a space half the size of a prison cell, to wield the thing. And veiled in a sepia gauze, courtesy of the light fixture above the medicine cabinet, is my mother, naked as Eve, dripping wet and cowering in the claw-footed tub, stillbirth emblazoned across her frontal lobe. But whose memory is this in which I can see these things so clearly yet can't place my father? His? Hers? Or mine?

I despised my mother's need to belittle my father in my eyes as much as I hated his refusal to deny wielding this belt. To accept her version as fact, which I did, and never believing his trademark "Aw, hell, Cauzette, you know I did no such a thing" meant embracing the possibility that it could all happen again. Together, my parents made it impossible to keep my father on the pedestal where I needed him most. And about that, all I can tell you is this: I'd be well within range of the truth if I said there were times I was mad enough to kill them both.

I'd been sleeping in the living room longer than I could remember, my mother making a nightly ritual of "fixin' up a pallet" on the sofa. In the early days, the kitchen chair she positioned to keep me from rolling off onto the floor simulated a perfectly good crib. Still, the shame of my not having a bedroom of my own was particularly hard on her. Other than dying and going to heaven, the dream of a nursery for her only living child was her lone investment in the promise of a better future. As far as I was concerned, this was a waste of wishful thinking; I much preferred my arrangement on the couch to the mildewed cave that was the front bedroom.

Conditions surrounding my parents' beer-and-baloney soiree made the crossing of some invisible line in their ongoing war of hard words and physical abuse a foregone conclusion. As much as I hated the discomfort of having my territory invaded by mindless adults, I dreaded even more my inability to escape the hellish crescendo I knew would follow when my father started chasing beer with whiskey.

But no refuge was to be found in the front bedroom, whose dark shadows and damp spookiness scared me witless. Wallpaper hung from the ceiling in stained, ragged strands, like a cross between witch hair and brown cotton candy. The jaundiced glow of the exposed overhead lightbulb fell far short of its four corners, where untold evil lurked. Should I find myself alone in that room, the cardboard windowpanes, creaky floors, and lumpy thirty-year-old mattress were the least of my worries.

Traffic to and from the party's beer supply rendered the kitchen in back of the house a useless hideout, likewise the bathroom where I could have played with my toy cars on the floor. Left to idle in the narrow hallway between the living room and the bedroom, I began to hatch a plan.

My intention to break up the party, before it reached the point that my parents had time and again proven themselves unable to return from without inflicting damage, didn't necessarily include subjecting their guests to bodily harm. I liked Doc and Dorothy Lawrence, Pete and Wanda Faye Conn, Paul and Cookie Chastain as sober adults. Just the same, the job of saving my parents from themselves called for drastic measures, and innocent bystanders couldn't be helped.

My father kept a loaded pump-action 16-gauge and a .22-caliber rifle stashed in the bedroom closet. Such an arrangement was as natural to him as breathing the night air. Childhood in the Depression-era backwoods of western Kentucky had left him ingrained with the notion—contrary to his wife's—that a boy was never too young to put food on the table. On the morning of my fifth birthday, I awoke to find him cleaning the shotgun. While examining his handiwork, he broached the subject for the first time. "Son," he said, affecting more profundity than I was used to hearing, "in this old world of snakebites and hunger pain, a man's aim's 'bout as close as he's gonna get to a paid-up insurance policy. They ain't many scores that cain't be settled with a load of buckshot." My mother argued rather convincingly that in East Houston in the mid-fifties, squirrel and rabbit were in such short supply that knowledge of small firearms was about as useful as the ability to speak

Portuguese. But she was told where she could stick Portuguese, and with that the discussion ended. Later in the day, he borrowed Little Willie Smith's shiny black '49 Ford Roadster and drove Grandpa Willoughby and me to a pine thicket north of Old Wallisville Road, where I was given my first lesson with a single-shot .22.

My decision to fish the .22 from the closet wasn't made lightly. To retrieve the gun meant entering the room alone, a chilling prospect even in broad daylight. But sensing the storm gathering behind the rising levels of alcohol, I figured those dark corners were no match for what would happen if the adults out there started screwing each other.

Aside from enhancing the gravity of my announcement that it was time to go home, I had no intention of using the gun. Based loosely on the Saturday matinees I'd seen at the Navaway Theater, where the good guy got the bad guy's attention by wielding a six-shooter full of silver bullets, my plan required the gun as a prop.

Hank Williams was singing "Lovesick Blues" when I stepped into the living room armed with my father's rifle. Dorothy Lawrence was the first to notice my arrival. "My Lord, he's got a gun!" she called out, a bit less dramatically than I'd have liked but compelling nonetheless. The focus of attention shifted instantly in my direction, and having all eyes on me sent a surge of power through my nervous system that left my mind a small blank canvas. From there, the script unraveled.

It was lack of preparation for this pivotal moment that provoked two serious blunders: one, inadvertently disengaging the thumb-activated safety on the rifle; two, pulling the trigger. The bullet exploded into the linoleum floor less than a foot from where Dorothy stood. "Lovesick Blues" came to a screeching halt, and my father pounced on me like he was Batman on pep pills. Sensing his first impulse was to beat me with the butt of the rifle, I braced myself for the worst. Instead, he hugged me so close to his heart that even through the ringing in my ears I could hear it pounding. Being squeezed so hard that I could barely breathe gave me a feeling of comfort. My peacekeeping mission was complete. There would be no fighting that night.

Shocking people sober and sending them home thankful to be alive is one way to break up a party. Although visibly shaken, my parents' friends showed no ill feelings. Cookie Chastain said she knew I was "a good boy and wouldn't hurt a flea." Pete Conn reckoned I "knew not to play with no more loaded guns." Doc Lawrence went as far as making a joke about my aim being so bad that I was "lucky not to have shot [my] dang pecker off." Hushed exits, however, told the story of how they really felt.

My parents never asked why I chose to wave a loaded rifle around a room full of people, let alone pull the trigger. Their joint lecture on involuntary manslaughter suggested they were filing the experience away under the harmless "Child Plays with Father's Gun" heading. I wanted to tell them my true intentions, that it was all their fault, that I was sick of being stuck in the middle of their stupid shouting matches, that their friends needed singing lessons. Seeing them work as a team held this impulse in check. At that moment, volunteering information seemed as great a waste of ammunition as the .22 slug lodged in the floorboards.

On the surface, a temporary halt in my parents' conflict and a hole in the linoleum was all I had to show for my shooting spree. Beneath that, my success was more far-reaching. Ten-plus years of knock-down-drag-outs were still to be accounted for, but from that day on my father refused to allow a loaded gun in the house, a decision that perhaps saved his life and my mother's many times over.

The House on Norvic Street

The cause for celebration that long-ago New Year's Eve was my parents' not-so-fond farewell to the rented house on Avenue P. Not being privy to the news they'd made a down payment on a tidy new four-room bungalow of their own, I was in no mood to indulge in the giddiness of the occasion. But to flash forward fifty years, given what I know of the crippling sense of disentitlement both my parents would struggle with for four and a half decades, getting blotto with a few friends before plunging for the first time into home ownership makes perfect sense. For my mother and father, getting off on the right foot when taking those first few timid steps toward their "golden future," a concept no less foreign to them than walking on the moon, was a terrifying proposition. To go from a one-room log cabin with a dirt floor to the threshold of some spiffy new cracker-box palace in twelve short years is heady stuff, and just thinking about it almost makes me wish I hadn't been so hasty in pulling out my father's gun. As witness to and harvester of my family's past, I'm mindful of something I once heard about the truth having no greater enemy than wishful rethinking, which in turn reminds me of something I once read on the wall of a truck-stop bathroom: "Just because the past doesn't seem fucked up in the present doesn't mean the present wasn't fucked up in the past." Amen. The truth then versus the truth now *is* a tricky business. But here the facts remain simple: J.W. and Cauzette, sometime connoisseurs of privation and domestic disturbance, did, if only for a while, overcome the limitations of their beginnings and, with yours truly in tow, head east toward that golden future—six miles east, to be exact.

According to Grandpa Willoughby, failed sharecrop farmer turned twenty-seven-dollar-a-week night watchman for the Port of Houston branch of the Hughes Tool Shipping and Receiving Company, a case can be made that the story of the house on Norvic Street began more than half a century earlier, in 1900, when Galveston was slam-dunked by the deadliest hurricane in recorded history. In the storm's aftermath, while its survivors pondered the rubble of what had been an up-and-coming international seaport, a team of entrepreneurial Houstonians was busy cajoling the special-funding branch of the federal government into donating two million dollars for a dredging operation that would convert a series of salt-marsh bayous into the world's largest man-made shipping lane. When the digging was done, the Houston Ship Channel stretched fifty miles inland from Galveston Bay to the corner of Wayside Drive and Navigation Boulevard, three blocks south of Avenue P. My grandfather put it like this: "After all them people died down there by the gulf, that crew of wildcatters jewed the government out of a shit-pot full of taxpayers' money and dug 'em a ditch all the way from Galveston up to Wayside Drive. If it weren't for that bunch, wouldn't none of us be where we are today."

The post–World War II housing project where my parents would stake their claim as landed gentry was the brainchild of an over-achieving land developer named Frank Sharp. His vision of a lower-income suburb, easily accessible if barely affordable to the workforce employed by the refineries and chemical plants lining the ship channel like so many poison gas–spewing space stations, sputtered into existence as Industrial Acres. In the early going his proj-ect failed to capture the imagination of its intended buyers. But when the war ended, Sharp lowered prices and soon poor fools like my parents were clamoring for any available property.

On a clear day, from the backseat of my father's Studebaker on Highway 73, the San Jacinto Monument was visible from two miles away. It stood nearly 570 feet tall—alone in the middle of a mosquito-infested swamp twenty miles east of downtown Houston, a giant star crowning its misplaced glory. In 1936, as part of some big wingding celebrating a hundred years of Texas independence, the San Jacinto Battlegrounds—where Sam Houston got the better of Santa Anna in what amounted to a twenty-minute shoving match over who was the rightful owner of this unruly territory—were enshrined in a ceremony dedicating the newly erected monument as a symbol of the Lone Star State's illustrious heritage. That the heroes of this so-called struggle for independence were alcoholics, opium addicts, and illegal slave traders seems to have been lost on the committee. Then again, in Texas, the immortalization of scoundrels had long been a profitable enterprise, a fact that no doubt weighed heavily in favor of the monument's construction. Spending four hundred thousand Depression-era dollars on a six-hundred-foot phallus memorializing a pack of thieves literally took the old maxim that everything is bigger in Texas to new heights. My friend Dabbo claimed it looked like somebody giving God the finger.

With the world's tallest freestanding masonry structure looming in their backyard, civic-minded residents began voicing their disen-chantment with the name Industrial Acres and in 1946 banded together to form Jacinto City. Within ten years Frank Sharp's brain-child was wearing its post-boomtown complacency like a worn-out shoe.

The water tower and rec-hall gym notwithstanding, the Jacinto City of my childhood was a one-story town. Scrub brush stood higher than most rooftops. Dwarfish middle-aged chinaberry trees towered like redwoods on the low-slung horizon. Whether in the whiteout of a high-noon summer sun or the cold gray raindrops of winter, life under these prairie skies had a settling-for-less quality that my parents found reassuring.

In fairness, citizens of Jacinto City in the mid-fifties were, for the most part, solid working-class people. Homes were modestly respectable and well maintained. A splash of landscaping here and an add-on there indicated that a modicum of forward progress still existed in the housing project's everyday cycles. Not so for the Crowell family. Among the more crippling side effects of my parents' disentitlement was a dirt-poor sense of themselves that made them far better suited for the maintenance of property not their own—particularly my father, whose mathematical wizardry and carpentry skills emerged only when he was employed by a third party, preferably at below minimum wage. Underfunded, overwhelmed, and out of their league from the git-go, my parents took to home ownership like horse thieves to a hanging judge.

The house on Norvic Street was one of a thousand or so cookie-cutter bungalows whose poor workmanship, lack of imagination, and cheap materials destined them for an early demise. Considering the six-thousand-dollar price tag, I'm as hard-pressed to imagine where my father came up with the down payment as how he managed the monthly mortgage.

My parents' little white dream house sat submissively on a forty-by-sixty-foot lot, the extent of its floor plan a living room, a kitchen, two small bedrooms, and a bathroom at the end of a six-foot hallway. No frills, no nonsense. Two parallel cement strips, twelve inches in width, led to the one-car garage at the back of the property.

In the transition from Avenue P to Jacinto City, my father managed to wrangle himself a dull-red 1953 Studebaker President, the first in a long string of used-car disasters in which he was unable to align tires and driveway strips with any degree of accuracy. Within a year, the deep ruts that had formed along the edge of the cement made the trip from street to garage as bouncy as a Baja road race. In summer months, when grass grew tall between the strips, he was forced to shrug off wisecracking punks riding past on their bicycles, calling, "Hey, mister, your yard needs a haircut." I hated them for taunting my father but had to agree our driveway looked like a giant green Mohawk.

The garage stood in the back right-hand corner of the property and was sided with the most easily breakable shingles available in the late forties. Once neighborhood kids discovered the joy of smashing holes in it, the garage's days were numbered. (I myself was Roy Rogers—holed up in an abandoned mining shack, surrounded by desperadoes and needing to get off a clean shot—when I plunked my first shingle.) Soon after the first few holes appeared at the eye level of a seven-year-old child, my parents threw in the towel. By the end of the decade, all that remained was the roof, the frame, and crumbled white shards scattered in the grass.

The house itself was essentially a tarpaper shack, also with shingle siding. A layer of tarpaper tacked to the two-by-four studs between the exterior shingles and the interior drywall supposedly served the dual purpose of water retardation and insulation. But when you consider that the natural laws governing water damage automatically tripled when you crossed the line into East Houston, leaving four hollow inches inside the walls was less than inspired. It's unlikely that Mr. Sharp had had planned obsolescence in mind when choosing this design—in fact, using tarpaper to avoid an accumulation of waterlogged asbestos suggests good intentions—but all things being equal, a handful of volunteer Texans stood a better chance of holding off 1,500 Mexicans at the Alamo than a house with a flimsy façade had of surviving the elemental onslaught of southeast Texas weather. In Jacinto City, when the rains came, mailmen needed diving suits.

Baseballs, bicycles, and bad luck didn't take long to put dents and dings in the outside walls that would expose the house's interior to its liquid foe. After a few short rainy seasons there was little siding left to dampen the downhill slide my mother and father had been on since the day they moved to Norvic Street.

The house's roof was a sheet of plywood covered with a layer of tarpaper and a mixture of hot tar and pea gravel spread across the surface and left to dry. Hurricane Carla would soon uncover the flaws in this plan. The living room and my bedroom held together surprisingly well. Had the leaks that began in the kitchen and my parents' bedroom been swiftly repaired, perhaps they wouldn't have become indoor waterfalls. My father saw it differently, holding the opinion that a cooking pan and a wash pot—or three cooking pans and a bucket—were a better solution to a leaking roof than needless repair. By the winter of 1962, my parents had to push their bed against the wall nearest the living room and strategically place a number 3 washtub, a five-gallon Igloo water cooler, an ice chest, and various pots and pans to catch the rainwater coming through the ceiling. On a clear night, stars could be seen twinkling through the holes in the roof.

Sheetrock hung from the kitchen ceiling like papier-mâché stalac-tites. Here, too, the sky was visible. Kelly Smith's mother had rea-son to enter the house on Norvic Street but once, and by the way she steeled herself before entering the kitchen you'd have thought it was a leper colony. Her purpose in crossing our dreaded threshold was to hurry up my mother, who was licking and sticking S&H Green Stamps into a book so that I, like Kelly, could snag a tennis racket that I'd never use. Mrs. Smith looked as though she would've puked her guts out if she'd taken a second longer to get back outside. My mother was paralyzed with shame.

As the holes in the kitchen ceiling grew bigger, she dispensed with the pots and buckets in favor of just sweeping the rainwater out the back door. She or I would stand there with a broom as it poured down around the overhead light fixture, and it's only dumb luck that neither of us got electrocuted as we went about our busi-ness on these endless rainy days. As the hardwood in my parents' bedroom floor warped into miniature brown mountain ranges, my father shrugged off the relentless deterioration with a snort. "I like the sound of the rain," he said. "It makes me sleep better." Assuming he was telling the truth, he must've slept like a dead man, given the bucketfuls that rained down not a foot and a half from his bed.

Summer nights in Jacinto City were an adventure. Evening fell dense as a jungle, and opportunistic insects thrived in hothouse conditions where humidity reigned supreme. Gunshots fired six blocks away would rattle the backyard fence, while eastbound freight trains took their nightly shortcut down the hall and out through the bathroom wall. Past midnight, five houses down, Ruby Gaines would yell, "Got-dammit, H.B., go home and get in the bed," thus alerting the entire neighborhood that Horace Boudreaux Chenier, the crazy Cajun peeping Tom, was out making his rounds.

How to make it safely through the wicked summer nights was a question that rarely came up among Jacinto City's sweltering denizens, though how to stay cool was under constant investigation. In a cockeyed stroke of low-cost ingenuity, Frank Sharp's suburban innovators hit on a brilliant plan to do just that: the attic fan. If there has ever been a more left-footed concept than this—a fan the size of a small, fat airplane propeller wedged into the hallway ceiling and working in reverse, sucking instead of blowing—I've yet to encounter it. A switch on the bathroom wall triggered the fan's slow assimilation of speed until, at full-tilt, the house shook with the rattle and roar of a B-52 bomber.

On paper this might've looked like a home run, but its practical application told a different story. Sixty-four straight days at ninety-six degrees and 92 percent humidity revealed the stupidity of inviting the outside indoors. With an attic fan sucking away, window screens had a life expectancy shorter than the Little League baseball season. In my parents' new house, by mid-July of the second summer, the bedroom screens were a mesh of crumbling rust. As with the holes in the ceiling, my father had neither the money nor the inclination to meet the problem head-on; and once the screens were gone, so was our last line of defense. Without any screens at all, the attic fan brought us face-to-face with one of Mother Nature's most bothersome creatures.

The Gulf Coast of Texas in 1961 was a breeding ground for mosquitoes more deadly and opportunistic than any others in known existence. That summer, front-page news focused almost entirely on the encephalitis epidemic rampant from Beaumont to Brownsville, and the purveyors of this dreaded disease were feasting on human blood and spreading the sickness around like Confederate money. One bite from the wrong mosquito and the unlucky bastard infected would lapse into a deep coma from which some never awoke. Locally, the condition was known as "the sleepin' sickness."

My father wasn't buying it. "Sleepin' sickness, my ass," he'd scoff at the news report on the ever-rolling black-and-white television screen. "I wish one of 'em would put *me* to sleep. I sure as hell ain't gettin' no rest with them noisy sons-a-bitches buzzin' around bitin' me all night long." Meanwhile, the attic fan served us up like hors d'oeuvres.

But I was taking the epidemic seriously and had *The Tingler* and *House on Haunted Hill*, the Vincent Price double horror feature my cousin Larry and I sat through twice at the Capitan Theater, to thank for my diligence. I knew for a fact that only a fool would fail to keep a sharp eye out for things supernatural. Seeing a human spine rise from a bathtub full of blood, or a giant crab monster luring unsuspecting victims into its seaside cave by crying out for help using the voices of people whose heads it had recently bitten off, furthered my resolve to never let my guard down. To blame these deadly mosquitoes on an abnormally rainy summer was to ignore all the signs pointing to their planned takeover of the world. Any self-respecting Vincent Price fan knew this was the reason they were putting us all to sleep.

I refused to be a hapless victim. Beneath a sheet, three blankets, and two of my grandmother's handmade quilts, I braced myself for the long night with the belief that the deadliest insect could never penetrate my fortress of layered cotton. Sleep, when it came, usually from lack of oxygen, was fitful. The moment I nodded off, the covers hit the floor, and most mornings I awoke with bleeding ankles. From the sweat-soaked womb of my nightly sauna, I listened to the mosquitoes' pre-feeding frenzy, a bloodthirsty swarm whose intentions were clearly audible: to start biting me the second I dozed off.

Insect repellents were a waste of time and money, a fact of life my father spent countless hours trying to disprove. With a can of Off! in one hand and a bottle of 6-12 Plus in the other, he fought a losing battle at every window in the house, emptying their contents for naught. Hurling insults—"Ya'll are just like them Mexicans at the damn Alamo"—and threatening to burn the house to the ground did more to dent the nightly onslaught than all the cans of Raid and Black Flag put together.

When at last my father's white flag was raised in defeat, my mother seized the opportunity to pour salt on his wounded ego. "Why, J. W. Crowell, you ain't been doin' nothin' in the world but makin' them skeeters mad," she told him with a smirk. "Now they're gonna take it out on the rest of us." She wasn't above high-handed admonishment when given a chance to have the last word. When I asked why he let her remark pass, my father responded with rarely seen resignation. "Hell, son, somebody around here's gotta win at somethin'."

Burning the circular incenselike repellent called PiC was a tonic for his flagging spirits. The black-and-white commercial for this product, shown between features at the Market Street Drive-In, depicted a cartoon mosquito with a squeaky voice saying, "P-I-C, don't believe it, it don't work." A giant wooden mallet with "PiC" written across its head would then flatten the bug, leaving Xs where its eyes had been—subliminal advertising for dumb asses, and my father loved it. Laughing all the way to the snack bar, he'd load up on packages of PiC they sold right on the spot.

I'll admit that watching *Sink the Bismarck* and *Run Silent, Run*

Deep through a cloud of PiC smoke did enhance the wartime feel of the battle scenes. But from where I sat in the backseat of the old Studebaker, the mosquito was telling the truth when he said it didn't work. I'd be choking on the smoke while my arms and legs were being gobbled like popcorn, and I made a point of saying so. But my father, unswayed, started burning PiC throughout the house day and night. For him, smoke smudges on what was left of the ceiling signified a moral victory. I came to understand that debating the merits of various insect repellents with him was as pointless as all that smoke. But by learning to go along with his futile attempts at supremacy in his own home, I found I loved my father more than I hated mosquitoes.

In its ongoing war with encephalitis, the Harris County Health Department unwittingly introduced a new brand of fun and games. The "Mosquito Dope Truck," as it was fondly dubbed, was responsible for one of the strangest rituals that Gulf Coast living could offer a child in the early sixties. Come dusk, from May to October, six days a week, a green round-nosed 1947 Army-issue Plymouth pickup with a diesel-driven fogging apparatus in its bed would make a left turn onto Norvic from Hart Street. The driver, obviously aware of his role in the evening's frolic, paused to let the truck's rumbling idle alert the neighborhood to its arrival. Then, like a giant smoke-belching prehistoric land crab, the truck crawled slowly up the street blasting blue boiling twenty-foot plumes of sweet-smelling DDT and triggering a tribal dance void of all inhibition. Barefoot heathen children, some with baby brothers or sisters on their hips, ran, skipped, rode bicycles, pushed scooters, pulled red wagons, roller-skated, bounced on pogo sticks, or walked on stilts to get close enough to inhale great lungfuls of the toxic blue smoke.

I kept my Indianapolis race car, made from a medium-sized cardboard box with a hole cut in the middle and bright red 8s painted on both sides, stashed in the one dry corner of the garage. When the truck's rat-a-tat rumble set screen doors slamming up and down the street, I'd dash out there, pull the homemade racer over my head, and lay strips of imaginary rubber as I joined the happily huffing throng. My friend Dabbo and I could always count on each other to go the extra two or three blocks to ensure a properly scorched respiratory system and nauseous buzz.

In my opinion, the mosquitoes scoffed at these genocidal foggings and in fact thrived on DDT. Still, it must be said that for a half hour or so afterward, they showed little interest in blood sucking. Eventually, when the narcotic effects wore off, the bugs and I would prepare for another nightlong skirmish.

In spite of their dominating the newspapers and airwaves, for me the Gulf Coast mosquitoes deserved second billing behind the region's most tenacious entomological headliner: the cockroach. I'm not referring to the clunky loners who present themselves like lost puppies, one or maybe two at a time, in the bathtub or behind the sink. No, "La Coo Coo Rotcha" (as Dabbo called them) were slender, brown, lightning-fast, and, at the peak of summer, teeming in the darkened corners and hidden crannies of our kitchen. To flick the light on there in the middle of a scalding July night meant entering a dimension where every available inch of surface space was swarmed by their translucent, root-beer liquidity, giving the table, chairs, stove, and refrigerator the look of a living, breathing, and grotesque organism. A mere 75-watt bulb sparked an exodus beyond biblical proportions in less than four seconds. This incredible disappearing act—millions of bugs gone, *just like that*!—was woven into the fabric of our lives on Norvic Street with the same indifference bestowed on buckets of rain and fatal encephalitis. It became commonplace to flip on the kitchen light, walk to the sink, and rinse out a glass that seconds before had been crawling with cockroaches, then drink your fill of water without a second thought.

Our nonchalance, in hindsight, seems robotic. Not once did one

of us turn to another and say, "Gee, there must be at least six million cockroaches scurrying around the kitchen. Doesn't that seem
strange?" Instead, we went about our lives as if honoring a
foresworn oath never to call the exterminator.

So the kitchen belonged to the cockroaches. The rest of the
house we shared with the mosquitoes.

Chinaberry Sidewalks

In yet another burst of cost-cutting brilliance, Frank Sharp's engineers came up with the bright idea of constructing, along both sides of the street, concave concrete troughs that served the dual purpose of sidewalk and shallow drainage ditch. As ditches went, these were excellent for the post-rainstorm races Dabbo and I contested with battleships made from discarded two-by-fours. Since the course emptied into something akin to a sewer system at the end of each block, considerable dexterity was required to pluck your ship from the raging rapids the moment it crossed the finish line, before it got flushed.

When Norvic Street was named host sidewalk for the 1960 grub-bug summer Olympics, jumped-up snot-heads from as far away as Flaxman Street (nine blocks over) showed up, seriously expecting to dethrone our legendary thousand-leggers, their miserable stable of losers contained in assorted hand-painted cigar boxes and coffee cans. D'Artagnan Doolittle—a name I partially plucked from an old Three Musketeers movie—would retire undefeated. He handed Wing Zay Wyklefunk, Dabbo's prized champion, his only loss in a photo-finish heartbreaker, D'Artagnan inching out the big guy by a nose, and the next day a size-13 steel-toed work boot belonging to Dabbo's daddy put an end to Wyklefunk's illustrious career. Anyway, when darkness halted the competition, the validity of chalk marks identifying the next day's starting positions were argued with clenched fists, and neighborhood mothers took turns breaking up the free-for-alls. With reputations on the line, a busted lip was a small price to pay for a good track position. As for the practicality of these sidewalks' design, two adults couldn't walk comfortably side by side, so pedestrians preferred the street.

One day in the spring of 1958, my mother had enlisted my help in planting three young chinaberry trees along the sidewalk's edge. Coaxing these saplings into thriving on our property was an exotic proposition, a concept that called for initiative previously unheard-of in the Crowell-Willoughby bloodline. For a while, I became sufficiently engrossed in my mother's unprecedented attempt at landscaping to forget the endless trips I'd made to the trees growing by the back fence to cut switches for my own whippings. Not until we stood back to admire the early stages of our handiwork did the notion of planting more trees for more switches for more whippings strike me as pure madness.

Perhaps the most Philistine of all southern customs is the one that sends children in search of a suitable tool for their own bloody torture. According to Grandma Katie, the ritual's therapeutic value lay in the journey to and from. For the spare-the-rod-and-spoil-the-child contingent, the heightened state of awareness brought on by the miscreant's sense of impending doom made every solemn trek to the chinaberry trees an invaluable tool of heathen reform, and the ass-blistering that awaited your dutiful return of little importance. I loved and trusted my grandmother more than anyone in the world, but her defense of this practice was pure hogwash, and I told her as much.

The only thought I could remember crossing my mind during all those switch-cutting expeditions was to choose as many weak, flimsy sprigs as possible in hopes my mother would lose interest in whipping me. Once, hoping that humor might dismantle her resolve to punish me for cussing or some other minor offense, I tied a white dish towel to a broken limb. She laughed and beat the hell out of me anyway.

In possession of a firm, fresh-cut switch, my mother was nothing short of a left-handed Zorro. She liked the sound and feel of sliced air. Her interest in raising bloody welts on the back of my legs bordered on the sadistic. To whip the daylights out of me and leave it at that was something she simply couldn't do. Until the markings on my legs and butt were examined and pronounced of a quality in keeping with her high standards, the tanning of my hide was never considered complete. I can't help thinking that it's a shame she didn't apply such perfectionism to other areas of her life.

Lacking imagination to match our industriousness, my mother and I named the trees J.W., Cauzette, and Rodney. Perhaps it was the intoxication of accomplishment that prompted us to christen the trees with our own names, or maybe the trees symbolized for the two of us a new chapter in our family history, in which case we wanted our names displayed front and center. Either way, our buoyancy was short-lived.

In matters concerning my mother, my father was a master of dismissal. And for me, a pat on the head and a "Well done, son" was as foreign to his nature as a taste for caviar. Approval was apparently beyond his ability to give.

From time to time, having stopped after work for a few rounds at whichever icehouse he was frequenting at the time, my father missed the driveway strips by a wider margin than usual and he and the Studebaker would come to a noisy, jaw-rattling stop.

Were my mother still alive, she'd be the first to admit that on many occasions she was hopelessly incapable of reading my father's mercurial disposition. "When it comes to your daddy, sometimes I don't know whether to shit or go blind" is, I believe, how she put it. Based on my ability to decipher, by sight or sound, the subtle and not-so-subtle variations in his driveway etiquette, I became the acknowledged expert in gauging the slant of his mood. "He drunk?" she'd ask. "Sounds like it," I'd answer. "How bad?" she'd want to know. "Not good," I'd conclude. On this day, judging by his revving the engine three times before switching it off—a signal meant to convey that he'd sooner crash the Studebaker through the garage's back wall than take an interest in whatever it was we numbskulls thought we were doing out here—I already knew what she would soon find out: out little tree-planting project was about to take a big hit.

Feeding off the dregs of whatever had been the cause of his vinegary disposition, my father appraised our gardening skills with sarcasm soaked in beer and whiskey. "Aw, hell," he sneered, "them shit-ass twigs don't stand a Chinaman's chance of growing out here next to the street."

Refusing to be bullied, I shot back, "You don't know nothin'. These are chinaberry trees, and if anything stands a Chinaman's chance of growin' out here, it's a damn chinaberry tree."

He fixed my mother with a cold stare. "Is this how you're teachin' him to act—"

"You leave her alone," I interrupted. "We were gonna name one after you, but we wouldn't do it now if you begged us. You don't deserve to have a tree named after you."

As much as I'd like to say this rebuff was intended to calm my father's hostile temperament, I can't. It was nothing more than dumb luck. By chance I'd struck a chord close to the heart of his schoolboy vanity. When it came to the possible lionization of his name, he couldn't resist any opportunity, no matter how small, to bask in the glow of hypothetical glory.

He softened, and to reward our beloved man-child for yet another of his dazzling mood swings, my mother and I reinstated his name. Unfortunately, in spite of my constant attention, his namesake and hers died, whereas mine took root.

· · ·

The first week of sixth grade, I come home from school to find a black panel truck idling in front of our house. No less puzzling than the sight of its running with no one behind the wheel is how little its curbside vigil alters the ebb and flow of neighborhood routine. On a street where shell-shocked war veterans ran naked with machine guns exploding the ground at their heels—Mr. Plowman, from down the block, had had hallucinations ever since he came home from helping storm the beaches over in France—a double-parked rattletrap choking on its own exhaust actually must have seemed pretty normal.

But in addition to its advanced state of disrepair, something about this truck, seemingly poised for a quick getaway, strikes me as peculiar. Faded signs stenciled with Battleground T.V. Repair linger on either side like sun-bleached petroglyphs. Cartoon murals illustrating the before-and-after effects of a house call adorn the rear-door panels. In one, a kindly-looking San Jacinto Monument, complete with a surgeon's mask and headlamp, zaps Reddy Kilowatt lightning bolts at the rabbit-eared antenna of two sickly televisions. In the other, the same monument does a flying-stethoscope version of the jitterbug while the much-improved televisions kick up their heels in eight-legged joy.

Seventh-grade algebra will be only slightly more difficult for me to understand than the possibility that this traveling TV medicine show might put my pajama-bottomed butt back in front of our set, hugging a bowl of soggy Cheerios and ignoring my mother's pleas not to sit so close and ruin my eyesight. But if there's any truth to be found in the van's weather-beaten graphics, restoring *Sky King* and *Fury* to their regular Saturday morning time slots is a matter no more complicated than dialing Orchard 6-2626, the office number given on the driver's door.

As was the case with the roof over his own family's head, my father's penchant for half-assed remedies precluded actually placing such a call. The lack of sport in proper procedures bored him silly; instead, he believed that from the cultivation of loose ends came the fruits of the unexpected. For example, how he stumbled onto this opportunity in the first place: "I was sittin' at a red light on the corner of Market Street and Federal Road studyin' how to get that dang thing fixed," he mused, "when that old truck come a-rumblin' through the inner-section. Well, sir, I made a right-hand turn outta the left-hand lane and chased him a mile 'fore I run him down. Told him my set was on the blink, had been for two months. And I be dang if he don't turn right around and follow me to the house and fix it while I'm sittin' there watching. That's how you get something done around here."

When the concept of TV repair finally hits home, it's with the force of a big gum eraser bouncing off my head. Any questions concerning the eyesore parked out front disappear like invisible ink as visions of Mighty Mouse saving Pearl Pureheart from Oil Can Harry fill me with the urge to see our blessed savior in action, so I take the sidewalk, yard, and porch in about four long strides.

Even before the slamming screen door pronounces me home from school, I'm stopped dead in my tracks by the Grand Canyon of butt cracks now on display in our living room. The owner of this anatomical anomaly is in the process of plucking some derelict tube from the dust-caked entrails of the cantankerous old Philco my father bought off some guy in a barbershop. Where his green khaki pants and shirt have been separated by the hands-and-knees positioning required to reach into the back of the television, there is now a gross white chasm.

A lumbering voice, a cross between Bronx brogue and Cajun bumble, sends words like "Now I gotcha" and "C'mon outta there" rattling around in the electronic gadgetry. When the head the voice belongs to emerges from behind the set, I nearly swallow my wad of bubble gum.

The color of orange soda water, a horseshoe-shaped hedgerow that looks more like clumps of used Brillo pads than sprigs of hair has attached itself to what looks like an oversized version of the plastic Cro-Magnon skull Mr. Weiss keeps on a shelf in the back of his classroom. Matching steel-wool eyebrows punctuate an impossibly white dome where one green eye stares down an exact replica of W. C. Fields's swollen red nose. The other eye, blond as buttermilk, alternates between a sideways glance and St. Vitus's dance. The demands on my attention have never been so clownishly divided. The very sight of him decrees that I try to focus on one eye over the other, but I can't figure out which one to go with.

When he rubs his catcher's-mitt hands together to commemorate a job well done, I notice just below his rolled-up shirtsleeves a pair of jailhouse-quality ship-anchor tattoos on his forearms. Noting my interest, he cranks up a mumbling chuckle.

Unable to muster a suitable response, I excuse myself and go spit my wad of gum into the commode. When I return, I can't decide if it's Popeye the Sailor Man, Jack in the Box, or Bozo the Clown assuring my father that *Gunsmoke* will once again be a stationary target and his Sunday night motion sickness a thing of the past. "I put some lead in yer picture tube's pencil," he says. "That oughta hold her still for a while."

While the repairman focuses his green eye on my father, his blond one sizes me up like a radar dish. I'm thinking up excuses to go to my room when he starts rattling off answers to questions he thinks I've been dying to ask. "Like to leave her runnin'. She runs like the dickens but she's hard to get started. Drawed up her advertizin' myself. I taken after my daddy's side and reckon you taken after your daddy's side, too. 'Preciate ya'll's business."

As I stand in the doorway watching his truck rumble away, the phrase "fallen into ruin or partial decay" comes to mind and I recognize it as the definition of "dilapidated," which I'd memorized in Mr. Weiss's class earlier that day. I wander farther out into the yard to gauge the strangeness of this repairman's visit and find the evening settling into a kind of barometric hyperstillness. I don't recognize it as such, but its eeriness has calm-before-the-storm written all over it. So I drift back into the house hungry enough to eat the fried baloney and sauerkraut my mother has no doubt made for the fourth night running. My father's admiring his newly resuscitated television when a news bulletin announces the impending arrival of Hurricane Carla.

This sends Jacinto City residents into a frenzy of preparation. Masking-tape crosses appear in windows, sheets of plywood seal up screened porches, new batteries make old transistor radios work just fine. Everybody stocks up on food and water, blows cobwebs off kerosene lanterns, and replenishes liquor supplies. So many people scurrying around in a frenzy reminds me of the Ant Farm Mrs. Cain keeps in the back of her fifth-grade classroom.

Such fastidiousness offends my father's sensibilities and is as unlike him as being a bird-watcher. He dismisses his conscientious neighbors as a nervous pack of limp-wristed do-gooders. Lighting up a Pall Mall and spitting tobacco strands from the tip of his tongue, he scoffs, "Aw, hell, I ain't afraid of no hurricane. It can blow the dang roof off for all I care."

His arrogance stirs a foreboding in the pit of my stomach that, once ignored, allows me to voice solidarity with his assessment of the men climbing ladders and crawling around under their houses as a bunch of pussies. "Look at all them 'fraidy-cats," I sneer not loud enough to be heard beyond our property line, and his "You tell 'em, sweet smell 'em," chuckled through a cloud of smoke, is all the approval I need.

A similar disdain for preparation will become the hallmark of my adult life, winging it at all costs my Achilles' heel and "damn the torpedoes" my battle cry. Like my father before me, I'm a spur-of-the-moment snob who looks down my nose at those who plan ahead. Family vans cruising down the highway with all their vacation gear securely fastened on the top bring out the worst in me, my gut reaction being to ram bumper car–style into the driver's side door and wreck both automobiles. A voice inside my head shouts, *I am my father's son. I came into this world unprepared, and I expect to die the same way. All you Boy Scout sons of bitches better learn to steer clear of J. W. Crowell's boy.*

I know my father has doubts about our house's ability to survive a direct hit from a full-blown hurricane; his contempt for more punctilious homeowners practically announces it over a loudspeaker. Loyalty, however, requires that I set my own misgivings aside and support his head-in-the-sand tactics.

Relief comes in the form of a phone call and an invitation to the Millers' for a hurricane-watch party, where two or more families huddle together beneath one roof intending to collectively withstand nature's wrath. In truth, it's an excuse for the adults to drink hard liquor, smoke cigarettes, and play dominoes. Eventually, with enough alcohol, the lines of propriety become blurred, and sexual innuendo rears its naughty little head. Passes are made, tempers flare, and fistfights nearly break out. When the indoor chaos reaches a peak, gusts up to 140 miles an hour can be counted on to refocus attention on more immediate concerns like survival. Adult participants fall into a pattern of drunken stupidity and intermittent sobriety that lasts as long as it takes a hurricane to "blow on through." For the kids, it's open season on making a mess of the house.

My father can hardly contain the joy of having solved his dilemma. I'm tempted to point out that, technically, it was solved *for* him, then decide against it. He thinks abandoning the house in favor of a let's-all-get-drunk hurricane party is the best idea he's had in years, and I see no reason to argue. The same can't be said of my mother. "I'd rather drown in my own backyard than be locked up with that bunch for five minutes," she tells him. Taking her dissent as the affront to his newfound buoyancy that it's intended to be, he snaps back: "I tell you what, Cauzette, you go on and get drowned out yonder. Me and the boy's goin' over to Floyd and Sally's."

Registering complaints doesn't come naturally to my father; ignoring the obvious is more to his liking. My mother's apprehension about weathering a Category 4 hurricane in close proximity with the Millers, paired with his need for her unquestioning loyalty, illustrates perfectly the conundrum they will spend their lives trying to unravel. His tendency toward unsubstantiated cockiness and her pinprick precision in delivering the right words at the wrong time make them doubly vulnerable to the bubble-bursting rifts that distinguish their marriage.

Ransacking kitchen drawers for a pack of smokes does little to hide my father's misgivings about casting the fate of his house to this gale. Translated, "Got-dammit, Cauzette, I know they's a carton of Pell Mell in here somewhere" means he knows that accepting the Millers' invitation to an alcohol blackout amounts to nothing more than shirking his responsibilities as a home owner, but that if his wife would just play ball every once in a while, the world would be a better place. A sucker for the pouting Crowell pathos, my mother will turn a deaf ear to her own better judgment and agree to go. If like me she heard him mutter, "If the house is still standin' when we get home, good. If it ain't, piss on it," she's keeping it to herself.

We're maybe halfway into the twenty-five-minute drive when the first few sprinkles land softly on the windshield, but something about their arrival hints at Carla's power. At a stoplight, my father leans forward, elbows flared, chest pressed against the steering wheel, and stares upward through the glass as if at the underbelly of a flying saucer. On the passenger side, my mother does the same. In the backseat, I try to hold my breath until the light turns green. Once the car's moving again, the rain has begun to fall in earnest. Through a kaleidoscope of reflected streetlight, raindrops burst like liquid fireflies on the back window, and my father asks, "Ya'll wanna just go back home?"

The Millers' house is large enough to eat ours for breakfast. A brand-spanking-new chain-link fence surrounds its manicured half acre like a silver necklace. Green latticed shutters flank the front windows, giving added glow to a fresh white paint job. The fifty-foot television antenna standing there in the backyard is known to get the best reception in northeast Houston. For a man who owns a two-truck wrecker service, Floyd Miller has worked wonders in creating an air of affluence around his family. Knowing my father's need to hide the shame of his own poverty, I'm hardly surprised to see him voluntarily deluded by the façade of a lesser man's accomplishments. I hate seeing him defer to Mr. Miller but have to admit that their house is better suited to withstand a hurricane than ours.

Besides, Andy and Mike, the Millers' sons, make the prospect of riding it out at their place far more appealing than staying at home. Three boys roughly the same age triple the opportunity for fun and games. The grown-ups can be grown up, and we can romp until we pass out.

When we arrive, the Millers are sitting in front of their television, watching local newsman Dan Rather's live report from Galveston. "It's gonna be a big 'un," Floyd says as he greets us at the door. "Y'all all better get on in here."

We settle in, eager to catch up on what had taken place in the half hour since we turned our television off. Andy, Mike, and I nod our heads at the screen an extra beat before slipping off to take advantage of the loosened house rules. To stay abreast of our impending doom, we call frequent time-outs to check what's happening on television.

High drama surrounds Dan Rather's inability to divine where Carla will make her landfall. Watching the first-ever live television broadcast of weather radar, I'm put in mind of the monster's face at the beginning of *Weird,* the weekly sci-fi horror program that comes on Saturday night after the ten o'clock news. Carla appears to be sitting out in the Gulf of Mexico and trying to decide whom to clobber first. It occurs to me she's playing eeny-meeny-miny-moe to decide where to strike. Thus inspired, I make up a poem and recite it in front of everyone:

> *Eeny, meeny, miny, moe*
> *Is Port Arthur where I should go?*
> *If I decide on Houston, ya'll*
> *Everybody's gonna really bawl*

Mrs. Miller and my mother muster a tepid round of applause. Andy hocks up fake loogies and Mike makes armpit farts to show their appreciation.

As the first night passes, I help Andy and Mike build a fort under the dining room table. My father and Mr. Miller get drunk watching the weather reports.

Early the next morning, the boys and I are cracking eggs, burning toast, and plotting a course of adventure in the storm's gathering intensity. But I have a problem with the coffee-swilling, Bufferin-chewing adults paying so little attention to the requests they're currently green-lighting. Granting eleven- and twelve-year-olds permission to risk life and limb demands precautionary measures, the very least of which should be "Y'all boys stay in the yard."

I'm considering speaking my mind when Andy and Mike appear decked out in matching yellow slicker suits. Their fireman-quality rubber boots, galumphing on the hardwood floor, fill me with a shame not unlike my father's. Bringing a raincoat and galoshes to a hurricane-watch party constitutes the kind of preparation he and I disdain, but I'm beginning to think maybe a little forethought isn't such a bad thing after all.

Having nothing weather-worthy, I find myself at the mercy of Mrs. Miller, who roots around in her closet for a while and emerges with a see-through plastic raincoat. I have no reason to suspect her motives, but there's something sadistic in the joy she takes in outfitting me like some old lady and belittling my mother by humiliating me. When she says, "Try this on, sweetie," and "This oughta work just fine," it makes me want to puke. But Andy and Mike are so fidgety to get going that I swallow my pride and put the stupid thing on. Once she ties the rain hat under my chin, I look like a refugee from Mrs. Flint's special-education class.

Complaining to my mother about how retarded I feel is useless; she's off on some toot about how cute she thinks I am. I want to tell her she can stick that crap up her stupid hillbilly ass, that Andy and Mike are the cute ones because they have *real* raincoats, but I don't want to give Mrs. Miller the satisfaction. Thank God for my father's ability to put this fashion fiasco into perspective. "Aw, hell," he says. "You look like shit, son, but it ain't gonna matter one bit when that hurricane gets through with you."

Outdoors, Mr. Miller's rusty three-pronged frog gig, a sawed-off mop handle, and a flimsy cane fishing pole become customized harpoons destined to bag Moby-Dick. The cane pole accessorizes my makeshift rainwear so naturally that I claim it as the perfect weapon to fit my needs. Looking like an idiot and sporting the least glamorous of harpoons, I'm beginning to share my mother's reservations about hurricane-watch parties.

An imaginary crow's nest atop the TV antenna offers a bird's-eye view of Carla's cleavage, if some fool seadog dares to make the climb. Desperate to overcome my status as an afterthought, I'm a third of the way up the ladder when whiplash halts my vision quest. The antenna will soon be coming down.

Damn the white whale! Ahab, Queequeg, and Ishmael have bigger fish to fry! Improvising a game of shipwreck on a stack of lumber by the back fence, we hoist our homemade Jolly Roger and it's promptly plucked from our midst. Horizontal rain pelts our faces like 20-gauge ratshot. Pine trees sway like tent-revival Pentecostals surrendering to their disapproving God. In the woods behind the house, a usually dry fork of Caney Creek floods its banks and sends copperheads in search of higher ground. This alone puts a damper on our adventures.

Quitting the snake-infested woodpile, we hit the streets in rescue mode. But in our search for the perfect emergency, lost kids, little old ladies, and small animals are nowhere to be seen, nor is any sign of life in need of saving. Still, knowing that the will to press on in the face of insurmountable odds is the yardstick by which great rescue teams are measured, we refuse to quit even though throwing caution to a twenty-five-mile-an-hour wind is one thing and braving sudden gusts of up to sixty quite another. Not until a walloping blast rips off my old-lady's rain hat and wraps it around a street sign do we begin to understand that Carla's telling us to forget about toddlers and lapdogs; it's time to save our own behinds. Taking stock, we're hit with the realization we most likely have strayed too far into the barometric no-man's-land to make it home alive. To strategize our own evacuation, we have to scream to be heard above what has come to sound like the world's largest jet engine.

And just when lack of organization and absence of leadership seems on the verge of abandoning us to the wind and rain, someone or something hits the world's largest Off switch. The tempestuousness of three seconds before is now a mild, late-summer morning. Andy and Mike stop dead in their tracks and cock their heads to one side like twin versions of the Jack Russell terrier on the RCA logo. They appear to be unscrambling some coded meteorological message that I, in my ridiculous outfit, am obviously too far down the chain of command to be privy to. I'm weighing the merits of controlled self-pity over pitching a fit when the voice of my grandmother, dead for six months now, shouts in my ear, *You need to get your hind end on home. This here hurricane's fixin' to come unwound.*

And so it does. The boiling charcoal cloudbank that has been idling overhead shoves itself in gear and pops the clutch on the beginning of the end of the world. Panic strikes the heart of our rescue mission, and congratulations on our community service will not be forthcoming.

Three blocks and six lifetimes later, my father meets us at the door. "Hot damn, boys," he says. "I was startin' to think I was gonna have to go out in that mess and haul y'all outta some bar ditch."

The black-and-white Dan Rather trapped inside the Millers' picture tube isn't the laid-back news anchor he will become as the century wears on. He's edgy and aggressive, with a jet-black pompadour greased to near-Elvis perfection. His boxy suit reminds me of the ones that Richard Nixon, the guy who's been trying to get elected president, always wears. For three straight days he's been ranting nonstop about the storm-to-end-all-storms, and neither one of them shows any sign of letting up. In fact, with each new phase of Carla's development, he raises his level of showmanship to match her growing intensity. And now that she's about to stomp a mud hole in two-thirds of the Gulf Coast, he's somewhere on the beach in Galveston broadcasting live from her Category 4 mouth.

"I reckon he wants us to know what we're in for," says my father, slapping the snap-button pocket of his cowboy shirt for another smoke. "The eyes of Texas are on that ole boy, and he's sure puttin' on a show."

Knowing that sooner or later it was bound to happen, we're nonetheless dumbstruck when the television screen goes blank and everything else electric in the house shuts off. Blanker yet are the stares we trade in the aftermath of Dan Rather's dematerialization. This is perfect television, and its drama couldn't have been scripted any better. My father's definitively unself-conscious "son of a bitch" raises the question that's on everybody's mind: What happened to him, and how do we keep this hellacious house-hammering hurricane from doing the same thing to us?

Huddled in the chalky glow of a kerosene lamp, both families observe a moment of silence for our fallen newsman. Connection to the outside world has been downsized to the scratchy, on-again, off-again reception of a transistor radio.

"It's sure good to know somebody out there's still alive," Mr. Miller says.

"Hellfire, Floyd," my father snorts, "they could've tape-recorded what we're hearin' on that radio."

Outside, Carla's pounding the house with what sounds like a custom-made battering ram, and she's still thirteen hours from reaching her peak. Inside, the party has hit the skids. My father and Mr. Miller take this personally. They're not the kind of men content to sit idly by while a storm kicks the living daylights—and all the electric ones, too—out of their neck of the woods, but their only recourse is to take yet another swig of whiskey.

"Boys, y'all need to go on and get some sleep, this storm's a long ways from bein' over," says a tipsy Mrs. Miller. In anticipation of our fathers' further deterioration, she and my mother are herding us down the hallway with our path lit by a lone flickering candle.

Count on bedtime to bring the end of the world into focus. In the far corner of the room, Andy and Mike's bunk beds are stacked against the wall between bare windows. I'm sure neither walls nor windows will save us from the howling winds and driving rain, and say so aloud. The Miller boys pick up on this thread and make short work of turning a long day's end into a whimpering quagmire. Their mother's too drunk to know she's being had, and mine's too preoccupied with my father's liquor intake to offer any real reassurances.

Worse than any vision of collapsing walls is being stuck in the bottom bunk with Andy, who thinks trying to stick his pecker in my butt is funny. I put a stop to this by crawling under the bed with the Lincoln Logs and army figures. In spite of my worries about attacks from various directions, I drift off to sleep comfortably with an old baseball glove and a dirty towel for pillow and blanket.

"Come on, son, wake up, we goin' to the house."

I recognize the words, and the voice, but what I don't recognize is where they're coming from and why they're so gruff. Even with a blistering, nicotine-scorched hangover, my father's voice usually has a lyrical quality that's totally absent in its present condition.

Finally awake, I'm staring at his upside-down face, his blue bloodshot eyes searching my crawl space for life. His crimson cheeks and ears put me on notice that any questions will only make matters worse. Whatever it is that made him fish me out from under these bunk beds at this unknowable hour is serious enough to drain his voice of its musicality. That's all I need to know.

Going home is fine by me, and anything would beat Andy point-ing his pecker at me. And I'd learned long ago that when my father makes his mind up, there's no reason strong enough to alter his course. Besides, my mother seems equally determined to clear the hell out.

The first obstacle we encounter is the six inches of water standing between the Millers' back door and our car parked twenty yards away. Second is how formidable a threat the copperheads and water moccasins treading water and searching for an entrance to the house pose to our getting in the car alive. I'm thinking of myself as a cross between Jesse Owens and Jesus Christ as I sprint out there across the water. My mother matches me stride for stride, her crippled leg not the slightest hindrance. My father's already firing up the engine.

The trip home takes over an hour, but it seems more like an eternity. Whatever pissed my father off has caused him to severely underestimate the intensity of the storm he's steering us into.

Raindrops pelt the windows like liquid lug nuts. Low-lying intersections are flooded halfway up the side doors. In a stalled Studebaker, we stand a better than even chance of getting washed down some raging bayou. It's more likely, however, that a power line will simply blow over and decapitate all three of us.

On the verge of panic, my mother breaks out speaking in tongues six decibels above the roaring hurricane. "Praise God, praise Him, the Devil is a liar. Jesus, come to us now in our time of need. Deliver us from the darkness that has descended upon this Earth."

The agitation is almost unbearable.

My father delivers his rebuttal with controlled meanness, his quiet seething the opposite of her shrill hysterics. "Got-dammit, Cauzette, if you don't shut that shit up I'm gonna put your ass out in the storm."

"J. W. Crowell, you'll do no such of a thing. And you'll not take the Lord's name in vain, neither, not in front of me and your son."

I lie low in the backseat. "Ya'll leave me out of this."

Then she's off praying again, louder. "Our Father who art in heaven and on this Earth, deliver us from the evil that is upon us!"

In the middle of her tirade my father snaps, slapping her hard with the back of his hand and driving the car into an intersection that's under three feet of water. The Studebaker stalls. That he'd just hit his wife is instantly relegated to back-burner status, since getting the car started again is now a matter of desperate importance.

"You steer!" he yells, motioning for me to climb over the seat and take the wheel. When he opens his door, a rush of water floods the floorboards, and the wind nearly rips the door from its hinges. In the driver's seat I'm thinking of World War II submarine movies: the walls sweating and the air stale as we take on massive amounts of water.

In the rearview mirror my father reminds me of Gregory Peck as Ahab in the part of that black-and-white movie where he's finally hooked Moby-Dick with his harpoon but has gotten tangled in the rope and is about to be drowned. He starts to push the car, little by little, out of the intersection, though with no chance of ultimate success. Sobered by the slap in the face, my mother calmly lights a Viceroy and acts as if her husband's just run into the 7-11 for a loaf of bread. I can't tell if she's convinced her prayers will be answered or else is just ready to drown.

Scrambling to her side of the car, motioning for her to roll the window down, my father poses the question I know he's been dying to ask since he climbed out: "Are you gonna do something to help or not?"

My mother's reply? "Yeah, I'll smoke my cigarette."

Considering what happens next, I have to think my mother's prayers, off-putting as they are, might well have been answered. From out of nowhere, yellow and white flashing lights appear in the fogged-up rear window, and three blasts from an air horn signal my father to get in the car and steer.

The tow truck pushes our drowned Studebaker for over three miles as my father pumps the accelerator and sweet-talks the engine nonstop. "Come on, now, you little red hotrod," he's cooing.

"Turn on over and fire up for ole J-Bo"—his self-appointed nickname.

In the middle of all this, my mother lights a fresh Viceroy and scoffs, "The Lord's done answered my prayers, J.W. If you had any sense, you'd just let him push us on in."

But my father won't be denied the right to zoom off in a huff. He flatters and begs and threatens to sell the flooded car for junk metal until it coughs and spits, a string of backfires announcing his triumph.

Despite hating it when he hits my mother, I love seeing my father enjoy this victory and think to myself that for someone who craves winning as much as he does, it's a shame it happens so infrequently.

"You tell the Lord he can kiss my ass," he gloats, refusing to acknowledge that her prayers might have been instrumental in the Studebaker's finally cranking up. Similarly, his dismissal of Mr. Miller, our true benefactor, had been comical in its arrogance. He simply rolled down the window, flipped him the bird, and roared off into Carla. When the tow-truck lights disappear, I ask out loud what it was that happened back at the Millers' house, but my parents, out of either exhaustion or relief, have withdrawn into themselves and aren't taking any questions.

When we arrived unscathed, my father's overly careful about lining up the tires on the concrete driveway strips, barely visible under a half foot of water, and this seems peculiar given what our expedition's been like so far. With a hurricane blowing full-tilt all around us, sliding to a sideways halt would seem a more fitting conclusion to this wild ride. But then I'm not the one driving.

My mother gets out of the car, wades into the house, picks up a broom, and starts sweeping floodwater out the back door. Then she pops the refrigerator door open with a screwdriver—my father's solution to its broken handle—and grabs a can of lukewarm Jax, drains half of it in one *glug*, wipes her mouth with the back of her wrist, burps loudly and, pointing the can at my father, says, "J. W. Crowell, next time you lay a hand on me, you better make sure you kill me, 'cause if you don't I'll kill you. I don't care if I have to wait till you fall asleep to do it."

How quickly my mother switches from Pentecostal purist to beer-guzzling shrew is one of life's deepest mysteries.

My father pushes his luck lightly. "Aw, hell, Cauzette, I didn't hurt you. If I meant to—"

"You better be listenin' to me, J.W. I swear on the Bible I mean ev'ry word I said. I'll kill you deader'n a doornail."

My parents chain-smoked while the house went toe-to-toe with Carla, my mother singing "What a Friend We Have in Jesus" and sweeping out floodwater. Meanwhile I slept fourteen hours in the comfort of my own bed.

When Carla finished, she'd converted our little house with a leaky roof into an indoor swimming pool. Outside, it looks to have survived the ordeal with little more than a black eye; inside, it's more like a fatal brain hemorrhage. The final collapse won't come for three and a half years, but when it does, there can be little doubt that Hurricane Carla delivered the blow that brought on the beginning of the end.

In 1965 my parents threw in the towel. By the time the bank got around to repossessing the property, they'd long since quit Jacinto City and the house had collapsed. Later that year, whatever was left got bulldozed to the ground.

The lot then remained vacant for thirty-three years. As an adult, I often had the urge and enough money to buy the property, with a vision of constructing a monument of some kind and dedicating it to my parents. But for reasons I could never explain, I balked at reclaiming the site of my childhood home.

In 1998, near the small town of Highlands, Texas, less than a mile from the San Jacinto Monument itself, my mother will be buried next to my father, who died nine years before. During the funeral service, I'll be overwhelmed by the desire to drive the fifteen or so miles into Jacinto City and buy the vacant lot at 10418 Norvic Street. Why, I'll wonder, had I waited so long?

With my heart racing ahead in anticipation, my wife and daughters will show their concern with soothing words and gentle reminders for me to breathe. The journey will seem to last another thirty-three years. When we arrive, a newly constructed home is proudly positioned where my parents' little white house had stood so tentatively. All that remains of the lives gone before will be in the northeast corner of the front yard: a chinaberry tree that once bore my name.

J.W.

Dim among the glimmerings of long ago there is a light. In its presence—the only source of light in a vast hall of darkness—there are countless people, absorbed and adoring, my father and me among them. It is old and otherworldly now, this light, and it fades a little with each year, a hint that perhaps it will soon be gone forever. But it is proof, for now, that I once saw the light.

Not long after my second birthday, Hank Williams made his next-to-last public appearance at Cook's Hoedown, East Houston's premier hillbilly nightspot. Rejecting the notion that I was too young to enjoy the experience, my father appointed me his preferred companion for the evening. Hoisted high on his shoulders, my legs straddling his neck, I felt my senses dawning in this new world like the first few pieces being fitted into a puzzle. The eddy of cool air wafting down from overhead awakened the feeling I was somewhere very different from my usual surroundings, the hush of anticipation in the audience stirring the suspicion that I was part of something incomprehensibly great. A thunderous man-made roar tested the building's rafters for structural weakness and overwhelmed my fledgling sensory receptors even further, but somehow I was made to understand that this kaleidoscope of sound, color, and chaos was nothing I need fear. And then there was the light. Two weeks shy of fading away forever in the backseat of a powder-blue Cadillac convertible, Hank Williams was suddenly spotlit and burning on center stage, the embodiment of a lone flaming star. Visions of a distant paradise bobbed in the wake of his brilliance. I'd have joined the light then and there were it not for the scent of hair tonic and Old Spice aftershave that tethered me to my father's shoulders.

The pulse of the music matched my beating heart perfectly, and I took comfort in this. And yet it's the memory of my father that holds in place the memory of seeing and feeling a Hank Williams performance.

My father idolized him, and reminding me I once saw "ole Hank" sing was something he never tired of. It was the part of his legacy he savored the most. Knowing he'd exposed his only son to the greatness in another man that he imagined in himself served to soften the hard fact that his own dreams would never materialize. Hank Williams *was* what my father wanted to be—a Grand Ole Opry singing star. Taking me to see him perform was his way of saying, *Look at me up there on that stage, son, that's who I really am*. This is the truest picture of my father that I own, though at times I strain to see it.

James Walter Crowell was born in 1923—the same year as his idol—to Iola Wilson of Cherry Corner, Kentucky, and Samuel Martin Crowell of McEwen, Tennessee. At the time of their oldest child's birth, the newlywed Crowells lived on the outskirts of Blytheville, Arkansas. Martin worked splitting railroad crossties, ten for a penny, but his official occupation was sharecrop farmer. After the crash of '29, Iola, Martin, and their four children found shelter in a canvas-covered sheep shed in the Blood River bottoms of Calloway County, Kentucky. Despite a nearly fatal bout with scarlet fever, my father subsisted, along with the rest of his family, on squirrel, rabbit, and the occasional plate of white-flour biscuits. In the peak years of the Great Depression it took Martin two full growing seasons to move his family from the sheep shed to a dirt-floor cabin on a nine-acre sharecrop tobacco farm. I once heard my father say, "I was born in nineteen and twenty-three, and I never slept on nothin' but straw till nineteen and forty-one, when Daddy took over Old Man Hoot Paxton's place down on the Tennessee border. It's a wonder I don't crow like a rooster."

By my mother's estimation, the Wilsons of Cherry Corner were the meanest, most racist white trash in all of western Kentucky. My great-grandfather, known as Lyin' Jim Wilson, was recognized as the unofficial mayor of Cherry Corner. When he died in 1960, late into his eighties, it was accepted as fact that he hadn't answered a direct question truthfully since his twelfth birthday and hadn't taken a bath since he accidentally fell in the Blood River in 1936.

Again according to my mother, Jim Wilson was even meaner than he was dishonest. His sexual preferences included daughters, sisters, granddaughters, neighbors' wives, and the odd farm animal. Lyin' Jim's notoriety wasn't so much a source of family shame as a line drawn in the sand: Step across at your own risk; we Wilsons are crazy as shit-house rats and would just as soon kill you as look at you.

The "Paw Jim" I remember was a baldheaded old coot with stubbly chin whiskers. Clothed in a filthy undershirt and Dee Cee overalls, he sat idly by the kitchen fireplace chewing a cud of tobacco. That he kept his arm down the front of his pants and grunted like a hog drew little notice in Iola's kitchen. She might have bopped him upside the head and barked, "Paw Jim, get yer meat hooks outta them drawers and let that damn ole pecker alone," but that clearly wasn't going to change his behavior. Once, when Iola smacked the back of his head, I saw him swallow a wad of chewing tobacco without even blinking.

Iola Crowell was her father's daughter, perverse and mean. On the subject of her oldest boy, J.W., she was a shameless braggart.

Proclaiming him her favorite, she made it known to anyone willing to listen that she didn't give two shits about her daughters, Nadine and Lurleen, or her youngest son, Red. Nevertheless, and for no good reason, she was fond of whacking my father across the side of his head whenever he passed within reach. When he'd ask her why she'd done it, her smug reply was always the same: "You needed it or else you wouldn't of dodged."

My grandmother excelled in four areas: beating her children, fighting with her husband, baking biscuits, and breaking wind, the latter being her greatest passion. She meditated on and honed the craft of farting, always striving for greater heights in artistic expression. As a composer of farts, Iola could have been likened to a backwoods Beethoven—sometimes bombastic and overdriven, sometimes light and whimsical, and a touch of the maniacal, at once blatant and subdued, was the hallmark of her best work.

As you might expect, she loved beans and served three or four kinds at every meal. Pinto beans, butter beans, navy beans, green beans, pork and beans, pole beans, jumping beans, it didn't matter. She referred to them all as forty-fours.

"Pass me the forty-fours, Martin."

"Which ones?"

"Why, all of 'em. You know that."

A gassed-up Iola required everyone present to admire her works great and small. Only my father had the courage to challenge her farting supremacy, which he did as an aside to his brother. "Shit, Red, cain't nobody get a poot in sideways 'round here when Momma gets 'em goin'."

Martin Crowell was a product of hard times and hard work. He was rail thin and had the largest pair of ears ever attached to a human head. Dee Cee overalls and a clean white shirt, the sleeves rolled up two turns, were the mainstay of his wardrobe. He kept a small round mirror on the mantel above the kitchen fireplace and rarely sat down to eat without combing his already perfectly groomed hair. My grandfather was a creature of small habits. I loved him, and so did my mother. My father kept a respectful distance.

Grandpa Crowell played old-time flailing banjo. The three songs from his repertoire I remember most vividly were "The Great California Earthquake," "Old Shep," and "Rabbit in the Graveyard." The ironic glint in the old man's eye when he sang about dogs jumping into rivers to save drowning boys was for me the distillation of musical joy and front-porch storytelling, and images of rabbits running across the freshly dug graves of the dearly departed kept me awake many nights.

Although he was sweet and shy and stubbornly quiet, under the influence of corn liquor Martin was nearly a match for Iola in pure meanness. But she had a killer instinct that he lacked, so when it came to familial dysfunction and domestic violence she had the edge. It's due to his physical strength alone—Iola outweighed him by a good forty-five pounds—that Martin was able to post a break-even record over the course of their long-running series of knock-down-drag-outs. Eventually, this classic rivalry mellowed into something resembling a draw.

Their oldest child loved school, and his aptitude for mathematics was a source of great schoolboy pride. His claim that he was once the undisputed math champion of Kentucky, though never validated or even explained, sat well with me. I was four and a half years old when I decided that if my father believed he possessed a near-genius faculty for math and "sinus"—his pronunciation of "science"—then so would I. For my amusement, he enjoyed staging acts of mathematical wizardry and, like a boy doing magic tricks, displayed the same ones over and over, all of them problems he'd shamelessly worked out a thousand times already. "Seven hundred and sixteen plus six hundred and five take away thirteen hundred and twenty-one leaves nought" thrilled me to no end, as did "Five tums sixty-two hundred divided by eight is thirty-eight hundred and seventy-five."

And so on. Thus my father allowed me to observe the Swiss-watch quality of his mind. He craved attention and preened after every ooh and aah he ever got.

The official cause of his death at age sixty-five was heart failure. This diagnosis was accurate; his heart did fail. Perhaps the brilliant cardiologist who made it was right to blame two packs a day for forty-six years and a serious bout with rheumatic fever, but I tend not to agree. Considering the delicate balance between the irrepressible spark propelling my father's lust for living and the brutal downside of his posturing, it's my opinion that a steady stream of disappointments, self-inflicted and otherwise, the first coming in 1934 when he was forced to leave school after seventh grade, did more to bring on his early death than all the nicotine, whiskey, and butter-soaked biscuits combined. Call it maudlin, manipulative, or simpleminded, but as I see it he died of a broken heart.

"I had to quit school and go to work," he said. "If I coulda got me an education I'd be a civil engineer over at Brown and Root right now." Alongside being a performing member of the Grand Ole Opry, the absolute pinnacle of success for my father would've been the words "Civil Engineer" capitalized on a college degree. Through hard work and commonsense experience, he was named superintendent at the Mid-Gulf Construction Company of Houston, and his level of expertise in the construction business made him equal to any civil engineer coming out of Texas A&M or the Rice Institute. But that was never good enough. The lack of a formal education and a degree was a source of constant shame that my father was never able to overcome.

The Great Depression had far-reaching effects on his life. Not only was it the main reason he had to quit school, it also instilled in him the notion that the number one priority in a man's life was keeping a steady job. And if it happened to be low-paying, common-labor drudgery that was subject to rainouts and unexpected shutdowns, "well, by God, those are the breaks."

Not going to Nashville to try to make it as a country singer was a by-product of this mind-set. Of course the argument could be made that if this were truly his destiny then nothing could've stopped him, and I believe that's true. This is where my father was both an enigma and savant. His passion for music was as insatiable as his need for attention, and he knew more songs than anyone I've ever met. His repertoire numbered literally in the hundreds, songs by Hank Williams, Jimmie Rodgers, Roy Acuff, Gid Tanner, the Louvin Brothers, Jim Reeves, Ernest Tubb, Johnny Horton, Eddy Arnold, Hank Snow, Harlan Howard, Dock Boggs, Bashful Brother Oswald, Mother Maybelle and the Carter Family, Grandpa Jones, Little Jimmy Dickens, Buck Owens, Woody Guthrie, Appalachian dead-baby songs, folk songs, cowboy ballads, Negro blues, gospel songs, talkin' songs, train songs, songs about cocaine and murder, jailhouses, froggies that went a-courtin', rosewood caskets, holes in the bottom of the sea, and love letters in the sand.

The Saturday night *Grand Ole Opry* on a neighbor's dry-cell radio, local barn dances, his own father's front-porch performances—that was the extent of his access to popular music. But lack of exposure to the outside world did nothing to hamper his ability to accrue words and music. He possessed an ability to absorb songs from the atmosphere. If he heard a song once, he knew it forever. Such was his gift.

My parents met at a Roy Acuff concert held in the Buchanan High School gymnasium in the fall of 1941. According to my mother, some ill-mannered farm boy had placed a grimy paw in the vicinity of no-man's-land. Worse yet, his slobbering advances were ruining her concentration on the show. In perhaps his first act of chivalry ever, my father came to Cauzette's rescue, challenging the boy to a wrestling match after the show.

With a showdown looming in his near future, the offender of my mother's virtue turned his attention to a consideration more important than the harassment of innocent girls: liquid courage. A challenge to his manhood warranted some serious drinking in order to ensure a victory come wrestling time, so the boy disappeared into the woods with a quart jar of homemade liquor.

Free to enjoy the show, my mother was faced with an even bigger distraction. "It was like nothin' else was in the world but your daddy," she told me. "I knew it right then and there he was the boy I was gonna marry. I went home and told Momma I was. I loved Roy Acuff, but I couldn't hear a word he was singin' after your daddy showed up. Your daddy was good-lookin', and he stood right up to that other boy. Turned out he didn't have to go wrassle after all. That other boy got so sot-drunk he was off pukin' in the woods when it come time to face the music. I got walked home that night by the sweetest boy in the world, and I ain't even thought about another man since."

Cauzette

In 1924, Buchanan, Tennessee, was little more than a primitive Christian outpost in the heart of west Tennessee farmland. Owing its lifeblood to a red-dirt crossroads a mile south of the Kentucky border, this sharecrop populace boasted the Shady Grove Baptist Church and Cemetery, a one-room schoolhouse, and a country store. But for a single gas pump in front of the latter, there was little to suggest that the twentieth century was nearing the end of its first quarter. My mother was born in June, the seventh of Solomon Taylor and Katie Lee Willoughby's eight children. Addie Cauzette arrived with the right side of her body partially paralyzed, the result—according to an old country doctor who didn't examine her until she was three—of a stroke suffered in her mother's womb. So from before birth, a pattern was set by which polio, acute dyslexia, epilepsy, the sudden death of an infant son, and a subsequent case of whacked-out nerves would join the lengthy list of maladies assaulting young Cauzette well before her twentieth birthday. In the seventy-four years and nearly four months marking her time on what she called "this crooked old Earth," my mother rarely drew a healthy breath. Still, to say that life wasn't fair for this awkwardly glib yet deeply religious woman would fail to take into account her towering instinct for survival. Thanks to this primal urge to thrive, she would leave this world at peace with the knowledge that physical existence was something for which she was born ill equipped. And I honor my mother by saying that it wasn't for lack of effort that an accommodation between her sensitive soul and the poorly fitting body she wore was so very hard to come by.

In an early snapshot, taken when she was eleven, a painfully shy girl in a hand-me-down cotton farm dress stares deadpan into the camera lens. A closer look reveals her deepest inclination, that she'd rather her back were turned to the unknown photographer.

It would be untrue to say that my mother didn't possess the fetching qualities of an attractive young woman. A picture taken on her wedding day shows a fresh-faced girl of eighteen in full but precarious bloom. A splurge of lipstick overrides the reticent clasp of a near smile, one better suited to a distant cousin of the Mona Lisa than a bride-to-be. Then there's the well-proportioned nose and high forehead framed by a brown tumble of curls and the almost-pointed Willoughby chin that sets off her soft, sensual eyes, the message behind them whispering that she's allowing herself a flight of girlish fancy while knowing it offers no real solution to being trapped in this particular body.

Double dyslexia and every learning disability yet to be diagnosed in the 1930s could not keep my mother from flourishing in Buchanan's one-room country school. "I like to never learned to read and write," she told me more than once in the daydreamy way she had of conjuring wisps of childhood joys. "But I can tell you this: If ever there was anybody born to go to school, it was me. If I close my eyes right now, I'm right back at that wooden desk listenin' to Mr. Garland talk about England and Abraham Lincoln and all kind of facts and figures that made pictures in my mind. Even with my right foot draggin,' I didn't mind walkin' them five miles back and forth, honey . . . and your grandma knew it."

Because of her abilities and disabilities, my mother was chosen in the summer of 1936 to attend a state-funded girls' school in Nashville and invited to enroll in the fall, tuition paid in full. Wanting desperately to go, she pleaded with her parents for weeks on end to allow her this one opportunity to make something of herself. Her pleas came to naught. The cruel injustice of her having to forgo education to work on a succession of failed sharecrop farms was the beginning of the long, slow dimming of my mother's natural light.

It wasn't her father who refused. Since she was of little use to him around the farm, "Sol T" (as folks called him) didn't care if she went off to boarding school or not, and having one less mouth to feed was a plus. It was Katie who barred the door. Her flimsy excuse—that no one at the school could take care of my mother's special needs—was belied by the glaring truth that she needed her daughter at home to deal with her husband.

It is an unfortunate truth that Cauzette was the only Willoughby who could reason with her father when he was raging drunk. She paid a high price for the distinction and mourned the loss late into her life. "They didn't need me on that farm," she told me a few weeks before she died. "Momma was too afraid to let me go." Like my father, she never fully recovered from the heartbreak of being denied her one chance to be somebody.

My grandfather was as highly motivated at drinking as he was disinterested in sharecropping. His preference for binges over hard work was renowned. Some said Sol T came by his ne'er-do-well status honestly, for his great-grandfather had drunk and gambled away one of the largest single-family landholdings in western Tennessee, including thousands of acres bought later by the TVA at a premium price in order to dam the Tennessee River and create Kentucky Lake. That Sol T beat his wife and ruled his household with drunken turbulence was a communally known fact. There were the odd sober intervals in which he managed to perform as deacon of the Shady Grove Baptist Church like the upstanding pillar of the community that everyone knew he wasn't. His skills as an old-time, do-re-mi choir leader rivaled his reputation as a sot. In the vernacular of this sharecrop culture, it was often said of him that "if he ain't off somewhere drunk, when it comes to leadin' the sangin' over at the church house, you cain't hardly beat Taylor Willoughby."

Meanwhile, Katie and the kids worked the farm.

The spring planting of 1942 on the sixteen-acre blemish the Willoughby clan had taken over the previous November was made especially insane when my grandfather disappeared on one of his corn-liquor binges. Under the best of circumstances, with windows of opportunity prone to snapping closed like coffin lids, getting a crop in the ground hinged on the concerted effort of every available body, young and old. If any farmhand alive in the mid-twentieth century didn't know this or, worse, didn't care, he was probably in prison. Or, like Sol T, off somewhere drunk.

Kenneth and Raymond, my mother's older brothers, were particularly put out by their deadbeat father, and their vow to whip the "son of a bitch's ass" if and when he made it home foretold serious trouble. With the nationwide call to war fanning the fires of more noble pursuits on the horizon—joining the Air Force foremost among those—busting sod for their no-account daddy sat about as well with them as the Japanese bombing Pearl Harbor. But running away to enlist was something neither boy could do in good faith, knowing that Sol T would rather see the farm go to hell than wind his pocket watch.

My grandfather turned up the fifth day of planting, threw himself onto a straw mattress bed, and slept for thirty-two hours straight and, upon waking, demanded that my grandmother "get the hell in the kitchen and fix [him] something to eat." A woman of exceptional kindness, despite her ruining my mother's dreams of education, she responded, "Why, Taylor, where in the world have you been? We been bustin' our backs sowin' the tobacco, and you off Lord knows where."

"I reckon it ain't none of your goddamn business or anybody else's where I been."

This booming belligerence served notice to his children that Sol T was awake and in the throes of a bad hangover, and they knew only too well the shadings of his hateful disposition. Kenneth, Raymond, and Cauzette dashed into action, intending to throw their bodies into the path of the ham-fisted fury they knew was about to be aimed at their mother. He struck with the lightning reflex of a coiled rattlesnake, my mother remembered, separating Katie from one of her few remaining teeth. And then, in the kitchen of what could loosely be called his own home, Sol T proceeded to get the hell beat out of him by his two oldest sons.

My uncles attacked like kamikazes, their father swatting back at them in teetering self-defense. My mother's death grip on one leg caused him to lurch around the room like the drunkard he'd so recently been, her shrill "Stop it, Poppa, stop it!" adding a touch of hysteria to the madness. In less than sixty seconds, this family tussle breezed past crazed frenzy into sheer insanity when my grandfather came within arm's length of the double-barreled 12-gauge hanging fully loaded above the kitchen fireplace. Sol T grabbed it, cocked one of the rabbit-ear hammers, pointed it at Kenneth's head, and pulled the trigger. A split second before the gun fired, Raymond threw a forearm against the underside of its barrel, sending a full load of double-aught buckshot flying past his brother's head. Considering that it blew a hole in the wall the size of a watermelon, Uncle Kenneth got off lightly with a lifelong ringing in his left ear.

The impact of the blast shocked my grandfather back to his senses. He dropped both the shotgun and his guard, disbelieving. When he did, Kenneth buried the blade of his Barlow knife in the old man's chest. But he missed his target, the steel entering a few inches above and to the left of what might've been called his father's heart.

Something inside my mother snapped. The shotgun blast sent the essence of her nonphysical self literally flying across the room, where from a vantage point normally reserved for ghosts she watched her oldest brother stab their father in a blind rage of retaliation, thus making her neurological meltdown complete. Her out-of-body experience was brought to an abrupt conclusion when she saw the knife slice through his tobacco-stained nightshirt. "Why, son," she would marvel when relating this story for the umpteenth time, "it was like my spirit just made a beeline back into my body. It made the loudest *thwack* you ever heard. After that, everything went blank. That was when I had my first convulsion."

Twenty-eight years of the most violent epileptic seizures imaginable was the price my mother paid for being the one person in her family who could handle this drunken beast. Those of us who helped her shoulder the burden of his excesses didn't get off cheap either.

Grandma Willoughby kept the lead watch on my mother's condition until she died in 1961. That's when I inherited her rudimentary epilepsy first-aid kit: an old rag for the grinding of her teeth and a spoon to keep her from swallowing her tongue as she writhed on the floor.

My father had a sixth sense when it came to my mother's epilepsy, and when one of her spells came on he had a knack for being gone. In fact, his absence was the main precondition for her convulsions. As far back as I can remember, she never once had a seizure in his presence. Epilepsy was the pink elephant in their married life as long as my grandmother and I were around to keep it covered up.

When I began fourth grade, my mother landed a job as a janitor at Jacinto City Elementary School. To bolster her self-esteem, "fourth-grade custodian" is how, when asked, she framed her lowly position. In her mind, "custodian" sounded a lot better than "janitor" and also camouflaged that she was squarely, shamefully, in the fifty-cents-an-hour wage bracket. I wasn't happy about her new job no matter what she called it, since it brought with it the prospect of her having fits right there at my school.

It's hard to escape unwanted attention when this scene unfolds: Mr. Wallace, the principal, or perhaps another teacher knocks discreetly on Mrs. Smith's classroom door and asks if I might be excused from class. This means my mother's on the floor somewhere, in the hallways or the janitor's closet, contorting violently, foaming at the mouth and grinding her teeth. And feeling thirty-one pairs of nine-year-old eyes burning holes in your back as you leave the room is nothing when compared to walking back into class and facing those stares head-on.

In this situation, adults were useless. They acted as if she were a dog with rabies and, fearing her bite was infectious, kept a prudent distance. Mr. Wallace gave me the impression that a man in his position couldn't risk getting down on his knees because it might wrinkle the creases on his gray wool suit pants; to deal with an epileptic in the clutches of a grand mal seizure, you might, in fact, have to loosen your tie and maybe even roll up your sleeves. The others kept back respectfully, like friends of friends at a family wake. That made wading through the garbage cans and dust mops to fish my mother's tongue from halfway down her throat exclusively my responsibility.

Keeping her alive was something I became good at. The time came, however, when I just couldn't do it anymore. On an otherwise normal day in 1970, unloading thirteen years of frustration, I told her: "I've had enough of your fucking convulsions. As far as I'm concerned, you can die during the next one. I'm through taking care of you." This venting actually worked. In the last twenty-eight years of her life, my mother had only two minor seizures.

Anyway, as the story goes, my grandfather hardly bled a drop from his stab wound, nor did he go to a doctor. Since he'd been guzzling corn liquor for four days, no doubt his blood carried the alcoholic equivalent of ten tetanus shots. Supposedly, my grandmother kindly smeared axle grease on the wound and then he stomped off to get drunk for another two or three days. My mother maintained that he never once acknowledged the incident. Judging by his nonchalance, nearly blowing his son's head off and then having that same son come even closer to killing him were practically everyday occurrences.

The tobacco and corn did get planted that year, thanks to Grandma and the kids. When Kenneth finished his work that season he left the farm, never to return. Rejected by the Air Force for medical reasons, he found a factory job in Independence, Missouri, that was short-lived because he spent four years there hospitalized with a rare heart-and-lung ailment. He was sickly for the rest of his life. And for me, frail health and a kindly demeanor define his character. I can easily imagine his brothers Porter and Raymond getting in a knife fight with their father, but to frame Kenneth in such a violent picture has always seemed troubling to me.

Various effects lingered from this incident in the spring of 1942: my mother's spells and, if less conspicuous, my uncle's heart troubles. Strangely, the chill between my grandfather and his sons wasn't at all obvious, and but for my mother's incessant telling and retelling of her family's darkest secrets, I might never have sensed how bitter their acrimony actually was. Still, given what I knew, in the presence of Sol T and my uncles I made it my business to locate every unblocked exit. With that bunch you just never knew when all hell would break loose.

Gone to Texas

J.W. and Cauzette were married September 6, 1942, in Evansville, Indiana, where a marriage license could be obtained and the wedding performed in less than an hour. She was eighteen and in love; he was nineteen and in a hurry. After Sol T allowed five dollars for expenses and my father kicked in the few dollars he'd made splitting railroad ties, their justice-of-the-peace wedding came off without a hitch. "I got myself a dress and shoes and had a dollar and a quarter left over," my mother once boasted of her trousseau. "Your daddy wore a suit he borrowed from one of the Starks boys that didn't fit him, but I didn't care. I thought he was the handsomest boy I'd ever seen."

Iola and my mother's brother-in-law, Westley Smith, made the trip to the altar with them. Westley, the only member of the extended family who owned an automobile, provided the transportation, and Iola graced the wedding party with her particular brand of perverse succor. Westley's own marriage to my mother's older sister was as short-lived as it was nasty. The notion that he was a man destined for higher rungs on the economic ladder, however, lingered long after their divorce, this to my least-favorite aunt's chagrin. Given the family lore, I have no trouble imagining that he added a touch of class to my parents' shoestring wedding. Iola was something else altogether.

"She made my life a livin' hell," my mother would say when recounting the early days of her marriage. "She hated me for takin' her favorite boy. She told me right in front of your daddy's face, I might get him for a while but she'd have him back before I knew it."

It was under these conditions that she moved with her new husband into her in-laws' dirt-floor farmhouse. "If it hadn't been for Martin Crowell treatin' me like I was something besides a farm animal, I'da never made it."

My mother's epileptic seizures further complicated her new life, and she lived in terror of what would happen if she were stricken in Iola's presence. Yet on this matter she was given a reprieve, less than two weeks into their marriage, when my father fell sick with rheumatic fever.

"It was the first time I had my husband to myself," she said. "Iola didn't want nothin' to do with him while he was sick. I never understood that. But I was glad she didn't. He was so bad off. I took care of him day and night. His poor balls swelled up till we thought they was gonna bust open. They hurt him real bad. He run a temperature round the clock. When he started gettin' a little better, we got him some crutches and started goin' off by ourselves in the woods. It was some of the best times I ever had with your daddy. We talked and talked back then. He was so sick and handsome, and he was such a sweet boy once you got him away from Iola. I was so in love with him I coulda just died. I didn't realize it till a long time later, but I didn't have a single one of my spells while he was sick. I didn't have time to. The next one I did have like to've killed me."

After my father had recovered enough strength to go back to work on the farm, my mother's greatest fear was made real: an attack with only Iola present to care for her. " 'Send for Momma' is what I kept tellin' her when I felt it comin' on," she explained, "but she just kept lookin' at me like I was a knot on a log. She ran and fetched your daddy is what she did." When they returned, my mother was lying semiconscious on the kitchen floor, the worst of the convulsions having passed. By her estimation, it was the closest he ever came to witnessing firsthand the hideousness of her affliction.

Two days later, Cauzette was back living with her mother and father, an arrangement that lasted into the summer of 1943. My father worked Monday through mid-Saturday on his father's farm, then would ride a mule fifteen miles to spend Saturday night and all of Sunday with my mother. At three-thirty on Monday morning, he'd get up in order to be back at work by daybreak.

In August the couple went in search of a new life. First stop: a one-room log cabin near Paris, Tennessee. My father found work as a butcher's apprentice, and by late fall they were living in a board-inghouse in Murray, Kentucky, where he was on the evening shift at the Tappan stove factory.

The previous fall and winter, my mother had experienced two failed pregnancies. "I couldn't seem to carry a baby no more than fifteen minutes," she told me. "And your daddy swore up and down I was losin' 'em on purpose." But she did finally manage to complete a full-term pregnancy, and Tex Edward was born on January 27, 1944. He died thirty-seven hours later.

Staring into some vacant yet familiar dreamscape, where the sharp pain of thirteen miscarriages is softened by visions of a heavenly playground for lost children, my mother, sifting through fractured images that documented her baby's all too brief passage through this world, introduced me to my brother time and again. "Oh, he was beautiful, Rodney. He had a full head of curly black hair and the bluest eyes you ever seen. While I only got to hold him for a minute or two, I can still feel him to this day. They had me knocked out most of the time, but I could hear him cryin' off in the next room. They said I almost died, too, and for a long time I wished I had. They never brought him back and nobody told me nothin'."

My parents dutifully accepted no explanation as the official cause of their baby's death. Years later, my mother admitted that at the time she'd never even heard of any such thing as a valid death certificate. So Tex Edward was buried in the Shady Grove Cemetery, and for fifty-three years the grave site was marked with a single red brick.

As a boy, I accepted the vagueness surrounding my brother's death much as we recognize poetic license as an accepted contrivance in the shaping of family myth, and I suspended my disbelief. It was as if I were heir to some genetic predisposition toward unworthiness. Permission to ask about the medical particulars might have been granted to other people, but for a long time, like my parents, I assumed I wasn't good enough to know.

The birth of my daughters shattered this delusion, and at my instigation my parents found themselves in a series of heated confrontations on the subject of Tex Edward's death. Having begun to view the fog hovering over his nearly unmarked grave as a personal affront, I insisted on knowing what actually killed him. But my mother had no idea what had happened, or why, and showed no interest in wanting to. My father simply refused to acknowledge my questions.

Forty years after my brother's death, frustration finally got the better of me.

"Goddamnit, don't you want to know what the fuck happened? Don't you think you deserve an explanation for the loss of your child? I sure as hell do."

My mother fixed me evenly with her gaze and voice. "Rodney J. Crowell," she said—apparently forgetting my profanity-laced vow to let her die before I'd nurse her through one more spell—"you've never talked to me like that in your life, and I'm not about to let you start now. Do you hear me?"

"Yes, ma'am, I hear you. I'm sorry," I said, surprised by my own vitriol. "I meant no disrespect, but—"

"Yes, son, I do want to know," my father volunteered unexpectedly, his tone a sure sign that these words came at no small price. "They ain't been many days gone by that I didn't wish to God I knew why. He was my boy, just like you . . . and I lost him. At the time my heart couldn't bear knowing why, and neither could your momma's. I went ahead and buried him but didn't want to know why. You go on and find out for yourself, if that's what you need to do. I'll be knowing it soon enough."

Not long after losing their son, my parents moved into a one-room apartment over a shoe-repair shop in Clarksville, Tennessee. My father found a job at Fort Campbell, but civilian work on a military base was a humiliating experience. A prideful young man, he felt compelled to explain to the soldiers he met that rheumatic fever had rendered him medically ineligible for military service. "I didn't want folks thinkin' I was afraid to be over there fightin' " is how he described his wartime shame. That job lasted five months.

Next came a six-month stint on a Detroit auto-assembly line. Throughout their time in Clarksville and Detroit, my mother endured a particularly agonizing period of epilepsy, and my father perfected his knack for being elsewhere when her seizures struck. "I had most of my convulsions alone," she said, "or with people I didn't even know."

Just before Christmas in 1944, my parents took a Greyhound bus back to Murray, Kentucky. With her marriage in a nearly hopeless state of disrepair, moving her few belongings into a boardinghouse similar to the one where she'd carried her lost child was devastating. Living more or less alone with the sorrow of the past two years and with no place to go but down, she hit bottom, *hard*.

"My nerves just went out on me," she explained decades later. "I didn't really wanta die, but I figured your daddy mighta been relieved if I did."

While my parents were living in Clarksville, my mother's father had quit sharecropping for good and moved with my grandmother to Houston. There he found the job market as much to his liking as the duplex apartment they rented on Avenue P was to his wife's.

When word reached them that my mother was languishing in William Mason Memorial Hospital's psychiatric ward, showing little interest in recovering from an intentional phenobarbital overdose, my grandfather took the next train to Memphis, where he caught the bus to Murray. A day later, father and daughter boarded a train in Memphis that would finally deliver her from this hell on earth she swore she'd never go back to as long as she lived.

In the summer of 1945, my father hitchhiked to Houston and showed up at Sol T and Katie's door with his suitcase and a Gibson guitar. Reconciliations were "nearly" instantaneous. When I say nearly, I mean this: Thirty-four months after the wedding, the father of the bride laid down the law about how he expected the groom to treat his daughter. Their showdown consisted of splitting a six-pack of beer and arguing about who made the better automobile, Packard or Plymouth. Neither of them owned a car.

As always, my father didn't take long to find a job. With what he earned delivering ice, the newly reunited couple set up housekeeping in the vacant duplex adjacent to my grandparents'—the beginning of a five-year period when my mother had the only man she would ever love and the one person willing and able to nurse her through the growing stream of epileptic episodes literally under the same roof.

And between her seventh and eighth miscarriages, my mother managed another full-term pregnancy. I was born in August of 1950. Two months later, my parents moved half a block east on Avenue P into the little shotgun shack where my version of this story began on New Year's Eve of 1955.

PART TWO

Altar Falters and Prayer Witches

It is a Sunday morning in the summer of 1955, and my mother's literally dragging me to the Emmanuel Temple Pentecostal church services. She's singing "What a Friend We Have in Jesus," and I'm spewing bile about my feet, still hurting from last week's trek. Hating these holy-rolling, speaking-in-unknown-tongues free-for-alls she loves so well, I do my best to make the trip more miserable than it already is. It's a testament to her faith in an angry and kind and vengeful and loving God that she sees this two-mile slog with her son kicking and screaming as a small price to pay for salvation. Shouting, crying, dancing in the aisles, writhing on the floor, and bowing at the feet of charismatic evangelists, anything short of snake handling—it's all a tonic for her troubled soul. We're almost always on foot and it might be raining, but if the Emmanuel Temple's doors are open, she'll be there, and so will I. I'm learning to take it in stride.

In contrast to the knockoff Craftsman and raised-clapboard houses lining Wayside Drive, the Emmanuel Temple stands as the East End's most exotic architectural structure. A grand, green-carpeted stairway leads from the sidewalk to its second-floor portico entrance. Behind its four arched double doorways and mock–Italian Renaissance façade, the temple boasts alternating pastors, Brother Modest and Brother Pemberton, locked in a high-stakes game of spiritual one-upmanship. Each lays down an Old Testament gauntlet no God-fearing member of the congregation will dare trespass for fear of turning into a pillar of salt.

My mother's criteria for a church worthy of regular attendance are fairly basic. The congregants and preachers must refer to themselves as "Brother" or "Sister," followed by their surname, identifying one another as members of the same spiritual family. The church must be within forty blocks of our house, that is, within walking distance. And, most important, the preacher must be inspirational. My mother has this to say about the only subject outside of raising me in which she's at all decisive: "A preacher who ain't on fire for the Lord ain't no 'count."

Brother Modest has Dean Martin's smoothness and a wavy head of hair, as black and shiny as his shoes. He likes his shirts starched stiff and his neckties knotted tight. His suits, though off the rack, have a tailored quality that complements his buttery voice and sanctified diction. He seduces his flock of sinners with nuance and innuendo, his style equal parts politician, lounge singer, and used-car salesman. One by one, these poor souls empty their already virtually empty pockets into the offering plate before heading down front to press their noses against his gleaming footwear.

Accepting nothing short of total obedience, Brother Modest makes it known that he alone can dispense forgiveness on behalf of the Supreme Being. My mother and I march down front and fall to our knees, she with her eyes closed, enraptured, mumbling prayers punctuated by "Thank you, Jesus," and me fidgeting to keep my eyes from popping open and giving me away as the heathen I prefer to be.

Interpreting unknown tongues and deciphering the messages hidden within is Brother Modest's special talent. I don't understand his references to Armageddon and Judgment Day looming like a Nazi border crossing around the next bend in the road, but sometimes I do enjoy the ensemble performances.

As if on cue, Sister Worthan or Kunkle or Crowell breaks out in spasms of heavenly nonsense, bringing Brother Modest vaulting from behind the pulpit. With one hand waving high in the air—a kind of spiritual lightning rod—he hovers over God's chosen vessel and divines for his congregation the encoded reprimand concealed in such commentary as "Yea toma con kewly con rishney shalla lama cundullo shondalay."

My mother has a schoolgirl crush on Brother Modest, whose unattainable charm and lofty posturing are irresistible to a farm girl with low self-esteem. I myself prefer Brother Pemberton's rockabilly version of hellfire and damnation to his superior and slick approach.

Cut from the Jerry Lee Lewis mold, Brother Pemberton gives the impression that he might burst into flames at any moment. With his greasy pompadour spilling down over his eyes, his necktie flying, his shirt hanging halfway out of his pants, his face turned to the heavens like a satellite dish awaiting God's direct signals, which once received will be spat at the congregation like bullets from a Gatling gun, Brother Pemberton in full flight is a sight to behold.

Attacking the congregants with direct accusation is his strong suit, and it's his willingness to include himself in what he calls "this worthless heap of flesh with the nerve to call itself Christian" that makes his full-frontal assaults so effective. "We might be the sorriest bunch of sinners ever to walk through church-house doors," he'd say (his favorite assessment of his Sunday morning assemblage), "but the thing that sets us apart from them watered-down institutions over yonder in River Oaks and Sharpstown is we got us a direct feed to the salvation hotline."

Early in his sermons, Brother Pemberton implies he isn't sure if he has enough pull with the Man Upstairs to keep us all from roasting in hell. This prepares the stage for his all-important battle for our salvation, a struggle from which, God willing, he will emerge scarred but victorious. He begins his petition on our behalf with a crack in his voice that matches the world-weariness in his soul. "Lord God sitting right now on Your heavenly throne, I come before You with a heart so burdened I can hardly bring myself to speak Thy holy name." When it comes to making a voice sound like teardrops, there's no one in Brother Pemberton's league. "Lord God, You see us down here like lost sheep following in the footsteps of the one who would lead us straight through the gates of hell into everlasting servitude: Satan! Yes, Lord, Satan, the Prince of Darkness. I say unto You this very day, the Devil is a liar and will not steal this flock as long as I have air to breathe and life in my body."

To italicize the dire circumstances we have allowed to befall us, and to bolster Brother Pemberton's resolve to continue negotiations on our behalf, Sister Kunkle and my mother float the occasional "Forgive us, Lord" and "Help us, Jesus" from behind paper fans bearing a portrait of the long-suffering, blue-eyed Galilean who died all those years ago so that we could get away with what we now stand accused of.

"It was Thine own Son who gave us Your word, Lord God, that, if we but knock, the door will open, and if we but seek, we shall find." At this point in his performance Brother Pemberton tends to rely on stock biblical rhetoric, but I don't mind. He's a strong closer and needs the filler to prolong the precariousness of our situation and set up his big finish. "In Ezekiel, chapter thirty-seven, verse twenty-three, You said: 'Neither shall they defile themselves any more with their idols, nor with their detestable things, nor with any of their transgressions: but I will save them out of all their dwellingplaces, wherein they have sinned, and will cleanse them: so shall they be my people, and I will be their God.' "

He pauses, and the congregation nods in recognition that two important questions have just been answered: Yes, he knows his scriptures; and no, it's not just some chump off the street who's conducting these high-level talks with the Creator of the Universe.

"You see before You this morning a little church full of lost sheep, Lord God. We are knocking on the door of Your forgiveness, seeking the answer to this question: Are we too late in asking that in Your name we be spared from becoming the instruments of Satan's ill will?" This part confuses the hell out of me, since it was my understanding that we'd already been signed up and were playing first string on the Devil's team. "It is by Thy grace alone that we will be allowed back into the garden of everlasting light, nevermore to wander in darkness." "Amen's" pop up here and there, sure signs of solidarity in the pews, every last sinner supporting the preacher's proposal for our rehabilitation.

When he feels the flock is his to do with what he will, Brother Pemberton rewards our sheepishness with one of his world-class altar falters. Depending on the severity of our transgressions, there are two basic variations. Leaning against the podium while fluttering his eyelids is the go-to falter for mid- to upper-level transgressions, and asthmatic gasps from as far away as the back row—and it's a known fact that my mother would rather take rabies shots than be caught sitting there—confirm its effects on the congregation. But whenever truly *rampant* iniquity looms, he slumps against the organ with his eyes rolled back in their sockets and tears at his shirt collar and necktie in nearly suffocating panic, and this never fails to bring a stunned silence to the Emmanuel Temple.

Much of Brother Pemberton's success in the salvation business is based on the principle that when a church full of reprobates is reeling from the effects of a shared hallucination, there will be silence in the pews. And when there's silence in the pews, there are sheep to be led. His illusionist's skill is so finely honed that with a simple shudder or twitch he can convince an entire congregation that it has just witnessed his soul take wing and fly from the shell of his weary body. Milling around in the lobby after church, I've heard grown men and women claim to have seen gold, white, and silvery-blue light streaming out of the top of Brother Pemberton's head. One woman saw seven angels arrive to assist in his untimely departure. Another swore the hand of God reached down through the ceiling to take him on home.

Despite having seen Brother Pemberton's altar falters performed perhaps twenty-five times, I still have no idea how a packed audience can go fifteen minutes without drawing a breath. Although I prefer the subtlety of his subliminal sketches to his broad, stage-two brushstrokes, my appreciation of the showmanship involved in shocking sinners senseless is complete. Creating a life-and-death situation out of something as mundane as lying about your age isn't easily done; it takes energy, dedication, vision, and will. If an evangelistic hall of fame exists, James Pemberton should be voted in on the inspired audacity of this act alone. I'm a total fan.

Then, before the altar falter can claim its victim, Sister Conn races from the front row, her arms outstretched, as if to snatch the preacher from the clutches of the angel of death. But with the same shrug of the shoulder he used the week before last, she's sent skulking back to the pews, a wilted symbol of collective shame. (Why she volunteers for this humiliation always puzzles me.)

Whether he's turning his back to us or on us is open to interpretation. We know our boneheaded refusal to walk the straight and narrow has brought calamity on our fearless leader, and being left to stew in the juices of our own demise suggests that on this occasion Brother Pemberton might *not* hurl a Hail Mary that saves our bacon just as time runs out. We also know that when you're facing an eternity of roasting like a marshmallow in the bonfires of hell, it's not a good idea to infuriate your lead defense counsel; so it doesn't bode well that this Sunday's written prayer requests focus on gambling debts, washing-machine repair, new cars, and tawdry love triangles. What we don't know is how long he'll be lost in limbo or even if, in fact, he'll ever make it back to finish arguing our case in the Lord God's high court.

Besides meditating on the relative state of our disrepair, the other activity sanctioned by Brother Pemberton during "the silence" is the flurry of paper Jesus fans. This is a good idea. Redistributing the heat of a summer Sunday morning gives us a preview of what hell will be like if he's unsuccessful in getting the charges against us dropped. Aside from a "Thank you, Jesus" or two, the pews remain as quiet as a morgue.

But considering the current state of our affairs, thanking Jesus just now strikes me as presumptuous. As to whether or not we're all going to hell, it's my understanding the votes aren't all in, so the possibility of being forgiven for our sins in advance is cause for serious head-scratching. Comforting though it might seem, if indeed we've already been forgiven, why put us through the wringer every Sunday morning?

Though it appears that Brother Pemberton might already have crossed over to the Promised Land, he still has his finger on the pulse of his congregation and knows exactly when the last holdouts are ready to accept a Pentecostal plea bargain. In the stillness of this deathwatch, ninety-one panic attacks rage in silence, and unauthorized prayers rise toward the heavens like helium balloons: *Please, God, don't let this soldier of salvation fall on the rusty sword of our sins. I promise I won't cuss, lie, cheat, steal, drink beer or whiskey, smoke cigarettes, take Thy name in vain, drive fast, covet my neighbor's wife, bear false witness, you name it, I'll never do it again. . . . Please, just let Brother Pemberton live.* Quarters destined for the offering plate become dollar bills. Old men and children who have come to the service with no intention of kneeling at the altar and accepting Jesus Christ as their personal savior are now honor-bound to bow at the foot of the Old Rugged Cross. Men my father's age, whose wives have dragged them as many blocks as my mother has hauled me, now droop in red-handed resignation. Come Wednesday night, sporting dress shirts and clean shaves, they'll be parked near the front row, three hours away from firing up their next Lucky Strike.

Something stirs the eerie calm, identifying itself quietly, distantly, like the rustling of leaves or some faraway freight train at three a.m.

The flutter of Brother Pemberton's eyelids sends ripples across the room. Signs of life emerge from the pulpit, slowly at first, then gaining in strength, speed, and resolve. The faithless gasp and reverse their field now that hope glimmers guardedly in the Emmanuel Temple. Sighs of relief reach the back row. Like Noah's dove, our faithful petitioner has returned alive, olive branch in hand, to confirm there is air to be breathed, light to be seen, souls to be saved, a Devil to rebuke, and woods to be gotten out of. Damn the doomsday doldrums, change is in the air. The Grim Reaper beats an empty-handed retreat, and Brother Pemberton lives to carry on the fight.

The handkerchief pulled from the breast pocket of his coat symbolizes not the white flag of surrender but one last lap to victory. The mop of his brow, the tuck of his shirt, and the straightening of his tie are bold gestures of righteous supremacy. The slide of his handkerchief into his hip pocket demands that we arise and listen up, as further instructions are forthcoming.

"I have been given a vision," he thunders, his voice filling the church with a godlike gravity. "God has spoken to me. His words were like the music of a golden harp. The light of His love was blinding, yet I could see the hem of His garment of the finest silk. He said this unto me: 'My son, all is not lost. The time has not yet come for you to die. Return and lead your flock back onto the path of righteousness. Do this in my name, and thy flock shall return to the eternal peace of my fold.' "

I have to bite my tongue to keep from yelling out: *Did God really say that?*

"The way has been shown to me by the King of Kings, brothers and sisters. You must go forth into the streets as witnesses. Testify to all whom you meet of the miracle you have witnessed this very day. Testify how the Savior gave life back to this broken body that only minutes ago lay shipwrecked on Satan's perilous shoreline. Do this and know you are forgiven. Do this and reclaim your promised place in the sweet ever after."

Hot dog, we got off with another warning ticket. Shoot, yeah, we'll go out and accost bankers and winos alike. How hard can it be? All it takes is audacity and the willingness to annoy. People need to know what kind of deal we've got going on over here at the Emmanuel Temple. Sin like the dickens from Thursday through Saturday, ride out the Wednesday evening and Sunday morning performances, drop half a buck in the offering plate, and give a good review on the street, then all charges are dropped. Three Hail Marys and two Our Fathers require less effort, but the showmanship leaves so much to be desired.

As reward for service above and beyond the call of duty, the newly revived congregation gives Brother Pemberton a kneeling ovation. The organ player and ragtag choir roll into a modified version of the old hymn "Softly and Tenderly," and we all join in.

> *Softly and tenderly Jesus is calling,*
> *calling for you and for me;*
> *see, on the portals He's waiting and watching,*
> *watching for you and for me.*
>
> *Come home, come home;*
> *ye who are weary, come home . . .*

Brother Pemberton can't sing, alas, practically strangling these sweet old words. It sounds as if his heart alone is forcing them through the deflated balloon of his vocal cords. I'm constantly amazed by the difference between his singing, akin to "Turkey in the Straw," and his speaking, more like "Great Balls of Fire." An image forever burned in my memory is of Brother Pemberton standing tall at the altar, Bible in hand, nodding and smiling approvingly as his flock of lost sheep mosey forth one and two and three at a time to kneel down and receive a big dollop of spiritual liniment to rub on the aches and pains of the morning's long ordeal, and all the while he's butchering the beautiful hymn "Just as I Am, Without One Plea."

With the service's success fresh in everyone's mind, Brother Pemberton says a closing prayer and makes his way to the exit, where he'll accept congratulations on another stellar performance as his exhausted audience spills out into the blinding light of a summer afternoon.

Though disheveled and preposterous, his sermons were nonetheless inspired and, for a five-year-old boy, even fun. When the chips were down and my family was far behind on the scoreboard of life, my money (not that I had any) was on Brother Pemberton to pull the white rabbit of salvation out of the Devil's top hat. Or thin air.

Meanwhile, Brother Modest's style gave you the impression that polished insincerity was the hallmark of God's inner circle, and much of the congregation preferred his chilly aloofness. For some he was also a symbol of hope, since he was as close to the middle rungs of the economic ladder as most Emmanuel Temple regulars were likely to come.

Brother Pemberton, on the other hand, seemed like somebody who'd been passed over for promotion, an underdog struggling against the evils of Beelzebub more for God's amusement than his own satisfaction. This made him just another underpaid worker, like everybody else. Simply put, the former appeared to make more money saving souls than the latter.

Certainly the church elders deemed Brother Modest the better bet to lead them to the Promised Land.

One Sunday, toward the end of Brother Pemberton's tenure as copastor, my mother and I were kneeling at the altar with our heads bowed; she piously, gratefully, sibilantly thanking Jesus for one thing or another. Bored to distraction, I snuck a look at who was kneeling beside me, and my eyes fell on a pair of brown and white, pointy-toed, bebop loafers. I stared at them with the kind of admiration I now reserve for Tom Waits and Mother Teresa, then took in a pleated pant leg and the bottom of a gaudy green plaid sport coat, my gaze traveling upward until I was staring directly into eyes that closely matched the brown and white of those two-toned shoes. Caught red-handed, my mind adrift and unrepentant, I braced myself for the inevitable, because surely a gaffe of this magnitude would provoke the wrath of God. Then Brother Pemberton did something that under the circumstances was the last thing I ever would've expected. He winked at me. With one bat of an eyelash, that poor man's Billy Graham let me in on the secret of a lifetime: He, too, was bored.

Now and then, in waking dreams, I find myself kneeling at the altar of the Emmanuel Temple. In my less cynical moments, I realize that God once spoke to me directly through an old-school, hellfire-and-brimstone preacher. In the wink of an eye, I saw a compassionate, tolerant, and nonjudgmental God of love and great humor. My own faith was planted as a seed that morning, and there are days its fruit sustains me still.

The move to Jacinto City brought my mother's churchgoing to an unceremonious halt. One day she was washed in the blood of the sacrificial Lamb, and the next she was stuck in some Godforsaken wasteland where charismatic Pentecostal preachers were as scarce as African Bushmen. For the first six months in what she called "your daddy's new hellhole," she struggled so hard to maintain her signature Christian buoyancy that even her husband took notice. One Sunday morning, in a rare but timely display of concern, he offered to drive her (and me) to the Emmanuel Temple for a much-needed shot in her gospel-starved arm. Of course he had no intention of attending the service; as usual, he'd spend the morning drinking beer with his buddies at the Texas Ice and Fuel Company a few blocks away on Harrisburg Boulevard. But his act of generosity, however limited, noticeably perked my mother up. Her post-sermon spirits were running so high that she seemed to neither notice nor care when he arrived thoroughly sloshed to pick us up forty-five minutes after the janitor had finished cleaning the church for the evening service. As time went on, though, these doses of her beloved Brother Modest grew more and more infrequent, and the lack of prospects on the spiritual horizon sent her into a prolonged depression.

Parishioners at the Emmanuel Temple knew my mother as a first-class amen sister, and she earned their respect by peppering sermons with the well-placed and punchy "Thank you, Jesus." That everybody counted on Sister Crowell to praise the Lord or proclaim the Devil a liar at ninety decibels and in perfect counterpoint to Brother Modest's suave delivery of the gospel gave her a much-needed sense of worth, and intuitive concentration kept her half a step in front of every word forming in his mouth. If a man or woman ever paid closer attention to what a preacher was about to say than my mother, he or she was unknown in the East End. It was because of her righteousness that I was shocked senseless when, during an exploratory visit to the shabby little Church of God on Pilot Street, she allowed her mind to wander during the preacher's monumentally long and boring sermon. Leaning sideways, she whispered sarcastically, "The Lord's movin' in the house this mornin', isn't He, son?" Before I could squelch the spasm, I'd committed the most unpardonable of all childhood sins—giggling in church. And unbelievably, it was my mother who'd made me laugh. Then, walking home from a onetime visit to the Assembly of God on Mercury Drive, she muttered, "Next time I need me a three-hour nap, I'll go back over to that shit hole." I had heard my mother use mild curse words many times before, but never in connection with the House of the Lord. I was starting to worry.

Perfunctory surveys of the Church of Christ on Market Street and the imposing and obligatory redbrick Baptist church on the corner of Palestine Street and Kirby Avenue only deepened her frustration. "Why, they ain't a church house in all of Jacinto City worth puttin' on a clean dress for," she grumbled. "I might as well go on and surrender to the Devil." Fortunately, her misgivings about finding a spiritual home in such a Godless vacuum were soon to pass.

Tent revivals—the Barnum & Bailey version of soul salvation—had begun cropping up around us like Bedouin villages, and the ones passing through southeast Texas at that time were owned and operated by some of the most highly skilled Devil-debunking outfits ever assembled. Starved as she was for a good old-fashioned Christian tongue-lashing, my poor mother didn't take long to fall for the disingenuous charms of a series of nomadic evangelists, and before long her passion for hellfire-and-cash-money hucksters was even more intense than her crush on Brother Modest.

She couldn't drive a car, due to her nerves, but that didn't matter. She finagled rides to and from the revivals with the tenacity of kudzu. Young, middle-aged, and old Bible-thumping women were only too happy to park in front of the house and honk their horns for Sister Crowell to come hear Brother So-and-So preach, sometimes fourteen nights running.

My father gave her a hard time about this, often adopting a prim, singsong soprano to mock her newfound sisterhood. "Cauzette, one-a them church heifers just pulled up. You better get on out the door 'fore that ole biddy drives outta here." And then, back in his natural voice, "I swear, I never seen nothin' like these goddamn women haulin' your ass around."

"J. W. Crowell, if you don't stop takin' the Lord's name in vain, you're goin' straight to hell."

"I'd just as soon go there as whichever tent y'all are headed off to."

The tent-revival period was a good one for me. Sunday night rides were often so overcrowded that I was allowed to stay home with my father and watch *Gunsmoke*. During the school year, weeknight revivals were subject to the fictitious demands of unfinished homework. Summer months were more vulnerable, since only Little League games constituted an excused absence. This new string of Brother So-and-Sos who'd so thoroughly captured my mother's imagination failed to make any impression on me. One incident, however, I'll never forget.

In the spring of 1959, my mother attended a weeklong revival twenty miles east of Houston in the small town of Highlands. Word got around the tent that Sister Crowell was epileptic; furthermore, that the poor girl had no control over when, how, or where she'd be struck down. The core group of prayer sisters associated with this particular revival took a disparaging view of such afflictions, and the consensus was that Sister Crowell was possessed by the Devil. In effect, my mother's affliction gave them a golden opportunity to rebuke the hell out of that bony-fingered vermin who preyed so unmercifully on her soul.

One afternoon, six of them showed up unannounced at the house on Norvic Street and filed in like a coven. Wearing lace-up, square-heeled old-lady shoes and stockings and identical World War II–era business suits, their hair tied in braided buns, each one looked like a cross between Eleanor Roosevelt and Ayn Rand. The ringleader, probably in her mid-fifties, introduced herself as Sister Shook and informed my mother that the power of prayer was the only thing that could free her from an eternity in hell. As long as she played host to the Devil, the ravages of epilepsy would be visited upon her, and it was guaranteed that she'd have no chance of entering the kingdom of heaven. Telling my mother this was hitting below the belt, and Sister Shook did it without blinking. From then on, she could do with my mother as she wished.

First she instructed my mother to lie down on the living room floor. "Young man, go get a pillow," the old prayer witch commanded. Assuming she was thinking of Momma's comfort, I warmed slightly but soon realized she wanted the pillow only to kneel more comfortably beside her fallen prey.

"Show yourself, Demon," she demanded. "In the name of God I order you to show yourself for the liar you are." The other prayer witches chanted, "The Devil's a liar." Again Sister Shook demanded, "Show yourself, Demon," and then all six of them started chanting the same thing over and over again, like some kind of weird Christian cheerleading squad. The rhythm and gathering intensity was starting to scare me.

Sister Shook was hell-bent on upping the ante. That she would bag the Devil this afternoon was preordained, and my mother's well-being was beneath consideration. Sister Shook's voice was like Thor's hammer, and each new command a thunderclap. "Show us your cowardly work, Devil. Let us see you work through Sister Crowell."

I eased in a little closer. She was inducing a seizure. "Don't do that to Momma," I said defiantly.

The old crone speared me with a look ten times more evil than the red-skinned Antichrist they claimed was messing with Sister Crowell. *"Silence!"*

She couldn't have shut me up more thoroughly if she'd cut off my tongue with a knife. This was finality distilled to its most base form. My lips were sealed.

The prayer witches kept the chant going while Sister Shook repeated her ultimatum. "Show us your epilepsy, you lying coward. In the name of God almighty I demand you show us your vileness, Satan."

Ever the good host, my mother obliged with as violent a seizure as any I'd seen. When she began to convulse, Sister Shook launched a well-rehearsed tirade of prayer into which the other witches fell effortlessly in step, like schoolgirls in a jump-rope line.

Oblivious to Sister Crowell's condition, these bitches turned the intensity of their exorcism to full blast. Writhing on the floor, my mother ground her teeth and frothed like a rabid dog, her bones bending in directions physically impossible without breaking. In fairness to the prayer witches, she did look like someone possessed by the Devil.

"Spit him out! Spit him out!" Sister Shook screamed as this psychic storm raged in our living room.

Torn between seeing the Devil walking around our living room or watching my mother die, I threw my lot in with the prayer witches. If she did spit the Devil out, she might have a chance of surviving the ordeal, so I fell wholeheartedly into their chant. "Spit him out! Spit him out! In the name of *God*, spit him out!" we roared in unison, like crazed football fans.

I can't imagine what the neighbors might've thought was going on inside our house, but surely six old women and an eight-year-old boy shouting at a thirty-five-year-old woman in the throes of a grand mal seizure to spit out the Devil must sound like insanity with a bullhorn.

The madness reached its crescendo when my mother actually did start to spit. At first the froth from the corners of her mouth was all she could muster. Then, like the first drops of a cloudburst, a few small gobs fell to the living room floor—until suddenly she began coughing up waves of slobber. And right before my eyes, Satan took shape in a puddle of spit.

The prayer witches went on rebuking the ever-expanding pool. When she could spit no more, the seizure drew itself to a close, and both my mother and Satan lay exhausted on the floor. Satisfied at last, the six old biddies abruptly led my semiconscious mother to the kitchen for a victory cup of coffee. Sister Shook nodded at the pool of spit on the floor and ordered me to clean it up.

Of all the things I'd done in my short life, whether by happenstance or direct order, wiping the Devil off the living room floor was the task for which I was least prepared. I was better suited for getting swallowed by a whale or murdered by a drifter than I was for this line of work.

A more resourceful child might have politely informed the old hag that she was welcome to clean up her own damn mess—I can easily imagine Dabbo pointing out that his ass was hers to kiss whenever she was ready—but on this day such charming irrepressibility wasn't mine to flaunt. Instead I put on my father's cowboy boots (their tops so tall that Satan couldn't bite me on the leg), flung a towel over the pool of spit, mopped the floor clean with an outstretched foot, and, taking every precaution not to get close enough that the Devil could jump in my mouth, speared the dreaded bugger with the end of the broom handle and sprinted for the front door. Hightailing it down the alley with Sister Crowell's banished tormentor flapping in the breeze, I spied Buddy Abel's back fence—the highest one there—and, without noticing his mother was hanging clothes on the line, hurled the Prince of Darkness to within three feet of her laundry basket. "Whoops, I'm sorry, Mrs. Abel," I yelped. "It was an accident. My flag came off while I was whirling it around." *No, please don't pick it*— Needless to say she picked it up. "Oh, that's all right. Just throw it back over and I'll take care of it." Truth be told, I was hoping the Devil *would* get inside this mean neighbor who talked down to my mother.

Suddenly I remembered the culvert at the end of the sidewalk and bolted for it as fast as my skinny legs would allow. Flying past Mrs. Boyer, who for the first time in ages didn't call out for me to stop what I was doing and perform some piddling chore her granddaughters easily could've done but rarely did, I called over my shoulder, "Hey, Mrs. Boyer, just practicing a little jousting." A man loitering around the culvert told me not to throw the towel down the drain, that it would cause flooding and he'd write my parents a pretty steep citation. I was on the verge of telling him I had reason to believe this was Satan we were talking about, that there was every possibility he was about to enter my body, when something caught my eye. Sitting there fenceless on the corner, Billy Duncan's house offered exactly what I'd been looking for: an exposed crawl space in the back where his father kept an old-fashioned push mower that, openly visible to passersby, could as easily been stolen as put to good use. Promising the man that my friends and I always paid close attention to what we threw in the sewer system, I tromped off in my father's boots and hid behind the Cheniers' chinaberry tree until he cranked up his truck and drove away. Two minutes later, with Satan resting as far underneath the Duncans' house as I could sling him, the job was complete. *Good-bye, you old Devil, now you live under Billy Duncan's house. Momma's gonna need a new broom.*

I arrived back home to find the prayer witches taking leave of my mother. *Good riddance, you self-righteous old bats,* was my verdict. *I can take care of Momma better than all of you put together. Besides, y'all are butt-ugly.* Before the car pulled away, I was washing my hands for the first time in my life without being told.

Christian's Drive-In

Public dining was a matter of considerable complexity for my parents. On their list of priorities, vein-clogging greasiness ran a distant second to the avoidance of crippling self-consciousness brought on by the harsh demands associated with being seated in a restaurant. Luckily, two drive-in eateries on the east side of Houston, Prince's on Wayside Drive and Christian's on Market Street, were, by design, indifferent to my parents' inability to grasp simple etiquette. Specializing in hamburgers, gulf shrimp, chicken livers, French fries, and soggy onion rings—all of it fried fast, served fast, and eaten even faster in the comfort of your own automobile—both establishments catered to their social inadequacies. And the price was right. Dinner for three for less than five dollars gave a man making $1.65 an hour a shot at a little high living now and then. My preference, though, were the concession stands at the Little League ballpark and the Market Street Drive-In Theater, corn dogs, snow cones, popcorn, cherry Cokes, and slowpoke suckers being more to my liking than burgers and fries.

My mother had no interest in the culinary arts, but she did have a knack for producing edible meals when there was nothing to be found in either the pantry or the refrigerator. Frying eggs in an aluminum pie pan on an electric iron, when unpaid gas bills prevented cooking on the stove, is one example. Roasting squirrel meat marshmallow-style over a junk-pile fire in the backyard is another; squirrel, however, is an acquired taste, and I could never get past the salt-and-crude-oil tang that defined its gamy flavor, even smothered in what my mother called grease gravy.

The main ingredient in her short-order repertoire was the ubiquitous can of recycled Crisco she kept on the stovetop. Her basic theory on cooking was this: If it's edible, fry it. Chicken, corn, sauerkraut, Spam, Vienna sausages, hot dogs, liver, dove, venison, potted meat, frog legs, catfish, frozen okra, mountain oysters (bull testicles)—you name it, she fried it.

My tenth birthday fell on payday Friday, automatically tripling the chances my father would come home sloshed. Thanks to a booming payroll-check subculture, East Houston was a breeding ground for small businesses known as icehouses. Left over from the days before refrigeration—when block ice was delivered door-to-door, first by horse-drawn wagons and later by truck—icehouses had evolved into operations that transformed paychecks into cold beer in one smooth transaction. My father's natural aversion to the banking system and his construction-worker's thirst made him a perfect customer. Arriving home drunk on Fridays was something he did with great regularity—sometimes playful, sometimes dark and dangerous. On this particular Friday, I could tell by the sound of the Studebaker wheeling in wide of the driveway strips that his mind wasn't on my birthday.

Whenever my father drank, his face and ears turned a deep shade of crimson. In a good mood, this accentuated his comical nature; when he was seething, he made spontaneous human combustion seem as cool and refreshing as ice fishing in Minnesota. The most accurate barometer of his mood were his eyes: happy drunk, they were clear-blue sunshine; pissed-off drunk, the color of muzzle fire from his pump-action 16-gauge. On my tenth birthday it was the latter, shot through with the white fire of anger mixed with payday beer and a half pint of Old Crow whiskey.

"Hi, Dad."

"I thought I told you to pick up all this shit outta the yard."

The shit consisted of my bicycle, lying on its side, and four cardboard squares we used as bases during morning and evening ball games. "There ain't nothin' to pick up."

"There is, by God, I'm looking right at it. You ain't blind."

"Those are our bases."

"I said clear this shit up."

"We got a game in the morning."

"Y'all are wearin' out my damn grass."

"What do you care? You never mow it. We're just doing you a favor keepin' it all wore down."

"Boy, you go gettin' smart with me and I'll give you somethin' to get smart about."

"The chinch bugs do worse than what we do."

"You ain't too big for me to wear your ass out."

"You don't even know it's my birthday."

As pissed-off drunk as he was, his true nature surfaced, if only for an instant, and a glimmer of sweetness sobered him a little. "Naw, I didn't forget your birthday. Hell, it's three days after mine!"

With a halt called in our battle of wills, we were both suddenly awkward and at a loss for words. In danger of having our soft underbellies exposed, he and I shifted our weight from one foot to the other while the world around us settled into a deepening silence. The question of what to do next was answered when my mother stepped out of the house and cheerfully suggested we go to Christian's for a birthday celebration.

Gene Christian, owner and chief fry cook, was a robust man whose foppish, perfectly atilt chef's hat, waxed moustache, and starched white outfit gave him a Salvador Dalí look. He relished putting his booming baritone on public display when announcing Little League games from the green plywood press box my father had built courtesy of his generous cash donations.

Mr. Christian made the most of his drive-in's prime location. Seventy-five feet of red and white awning, in front of the little wooden shack he'd converted into the guts of his operation, was hard to miss. An oyster-shell parking lot served to alert his carhops to new arrivals, the hum of V8s and the crunch of shells beneath whitewall tires announcing a booming business.

The best jukebox in the world sat on bottle crates against the front wall of Mr. Christian's spruced-up little shack, and he kept it loaded with 45s by Santo & Johnny, Chuck Berry, Slim Harpo, Elvis Presley, Cookie and the Cupcakes, Fats Domino, Smiley Lewis, C. L. Weldon, and Jimmy Reed. It was on that jukebox I first heard Clarence "Frogman" Henry's "Ain't Got No Home" and Bill Doggett's "Honky Tonk." Today, when I hear Bruce Channel's version of "Hey! Baby," I see the bright red and yellow CHICKEN LIVERS, 99 CENTS sign in Mr. Christian's window. Rhythm and blues and humidity is nature at its best.

Any illusions I had about a birthday celebration evaporated about as quickly as the half pint of I. W. Harper my father polished off while my mother put on a clean pair of pedal pushers and a ship-to-shore blouse.

In the interest of maintaining her Christian self-image, my mother chose righteous indignation when it came to alcohol and loose women. When I pointed out the hypocrisy of denigrating "floozies" when she herself was known to chug beer occasionally, she adamantly refused to acknowledge that guzzling a six-pack of Jax for the purpose of knocking herself unconscious before the onset of a grand mal seizure could possibly be construed as licentious behavior. She viewed her drinking as self-defense. But whether it was for numbing the effects of epilepsy or joining her husband in escaping a tedious existence, the results were never pretty.

When our little birthday party in the red Studebaker rolled up under Mr. Christian's awning and my mother ordered a can of Jax to go along with her onion rings and fried chicken gizzards, I knew trouble wasn't far behind. The can she knocked back in the few minutes it took for our food to arrive and the two she killed by the time she finished eating suggested that she was going toe-to-toe with my father.

The jukebox might have been malfunctioning, but I'd rather think some blues-crazed customer in love with the new Jimmy Reed record kept playing it over and over again simply because it felt so good. In a voice half-slur and half-whine, poor Jimmy complained relentlessly about how some woman was treating him like shit.

> *Got me runnin', got me hidin'*
> *Got me run, hide, hide, run anyway you want to let it roll*
> *Yeah, yeah, yeah,*
> *You got me doin' what you want me*
> *So baby why you want to let go?*

As confused as Jimmy was about what his baby wanted him to do, I was twice as confused about what to do if my mother kept chugging beer.

I loved Jimmy Reed. To me his records sounded like grown-up sex: hypnotic, erotic, exotic, and, after twenty-five straight plays, psychotic. That's how "Baby What You Want Me to Do" sounded that night, demanding that I pay attention to its every nuance. More than anything I wanted to relax and listen to the song, but all hell was breaking loose inside the car.

Going toe-to-toe with my father did not involve standing up to him with the resolve of a wise and powerful woman. No, she favored the spineless, pathetic approach. Slurring her words even more than Jimmy Reed, she said, "I know you hate me. You've hated me since the day you met me. I'm a cripple. I have convulsions and you cain't stand me for it," lines that were tailor-made to tweak my father's revulsion. "J. W. Crowell, if you was any kind of man, you'd come out and say how much you hate me. Your own son knows you do."

"I don't know nothin' about nobody hatin' nobody," I said. "Y'all leave me out of it." This wasn't quite true: I hated my mother's willingness to be a doormat, for inviting my father to step on her, and hated him for accepting the invitation.

> *Goin' up, goin' down*
> *Goin' up, down, down, up, anyway you want to let it roll*
> *Yeah, yeah, yeah*
> *You got me doin' what you want me*
> *So baby why you want to let go?*

While Jimmy kept trying to figure it out, my mother danced like a mongoose around the coiled cobra of my father's temper.

"I know you been screwin' Jackie Winston, and I know you got a son walkin' the streets of Houston right now without your name."

"That's enough, Cauzette. You don't know when to shut up."

"You shut me up a long time ago when you said, 'I do.' Don't you think I know you'll screw anything that walks?"

> *Got me peepin', got me hidin'*
> *Got me peep, hide, hide, peep, anyway you want to let it roll*

Biting her fingernails was a habit my mother indulged to the hilt. "It's my nerves," she claimed, and she took nervousness to new heights—"down to the quick," as she put it—until her fingertips were a throbbing bloodred pulp. Considering this, it's hard to imagine how she could produce claw marks on the side of my father's face. But I saw it happen as Jimmy wailed on.

The time bomb suddenly exploded. My father punched her in the face, hard. Unfazed, she kept scratching away at his face and screaming, "Go on and hit me. Show everybody what a big man you are. Go on, knock my teeth out. I know you hate the ground I walk on."

These were eight-year-olds in drunken thirty-something bodies powered by pent-up rage. If experience had taught me anything, it was how to defend myself from their periodic need to hurl themselves into the inferno. But in the cramped quarters of the Studebaker, the flames were dangerously close to torching my self-preservation. Survival, from my vantage point in the backseat, was fast becoming an issue.

In my parents' world of downward spirals, outside influences—like the carload of customers parked next to us, or concerned carhops asking if everything was all right—were less effectual than a kite in a hurricane. Quelling these prizefights called for more drastic measures.

Clarity came from a familiar source inside my head. *If you want this to stop, get their attention.* It occurred to me the Dr Pepper bottle in my hand could end this brawl once and for all.

"Look what you made me do!" I yelled above the din of their vitriol, and was surprised when the fighting stopped instantly and both my parents granted me a haggard glance. Then, with the stage set, I busted myself over the head with the bottle, opening a three-inch gash just above my hairline.

I got the full cartoon effect. It felt as if I'd split my skull into two pieces. I saw stars. Drunken birds tweeted, chirped, and crash-landed on the seat next to me. Guardian angels swooped down for a closer look, winced, and sped off in search of scraped knees or bumblebee stings. Jimmy Reed's harmonica sounded like an ambulance somewhere across town promising to drop by and check on me when it got a chance.

When my brain began to unscramble, the images of my mother and father—jaws resting on their breastbones, their faces the color of a Ku Klux Klan sheet, their eyes lobbying for confirmation that indeed I'd just coldcocked myself with an empty soda bottle—came into focus. My whacking myself on the head had successfully halted their madness, and their shocked sobriety and my nauseated wooze left us in a three-way trance. The scene is like a Polaroid photograph that I view from the inside out.

Right before, Mr. Christian had been leaning in the driver's side window, thinking that by taking the humorous approach he might break up the fracas. I'm pretty sure I heard him say, "Whoa, there. I reckon y'all didn't hear the bell. The judges scored it a draw."

When he heard and saw the bottle bounce off my noggin, he jerked my father's door open, yanked him out of the car, and retrieved me from the back.

I'd regained my bearings enough to know that, despite my bloody forehead, no real damage had been done, but to be on the safe side I decided to pitch a crying conniption—my best hope of keeping my parents' attention turned away from the dog-and-cat fight I felt sure they couldn't wait to jump back into.

Mr. Christian's ballpark voice boomed, "Now, son, you be still and let me see if any of your brain's leaking out with all that blood." He pulled my scalp wound apart with his huge thumbs and pronounced me fit to fight another day.

Having regained his senses, sobered and sheepish, my father made a hollow stab at re-establishing himself as a capable citizen and father. "It's all right now, Gene. I can take care of this."

Mr. Christian growled, "J.W., I always thought you was a pretty good ole boy and a good customer. But I'm telling you right now, if I ever catch you beatin' up that boy's momma again, there won't be enough left of you to haul off with the garbage."

Not one to take challenges to his manhood lightly, my father, standing five foot eleven to Mr. Christian's six three, managed to place his nose and chin squarely against his adversary's. "I tell you what, Gene. I can come back here after a bit, and we can talk this out man-to-man. But right now I gotta go take care of my boy."

Jimmy Reed's harmonica shrieked like a referee's whistle, but neither of them seemed willing to budge. Both, in fact, seemed comfortable with the stalemate.

My heart leapt up in my chest at the sight of my father standing up to Mr. Christian, even if he was the one who started the trouble. Hearing him call me "my boy" was better than ten apologies or any present he might've bought me. How hateful he'd been to my mother and how recklessly he'd behaved on my birthday no longer seemed to matter. Having him hold me in his lap while the emergency-room doctor put four stitches in my scalp was the best gift imaginable.

Whether it was destiny or misfortune that caused my parents to join their lives together, I don't know. It could be that their collision course was a foregone conclusion long before my father stepped up to defend my mother's honor at that Roy Acuff concert all those years ago.

The Buck Family Chronicles

Dabbo Buck's arrival on Norvic Street in the spring of 1958 marked the beginning of a new era of full-tilt, living-on-the-edge childhood. Rusty nails, broken bones, and rabies shots tripled within the first month of the Buck family's materialization in the house catty-cornered to ours. Their impact on the neighborhood's noise pollution was instant. For them, racket was part symphonic composition, part improvisational jazz, with Sherman, Margie, Dabbo, and Dianne each a virtuoso in the art of raising a ruckus on the poorly tuned instruments of day-to-day living. Their integration into our ebb and flow was akin to that of a brick thrown through a plate-glass window, and there was no option of getting acquainted at your own pace. Where once had stood an empty house and a For Sale sign, there now were slamming doors, shotgun blasts, contusions, and concussions.

Margie Buck had been in the habit of chewing Days Work tobacco and spitting the juice into a Folgers coffee can since she was ten years old. She told me so herself, in an introductory monologue that highlighted the biographical importance of her four-year reign as the junior hog-calling champion of Jackson County, Tennessee.

Larger than life and of an indeterminable age—anywhere between thirty-five and sixty-five is my guess—she loved sitting on the front porch in her pea-green aluminum lawn chair and, depending on her mood, surprising Dabbo with a poke in the arm or a bop on the head whenever he passed within arm's length. Margie Buck was as loud as she was self-sufficient and mean as a water moccasin. She took a liking to me and the feeling was mutual.

Born and raised in the backwoods of western Tennessee, near the town of Jacks Creek, Margie, the adult, was a big-boned, swarthy gal whose stringy, silver-streaked hair was permanently braided on top of her head. Three cotton farm dresses, an old nightgown, and a pair of white size-13 sandals were her entire, year-round wardrobe.

At calling her children in from their neighborhood rounds, Margie Buck was without peer. "Cleeve Beniard Buck," she'd yell, rattling windows with Dabbo's given name, "you better get in this house right now, you little shit-ass, or I'm gonna track you down and gut you with your daddy's buck knife." She liked to yell, simple as that, a world-class hog caller and proud of it. Anybody who didn't like it could kiss her hillbilly ass.

Earsplitting nuance placed her summons in one of two categories: stay of execution or the electric chair. For Dabbo, the clue was found in her treatment of his middle name. He'd come scampering out of the bushes happy as a dog eating leftovers whenever his mother heightened the "ard" in "Beniard." Otherwise, he stayed hid.

Once, for fear of the bodily harm foretold in her flat pronunciation of "Beniard," Dabbo lay motionless beneath a parked car for three hours. For the benefit of any puritans in the neighborhood, she added, "You better get your skinny white ass in this house, or I'm gonna cut your balls off with your daddy's straight razor."

From the backyard, I'd heard her all-points bulletin and had a pretty good idea where the accursed fugitive might be found. Careful to avoid detection, I pushed through the honeysuckle bushes and crawled under the old Packard Mrs. Boyer kept parked in front of the house next door to ours and joined Dabbo in hiding. We lay there stock-still and silent as ghosts, our nostrils raising puffs in the cat shit and dirt, while Margie ran through her repertoire of death threats. Forty-five minutes later, she gave up, went in the house, and locked the door.

"Dabbo," I whispered, "I gotta go home. What you gonna do?"

"Lay here till she's sound asleep, then I'll get W'anne to let me in at her window." (Dabbo had a speech impediment that mangled his older sister's name, Dianne.)

An hour later, after I'd taken a bath and made sure my parents were in bed for the night, I slipped out the back door and found he hadn't moved. "Dabbo," I croaked, "why you still layin' under—"

"Sssh." He cut me off, placing an eight-year-old finger over his mouth. "I knew you'd come back," he whispered. "You gotta go look in Momma and Daddy's window. If they're asleep, scratch on W'anne's screen and get 'er to let me in. If Momma ain't asleep, I ain't movin' an inch."

Ever the dutiful friend, I stole across the street barefoot and in clean underwear. Crouched beneath their bedroom window but lacking the nerve to peep, I took Mr. Buck's herculean snoring as proof that he and Margie were fast asleep. Having counted to two hundred by fives without hearing anything but rumbling snores, I assumed the coast was clear and scurried around to the back of the house, where Dabbo and his sister shared a bedroom.

A scratch on the screen brought the left side of Dianne's face into fuzzy focus in the lower right-hand corner of the window frame. After silent arrangements were made for her to unhook the screen, I ran tippy-toed back across the street to the car.

It wasn't until I gave him the all-clear sign that Dabbo, after three hours of playing possum, crawled out from under the Packard. Dusting himself off, he nodded across the street. "You gotta help me climb in the window."

The temperature of the night air dropped a few degrees when I knelt on hands and knees, Dabbo standing upright on the middle of my back. The grass was dew-drenched and cool, shimmering in the moonlight as my friend negotiated re-entry with his uncharacteristically compliant sister. A slight breeze rustled the stillness, and the night settled into a deeper quietness, and, in a house down the alley, a light sleeper cleared his throat. He might as well have hollered, "Wake up, Margie, Dabbo's climbing in the bedroom window."

Dabbo was halfway through when the light snapped on inside the bedroom. His mother grabbed him by the ear, cackling like a broom-riding witch. "I got you now, you little sack-a shit, and I'm gonna beat the daylights outta you *and* that little fart from across the street."

I don't recall racing home in my underpants. The next thing I remember is that I was in bed with the covers pulled over my head, listening to the sound of my heart pounding in my chest cavity. And I didn't budge until long after the sun came up the next morning.

I didn't see Dabbo around for a few days. Assuming the worst, I waited for Margie to charge across our front yard, vowing to cut my gizzard out, but she never came. Three days later, figuring the suspense was more likely to kill me, I summoned the courage to cross the street and knock on the Bucks' door.

Dabbo answered in apparent good health.

"What happened?"

"Nothin'," he said. "She just wanted to scare the pee outta you and me. They were watchin' us the whole time. Daddy was in on it. He said he laid there in the bed fakin' snores and just about dirtied his drawers. Momma wouldn't let me come tell you 'cause it would take the fun outta keepin' you in suspenders. We been waitin' on you to come on over ever since."

Margie shuffled smugly onto the porch. Making a big deal out of plopping down in her lawn chair, she winked and spat a thick drivel of tobacco juice into her coffee can. "Y'all gonna have to get up pretty damn early to put one over on Margie Buck. And that's the truth if I ever told it."

.   .   .

Sherman Buck was the tobacco-chewing second-in-command of the household across the street, a cement finisher of the highest order and a man known to waste neither words nor motion. Khaki pants, concrete-dusted work boots, fisherman's cap, long underwear, and flannel shirt—the sleeves rolled up two turns—were his outfit for every occasion. His contributions to the family's noise quotient were made five, sometimes six, mornings a week at five-thirty when, without fail, a turn of the ignition in his '53 Ford pickup produced a chain of earsplitting backfires that announced it was time to go to work—only then, and the rare occasions when he spoke.

His voice combined the sounds of a bad muffler, a dump truck full of gravel, and the full-on, full-off blast of a foghorn. I heard him raise it in anger but once, standing a few feet away when he spat the full name of his son from his mouth like a full load of 10-gauge buckshot. Dabbo was bagged with one shell.

Mr. Buck was born in the hill country of central Texas; his father was a blacksmith and his mother a Comanche Indian. He had a natural aversion to words that I envisioned as the elegant by-product of his mixed breeding and the hard life his family had chiseled out of the horse-and-livestock trade particular to San Saba County, the faraway land where he grew up.

The only time I can recall him stringing more than a few simple sentences together was when he told Dabbo and me the story of an incident that took place when he was twelve years old and chopping wood with a double-blade axe. He dredged up this memory in order to demonstrate the virtues of concentration. While building a backyard duck blind, Dabbo had smashed his thumb with a ball-peen hammer and, with me in tow, run off to seek comfort from the first available adult, who happened to be his father. Mr. Buck sat silent as a statue while his boy wailed in his lap, and when the howling ceased and the tears dried, he said, "Listen here, son, I was twelve year old and working on a stack of firewood, and blamed if my mind wasn't off somewhere doin' somethin' else. What I done was bury that axe blade between the big toe on my left foot and the one next to it, halfway up to the ankle." Leaning back in his chair, he took a long, slow swallow from his ever-present jar of sweet iced tea, "Well, sir," he said, "my daddy pulled that blade out and cut my shoe off with his pocketknife, then poured black pepper in that great big slice. And I tell you what . . ." He waited a long beat to let the image of blood and black pepper seep into our imaginations. "I coulda caught any deer in Texas! I run six miles, one shoe on, one shoe off, 'cross some of the roughest country this side of the Pecos. When Daddy caught up to me, he was ridin' an old mule name-a Sadie. 'Boy,' he says to me, 'you done made me have to go doctor that foot all over again.' Damned if he didn't hold me down and pour the rest of that pepper in the gash and wrap my foot up tight with twine. He said he reckoned thataway my foot'd grow back together. I rode back to the house on ole Sadie, foot just a-throbbin'. Sure enough, the blamed thing growed back good as new. I never did go see no doctor. Hell, they wudn't one for twenty-five mile. Daddy cut down a saplin' and made me a crutch. I was back doin' chores in a day or two."

As a river fisherman, Sherman Buck was unrivaled. He could drag alligator gar and catfish as long as your leg out of a dry creek bed. Rain-soaked riverbanks awakened something primal in him. When he was fishing, his construction worker's slouch was overwhelmed by the regality associated with visiting dignitaries and war heroes. On muddier and swifter rivers, not even natural forces like gravity seemed to register on Dabbo's father.

The Brazos flows through the watermelon farmland west of Houston like a downsized Mississippi before emptying into the Gulf of Mexico, with the towns of Navasota, Hempstead, San Felipe, Richmond, Rosenberg, and Sugar Land lining its banks at a respectable distance. Mr. Buck's fondness for this wild and unpredictable river was infectious. Dabbo and I disdained the San Jacinto as fat and lazy, and the Trinity as nothing more than a trickle of tad-poles. The Brazos was our river of choice.

Crossing the Brazos brought a steady climb in landscape reach-ing up onto the Edwards plateau. Farther west was Old Mexico and the Rio Grande, where, according to *The World Book Encyclopedia*, a world-record alligator gar—270 pounds—was caught in 1936. Dabbo and I were staunch in our belief that beneath the Brazos's muddy waters, gar twice that size were lurking one cast away from his father's deep-sea rod and open-faced reel.

Flash flooding here was a common occurrence. Summer storms and gully washers could, over two or three days, turn the river the color of café au lait, with whirlpools and deep eddies everywhere. Negotiating her banks at such times required the kind of concentra-tion my friend and I sorely lacked.

In preparation for one of our big fishing trips, Dabbo and I finagled an excursion to the Sears, Roebuck. With all of twenty-seven cents between us, we begged and pleaded and eventually eroded his mother's resolve not to contribute to expeditions she considered "too damn dangerous for y'all little snot-nosed heathens." Our tenacity was rewarded with a ride in her nearly brand-new, sky-blue '59 Chevy Impala, since Margie was always on the lookout for opportunities to rub her neighbors' noses in the dirt. A shopping trip suited her just fine.

The Sears out on Wayside Drive was an airport hangar disguised as a department store, so Dabbo and I had little trouble giving her the slip. Faking interest in back-to-school clothes just long enough for Margie to be drawn into discussing the finer points of the lay-away plan with a clerk, we stole off for the Outdoors department. Less-deluded thieves might have known that the spinning lures, lead weights, pop corks, plastic worms, and forty-pound test line we stuffed into our pockets would cause unforeseen problems—the treble hooks, for example, were stabbing me in the leg. And shoving packages of plastic soldiers down the front of our pants made us only slightly less conspicuous than the Michelin Man.

Had another minute passed, surely second thoughts would've prevented the coming debacle. But by then Margie was yelling, from halfway across the store, "Y'all get on over here, we goin' to the house. So bring whatever it is you need. I ain't fixin' to wait on you little shits."

"Aw, we couldn't find nothin'," Dabbo lied. "We might as well get on home."

Bunched behind the folds of Margie's cotton dress, the two of us moved as one past an oblivious cashier, our nonchalance as suspect as the bulging pockets nobody seemed to notice.

"Looks like the coast is clear," Dabbo whispered.

With the glaring white freedom of a hot summer's day less than ten feet away, we followed his mother toward the Exit sign. As if welcoming us to the world outside, the automatic doors swung open and allowed us to transport a small mountain of contraband across some invisible line that differentiated shoppers from shoplifters about to be caught red-handed.

A tall man who was dressed like a shabby bank teller tapped Margie discreetly on the shoulder, indicating he'd like a word with her.

"He looks like old Ichabod Crane," Dabbo whispered.

The gawky man's sharp glance made it clear he'd overheard this remark, and that we were up shit's creek.

When it dawned on Margie what we'd done, her mouth flew open and a giant wad of Days Work tobacco splattered on the side-walk. Then came a breathless fit only she could've thrown. "I'm gonna kill you little bastards. Then I'll whip y'all so hard you ain't never gonna sit down again. Now, I'm countin' to ten and y'all can march back in there and put ever' bit of that shit back where you found it, and if you ain't back here by ten I'm gonna cut both of y'all's balls off."

Considering the amount of goods we'd stolen, a count of ten

would be cutting it close. Luckily, Margie's ongoing stream of invective gave Dabbo and me just enough time to return everything and hotfoot it back to the automatic doors before nine and a half turned into ten.

Then it was the Sleepy Hollow guy's turn. "Do you boys know I could be taking you to Gatesville right now?" Using the threat of reform school to intimidate us was a complete waste of time, since Dabbo and I were too busy blinking at the massive protuberance bobbing in the middle of our captor's neck. Here's the thing: For first-time juvenile shoplifters, an Adam's apple that looks like a sewer rat swallowed by a water moccasin is ten times scarier than prison.

After Margie and Ichabod had a heated discussion, the possibility that we hardened criminals might still have some stolen goods stashed away on our persons was next on the agenda. Dabbo and I were led into a windowless room and told to strip down to our Fruit of the Looms. Why an eight- and a ten-year-old boy would want to hide treble-hook fishing lures in their underwear is a question Margie wasn't too shy to ask. We just about peed ourselves watching the man's Adam's apple bouncing up and down like a hamster on a pogo stick when Margie switched to offense. "Listen here, Mr. Sears and Roebuck Head of Security, if there's any lookin' to be done down them boys' drawers, I'm damn sure the one who'll be doin' it."

"I tried as hard as I could to cut a fart when we was standin' there with him lookin' at us," Dabbo said afterward, "but I couldn't get one out. Wouldn't that of fixed his wagon, me fartin' like that?"

To ensure that we were tried as repeat offenders if we were ever caught stealing again, Sleepy Hollow called the store manager and a salesclerk into the interrogation room as witnesses to our crime spree. The manager made a halfhearted speech about how, with the merchandise returned to where it belonged and our sworn oath to repent, he was willing to forget the whole thing, so against Ichabod's protestations we were released into the custody of one hugely pissed-off mother. Suddenly the idea of Gatesville State School for Boys had considerable appeal.

"Y'all don't deserve no cool air," Margie fumed, refusing to turn on the air-conditioning in her new ride. "Might as well get used to the hell both of y'all is fixin' to catch." She reached over the seat, eyes completely off the road, and whacked her son across the top of his legs at the end of each new charge. "I didn't raise you to be no thief." *Whack!* "Don't you never let me catch you stealin' again as long as you live." *Whack!* "Do you hear me, Cleeve *Ben*iard Buck?" *Whack!*

Dabbo got the rest of his whipping when we arrived back home. Of course my mother commanded me to cut a fat switch off one of the chinaberry trees in the backyard. Seeing no use in prolonging the inevitable, I cut a good one the first time out. With my jeans around my ankles, she whipped me over and over, covering my legs with five skinny red welts for every piece of merchandise I'd tried to steal. Finally, there was the whimpering letter of apology we had to write to the Sears, Roebuck, offices up in Chicago.

Nevertheless, we did salvage our fishing trip once Mr. Buck came to the rescue. "Aw, let 'em come go fishin'," he said. "They done learned their lesson." So on Saturday morning, two hours before daylight, I was plucked from a morose sleep by my mother's chirpy "Rise and shine and give God the glory." She herself had just been jarred awake by Margie's scratching on the window screen, half-shouting that she figured it wouldn't hurt to let the boys go on and do a little fishing. Fifteen minutes later, the giddy parolees were perched on lawn chairs in the back of Mr. Buck's pickup, aping the '53 Ford's backfires with armpit farts. The river called, and no doubt a world record of some kind.

Judging by the Brazos's disposition, rain had been falling steadily for days. The wagon road leading to Mr. Buck's favorite spot was drive-shaft muddy, and as we drew nearer, raindrops the size of marbles forced us to abandon our post in the back of the truck and crawl into the cab.

"Y'all listen at me," Mr. Buck boomed above the rain and thunder. "This here riverbank's slicker'n snot, and I don't want to see you boys drowned. Stay where the bank's flat, and I won't have to go in after ye."

We did exactly as we were told . . . until boredom set in.

With neither of us getting a nibble in the first ten minutes, the rush of the river compelled us toward tomfoolery, and our fishermen's discipline dissolved in the rain like sugar cubes.

Mr. Buck worked downriver slinging cut bait on a leader, a heavy lead weight pointing the direction of each cast. Wielding his deep-sea rod like a sword, he gave the impression of a man fully expecting to pull out a fifty-pound catfish—an optimism matched by the tenacity with which he negotiated the riverbank.

Our hopes of landing a world-record alligator gar quashed, we headed upriver improvising games of chance, imagining ourselves Indians on the warpath, tempting fate along the high bluffs we'd been warned to stay away from. One embankment, however, caught our eye: eight feet high and dangerously steep, with a narrow ledge perhaps two feet above the rising current. Only Dabbo could've hatched a plan to slide down onto the ledge, and with my help he managed to do just that—though I couldn't guess what he planned to do after he was down there or how he planned to get back up. After all, the only thing between him and drowning was the tree limb I was holding from the top of the bank. Then again, seeing as how he is one-quarter Comanche and my great-great-grandmother was a full-blood Cherokee, we might have argued that the odds were decidedly in our favor.

Once he'd gained proper footing, we started a tandem trek upstream, him on the ledge below, me on the bank above, a rotting six-foot tree limb connecting our fate.

"Holler if you see any snakes," he called from below.

"They're all someplace dry."

One step later the embankment collapsed beneath my feet. As part of the landslide, I wrapped my arms and legs around Dabbo as we plummeted into a high-speed liquid escalator, its next stop the Gulf of Mexico. The two of us tried dog-paddling as one toward safety, but without success. Whirlpools retarded our lateral progress, imposing their downward spin cycle before flushing us out into whatever came next.

"Let go of me!" Dabbo screamed as loud as his lungs would allow.

"*You* let go of *me*!" I yelled back.

Even though treading water together was entirely counterproductive to our efforts to stay afloat, neither of us showed any inclination to let go, and I maintained my death lock around Dabbo's neck. Oddly, while I was scratching and clawing and swallowing water, I also felt as if I were floating down a lazy river on a rubber raft. A voice inside my head, curiously not my own, and therefore authoritative, was urging me to relax and enjoy the ride.

The river kept leaking into my stomach and lungs, but I found myself more and more inclined to embrace the passive acceptance this strange voice advised. Its reassuring warmth made the idea of letting go seem the most sensible option.

My mind made the decision to surrender, yet before it could send the message to my body a strong, big-boned hand grabbed my arm and yanked me from the river with Dabbo clinging to my torso, and Mr. Buck dragged us onto a flat, sandy bank. Knowing the river so intimately, he'd positioned himself on a sandbar and waited for a onetime shot at saving our behinds.

Sprawled there like fresh-caught catfish, Dabbo and I reacquainted ourselves with breathing, coughed up chalky-colored water, and braced ourselves for a hard reprimand.

"I thought I done told y'all to stay off of them high banks."

That said, Sherman Buck picked up his rod and plopped a big chunk of bait into a deep channel near the far side. Satisfied with his cast, he relit his hand-rolled cigarette and took a deep drag. Rain was pouring off the bill of his cap down his chest, but the cigarette stayed dry.

On the trip home the sun came out. Steam rose from the black-top, bound to reassemble itself as yet another rain cloud. We stopped at a roadside watermelon stand and were greeted by the smell of fresh sawdust and the sight of sweet Navasota stripers iced down and ready to be served by the slice.

The sunlight filtering through an oak tree and the sprinkling of salt on a cold slice of watermelon softened the experience of having almost drowned, and sitting at the picnic table spitting seeds, I found myself drifting down a peaceful river of thoughts. Now nobody had to tell me everything was going to be all right.

Presently, a rumbling, rattling voice filtered into my daydream. "Finish off your piss-chunk, boys, we need to be gettin' on home."

Ricky Schmidt and the Norvic Street Freedom Fighters

In the spring of 1961 a new craze took Norvic Street by storm. Overnight, or so it seemed, Dabbo, Ronnie Thomas, David Warren, and I had become obsessed with a potentially dangerous activity, and the number of errant feathered missiles whizzing along ill-advised flight paths went from zero to red alert. As usual, our parents had more pressing concerns than the safety of preteen males.

Archery, truth be told, is too fancy a word to describe what the sport became in our grimy, foolhardy hands. As so often happened, Dabbo defined the gist of the phenomenon best when, after yet another close call, he mused, "If one of us don't get killed, shootin' off bows and arrows is more fun than pootin' in church." Thus did our favorite new pastime become known on the street as "bows and arrows."

The resources to outfit a reckless band of would-be William Tells came from a system of recycled barter by which empty milk jugs and Coke bottles could be transformed into bubble gum, jawbreakers, baseball cards, and trips to the public swimming pool. With the return deposit on a gallon milk jug set at a quarter and on soda-pop bottles at two cents, a little spending money wasn't hard to come by. S&H Green Stamps, however, the miraculous by-product of shopping at the Minimax and Lucky 7 food stores, were the backbone of our arsenal. In many households, Green Stamps were the primary source of disposable family income, and this was the currency that produced the wooden bows and dull-tipped practice arrows that were wreaking minor havoc around the neighborhood.

My mother saved Green Stamps like my college education depended on them. She took comfort in knowing that, as long as my father could buy food, there was a better than average chance Santa Claus would find our house come Christmastime. Other than the Bible, which I suspect she never fully sank her teeth into, Green Stamp catalogues were her reading matter of choice. She gazed longingly at drab photographs of TV-dinner trays, basketball hoops, vacuum cleaners, bunk beds, pressure cookers, Skilsaws, desk lamps, wall clocks, golf clubs, and camping equipment as if she were looking at film stars in a movie magazine. All because of little green stamps, a wonderful selection of shoddy merchandise was sometimes attainable in a life otherwise devoid of entitlement. Four and a half lick-'em, stick-'em books, negotiable at the Galena Park outlet, could turn a ten-year-old boy into a modern-day Robin Hood or a woman of thirty-six with very few cooking skills into Betty Crocker. In my mother's world a little green stamp was the only precondition for making dreams come true, unless, as was often the case, the dream item was out of stock. Were I to meet whoever invented these stamps, I would pledge them eternal gratitude for offering my mother hope in times of despair.

Around the time bows and arrows were taking off, a new family appeared in the neighborhood. Word spread fast that the father, a genuine member of the German army and a rich dentist to boot, had, as part of a nasty divorce settlement, moved his American-born wife and their children, a boy and a girl, into the house next door to ours.

I took an instant disliking to Ricky Schmidt. The big deal he made about being two years older than I—I had two full years on Dabbo and still we were equals—was my first glimpse of the Schmidt family's twisted sense of offensive defense. To say the stigma attached to being of German descent in postwar Jacinto City made his integration into our tight-knit society no less abrasive than one of his father's drills, however true, falls short of explaining the dark side of his nature. Forces more sinister than blind prejudice and wartime resentment were working against him.

I blame my mother's dogged insistence that I "go the extra mile to make that new boy feel welcome" for our robotic pairing. "Bless his heart," she mewled, before sending me off to make nice with the bully next door. "I can tell he's had a hard old way to go."

Dabbo in particular was incensed that the spawn of a "Kraut machine-gunner" should take up residence in our tiny corner of the universe, and considered my consorting with the enemy an act of high treason. My attempts to explain that it was all my mother's idea fell on deaf ears. By his estimation, the Nazis had reconvened on our street and his best friend had joined up.

Early in my forced friendship with Ricky, I became part of a father-son ritual that perhaps sheds some light on the deformation behind his churlish façade. Two Saturdays a month, Mr. Schmidt used his visitation rights as an opportunity to terrorize his son. Being Ricky's designated new best friend, I was required to attend this bimonthly bloodletting.

Come visitation Saturday, Ricky and I were driven to the sludge-filled reservoir dividing Galena Park and Jacinto City where, from positions high on the retaining wall, his father indulged a perverse passion for throwing dirt clods at us. With these exploding at our feet, whistling past our heads, or landing with a hollow *ka*-thunk in the green goopy chemical muck dredged from the ship channel and left to stagnate in the white-hot Texas sun, we were reduced to huddling like refugees on the dirt road lining the water's edge.

Grappling with how to defend myself against the heartless German soldier masquerading as Ricky's father brought me face-to-face with the cruel realization that in a world of bloodthirsty predators, a ten-year-old Mickey Mantle fan was as close to easy pickings as you could get. I offered a silent prayer that my father might suddenly appear to vanquish this beast throwing dirt clods at my head. That it went unanswered, I chalked up to being in the wrong place at the wrong time. Of the situation on the reservoir, it could be said that had our ability to dodge incoming fire not been honed with routine practice, things could've been a lot worse.

When he tired of war games, Mr. Schmidt rewarded our cowardice with ice cream cones at Zesto's. From there we were dropped off unceremoniously in front of Ricky's house. Ashamed and bedraggled, we parted company with an unspoken vow to keep what happened on the levee a secret. Ricky knew that I knew that once inside the door he'd collapse into his mother's apron in tears. Why he elsewhere kept a brave face to protect his father is, doubtless, money in the bank for some expressionless Jungian getting rich by unmasking second- and third-generation sociopaths. But come to think of it, why was I, too, protecting Mr. Schmidt?

One afternoon, while enjoying the late-summer coolness found only in the dirt beneath Mr. Carnew's house, which, being built on blocks, offered a handy crawl space for use as an underground headquarters and bunker against the hot and hostile world outside, I related the story of Mr. Schmidt's perversions. David Warren and Ronnie Thomas offered wide-eyed "Unh-unh's," "He did not's," and "No shit's" as a show of incredulous accord. Dabbo, on the other hand, remained mute.

"What you thinkin' about, Dabbo?" I asked.

A long silence.

When at last he spoke, it was to announce a strategy guaranteed to rid the neighborhood of Nazi undesirables forever. To accentu-ate the hushed connivance of his scheming, Dabbo shot a quick glance over both shoulders before vowing, "We're gonna fix his grenade-chuckin' ass, and y'all can bank on that."

The plan itself was simple. Come Saturday, Ronnie, David, and Dabbo would hide out on the reservoir. And when Mr. Schmidt resumed his ritual, the newly formed Norvic Street Freedom Fight-ers would strike a blow for liberty the likes of which the world had never seen. The orders he gave me were: "You just go on actin' like nothin's gonna happen. And once we got him on the run, you join our side."

Having the old Dabbo back was a boon for all the Freedom Fighters. David was so moved by his commitment that he suggested they camp out overnight on the reservoir to ensure the element of surprise. Ronnie saluted the idea as a key to victory, adding that David should be promoted instantly to Lance Corporal. But as good as it felt being back on Dabbo's team, there was something about his plan that left me unsettled. After all, I'd seen Herr Schmidt in action. Behind a pristine pair of Buddy Holly horn-rims lurked the steel-blue coldness of Hitler's most depraved storm troopers. Caught staring into the rearview from the backseat, I'd had my daring rewarded with a knowing wink and menacing smile. *Yes,* he said telepathically, *I am what you think.* I knew the man's secret self but my battle-ready friends didn't, and I regretted bring-ing them into this mess.

Saturday morning dawned with more than the usual amount of dread. While waiting for the honk of Mr. Schmidt's horn, I devel-oped a case of the jitters my father couldn't ignore. "What the hell you got to be so dang fidgety about?" he snorted, sending blue jets of Pall Mall smoke streaming from both nostrils. This set me to thinking about the snorting-bull trademark on Grandpa Willoughby's Bull Durham tobacco pouch. Drawing comparisons between my old man and a pissed-off bull soothed my anxiety about what would happen if Dabbo's planned offensive went awry. Glad for the distraction, I plopped down on the couch, almost relaxed.

On weekends, when my rambunctiousness grated on my father's nerves, he usually, without looking up from his paper, would yell for my mother to come do something about the "wild Indian" she was raising in his house. To this she'd yell back, "Tell him to go out in the yard and play." This banter would continue back and forth, neither of them addressing me directly, until something in the natural course of the day called me out of doors. But on this particular Saturday, something caused my father to assess my fidgeting differently. Letting the sports page fall to the floor, he leaned forward in his chair for a closer inspection. As far back as I could remember, he'd never examined the subtleties of my behavior this carefully. Slowly, almost considerately, he asked, "What is it ya'll do when you go off with that bunch next door?" For him to be anything but brusque when questioning something was unheard-of. I was dumbfounded. The day had at last come when he sensed something was going on in my world that needed fathering. Feeling him probe my secret concerns worked on me like an opiate, and I gave myself fully to the moment. Tears started welling and I was prepared to welcome the flood—but this was interrupted by the sour *blat* of Mr. Schmidt's horn. "Aw, nothin'," I lied.

This morning, for some reason, Ricky tried hard to steer his father away from the reservoir, dropping hints about needing a little batting practice and how it might come in handy to shag some flies over at the ballpark. Instinctively, I chimed in with some lame-o crap about it being half-price Saturday at the skating rink. The thing I most disliked about Ricky, apart from my mother's pigheaded insistence on pairing us up in the first place, was his inability to grasp the obvious, which in this case was the sad and simple fact that his father had little interest in him save for throwing dirt clods at his head. It wasn't my place to say as much, but I had. "We might as well go on and get us some batting helmets for when your daddy picks us up" is how I'd put it the day before. Inexplicably, this bit of sarcasm drove the truth home for my fellow captive. After striking out on baseball, Ricky all but got down on his knees in the car and begged his father to take us to the zoo. Nothing doing. We were driven straight to the reservoir. Silently, I cursed the both of us for our spinelessness.

This morning Mr. Schmidt abandoned his usual frontal assault in favor of the more sporting method of lobbing much bigger dirt clods in the high-arching trajectory of a mortar shell, which deployment prolonged the anticipation of a direct hit and, in turn, his enjoyment of our degradation.

When the Freedom Fighters made their charge from the paved road beyond the reservoir wall, Mr. Schmidt was admiring the lazy arc of a massive clod bound for the top of his son's noggin. On the run, Dabbo smacked our tormentor squarely between the shoulder blades with a sun-baked dirt clump the size of a golf ball. The sharp *thunk* echoed across the putrid waters like a rolling clap of thunder. Then Ronnie opened fire, infantry-style, taking potshots with a Daisy air rifle, the unmistakable mini-thuds of BBs signaling direct hits to his enemy's kneecap. David got in on the action with a slingshot and pocketful of chinaberries; the white splatter marks on the back of Mr. Schmidt's green polo shirt later proved that he'd found his target.

I was tempted, at first glance, to label the Freedom Fighters' opening salvo a resounding success. Instead, I prayed my pals would hold off on the victory celebration. Soon they'd see Mr. Schmidt reduce the effects of a royal bushwhacking to a mild inconvenience, and come to understand what I already knew: Klaus Schmidt was no ordinary foe. Recovering from a well-executed blindsiding was, for him, a piddling process. Mild disbelief gave way to a survival instinct that had military training stenciled to its core. In a display of lightning reflex, the former soldier shoulder-rolled down the sloped retaining wall and landed in a warrior's crouch on the dirt road a few feet from where Ricky and I were huddled together. When he came up grinning like the know-it-all mass mur-derer whose picture I'd seen in the newspaper, I ran as fast as I could away from the site where I knew he planned to fight to the bitter end.

Quick as a snakebite, Mr. Schmidt nailed Dabbo in the groin with an actual *rock* he'd scooped up off the retaining wall, which Dabbo now scampered behind with a painful yelp. With him down, Mr. Schmidt focused a hard-rock counterattack at Ronnie, also hid-ing behind the wall. David he sent scrambling with just a steely gaze.

Our battle strategy hadn't taken into account the probability that father and son would join forces. In fairness to Dabbo, I'd have bet money against it myself. I'm inclined to think that for Ricky it was more of an involuntary reaction, not a true warrior's instinct; yet remembering how Mr. Schmidt threw himself into battle, it's hard to imagine the long-suffering son not pitching in. In any case, there's no doubt that his falling into step with his father had an effect on the skirmish. Technically, Ricky added little firepower—his rock-throwing abilities were barely a cut above his sister's. On the other hand, his enlistment seemed to double Mr. Schmidt's resolve to annihilate the Freedom Fighters. The newly united fam-ily duo was turning the tide, and if momentum continued to shift in their direction the war would soon be over. A whose-side-are-you-on interrogation loomed in my neutral corner like one of my father's unpaid bills.

My rejoining the Norvic Street Freedom Fighters was destiny ful-filling itself. I'm glad to say it was more for the love of my friends than my hatred of Ricky's father that my long-overdue decision to fight back arrived with such clarity. From my eye-level position on the right flank, fifteen yards from where Mr. Schmidt crouched, I saw I had only one option. Imitating Rocky Colavito—the best throwing arm in baseball—I pegged a perfect hard-rock strike to the side of his neck, a wallop that sent his black-rimmed Buddy Holly glasses flying and the sadistic bastard crawling on all fours.

Ricky threw himself into an all-out temper tantrum right there on the banks of the most toxic waste site in the state of Texas. "No fair! Y'all cheated, he's supposed to be on our side!" he hollered, kicking dirt and waving his arms like a stranded motorist trying to flag down passing cars. With Ricky making a sitting duck of himself, Ronnie fired a single BB that bit into his left thigh, the sting of which tripled the intensity of his hissy fit. The momentum suddenly swung back in favor of the Freedom Fighters.

On the battlefield, while Ricky bounced around on one leg protesting my defection, his father groped in the dirt for his glasses, which were now resting peacefully at the bottom of the die-if-you-dare-enter-these-waters reservoir. Who would've thought he couldn't see four feet in front of his face without glasses?

Dabbo chose that moment to call a cease-fire. Having scored the battle's decisive blow, I took the place of honor on Ronnie Thomas's handlebars and was delivered home a war hero and patriot.

Heavy-handed punishment was doled out unsparingly. My mother whipped me with a chinaberry switch until my legs bled, and when the switch became too frayed to inflict pain she grabbed a hairbrush and continued to beat the hell out of me. But I didn't mind that dull pain; it was the sting of the switch I'd never get used to.

Though she exhausted herself trying to beat an admission of guilt out of me, I remained unrepentant. When I flatly refused to apologize to Mr. Schmidt, she made a valiant attempt with a third whipping, this time with a coat hanger. Still unable to produce the desired result, she then sent my father into my bedroom to pry a confession out of me. Wincing at the sight of my legs, he declared, "Damn, son, your momma's done wore your ass slap out." And for the first time I can remember, he sat down on the edge of my bed. Lowering his voice so my mother couldn't hear from the other side of the door, he said, "You go on and dry up that cryin.' Your momma don't need to know nothin' about what we fixin' to talk about in here." He lit up a Pall Mall, pausing for his trademark blue-smoke exhale and thus giving me a moment to adjust to the notion that he had no plans of picking up where my mother had left off. He patted the bed for me to sit down beside him. "If y'all was shootin' BBs and throwin' rocks at that outfit next door, I reckon y'all knew what you was doin.' I cain't say if what y'all did was right or wrong, but I'll tell ya one damn thing: I flat out wouldn't trust that boy's daddy as far as I can sling him. If what went on down yonder at the levee is somethin' I need to be knowin' about, you go on and tell me."

Twice in one day my father had stepped outside himself with careful regard for the complexities behind my propped-up façade, and each was an act of kindness strong enough to keep me going for another ten years. Thinking my chest might explode with the pride of being the son of this good and decent man, I looked him directly in the eyes and said, "The son of a bitch had it comin', Dad."

In time, an unspoken truce settled over Norvic Street. The beginning of the new school year imposed a non-negotiated peace on both factions. Though still in a bad mood over her failure to beat contrition out of me, my mother showed signs of warming to my theory that the reservoir skirmish had turned a negative into a positive. After the heart-to-heart with my father, I felt vindicated enough to declare that reuniting an estranged father and son in the preservation of their bloodline, lost cause or not, merited celebration instead of switch whippings. My mother, I could tell, wasn't so sure.

Within a week of the ambush, the Schmidt family moved a half block east and a short block north to a house on the corner of Flint and Wiggins streets. To hear Dabbo tell the story, the Freedom Fighters had driven the entire German army out of Jacinto City. My pointing out that the Schmidts were alive and well and still living less than a hundred yards away did little to diminish his sense of triumph, and his gloating couldn't have been more pronounced if they'd all moved back to Berlin. But Dabbo's prediction that Mr. Schmidt's "grenade chuckin'" would soon be over proved prescient. That day's dirt clods were the last he ever threw at me, or, so far as I know, at his son.

Ricky bemoaned the Freedom Fighters' coup until the day he turned up flaunting a shining black fiberglass bow and a quiver of razor-tipped hunting arrows. Not one to pout when he could be rubbing our noses in the wimpiness of our wooden bows and practice arrows, he announced his sleek new equipment made him the undisputed King of the Universe. His newfound superiority might have been bearable were it not for the custom-made hand grip and the three-fingered deerskin shooting glove he wore on his right hand. Undone by these flashy accoutrements, we sank deep into an envious funk.

By the end of a second day's belittling, Dabbo had had enough. "I ain't gonna put up with this dookey anymore," he drawled. "Me and you fixin' to go on over to Market Street and collect us some Coke bottles. We gonna have to get us a razor-tip arrow if we're ever gonna shut that shit heel up."

Thanks to the steady stream of motorists flinging empty soda bottles in the slag and creosote weeds half-surviving along the railroad tracks, Market Street Road was an Eden of quick-fix cash for those willing to harvest that sordid fruit. We spent an unseasonably cool September Saturday scrounging the tracks for empty bottles, pausing now and then to congratulate ourselves on the growing size of our haul. Unfortunately, our spirits took a nasty plunge when the return deposit on a grocery sack full of soda bottles and the milk jug stolen from Mrs. Boyd's porch tallied less than half the price of a single razor-tipped hunting arrow. Following Mr. Buck's advice on how to make up the shortfall, we spent two weeks, after school and on weekends, searching vacant lots and back alleys for generators, tire rims, lead pipes, drive shafts—anything metal, large or small, that could be hauled back to Dabbo's garage in a rust-corroded red Radio Flyer wagon. When Mr. Buck figured we'd accumulated enough scrap iron to bring five dollars on the salvage-yard scales, we loaded the twisted heap into the bed of his pickup.

True to his word, he hauled it—Dabbo and I riding high atop our good fortune like World Series heroes—to Green's Bayou Salvage Yard, where a cashier's check was made out for $4.34. With this added to the $2.20 we'd cleared on the soda-bottle venture, Dabbo and I went in partners on a $5.89 hunting arrow and used the left-over change on celebratory packs of Twinkies and nickel Cokes. Thrilled by the success of the arms deal, Dabbo reckoned our purchase was key to restoring the balance of power on Norvic Street, putting me back on top as boss of the neighborhood, with him as my right-hand man. In this perfect world, he considered himself a modern-day "Sir Lan Sir Lot" and me a version of "Old King Alfred."

"Now that we can keep Ricky from messin' everything up," he exclaimed, "we might start back havin' some fun around here."

On his best day, Ricky Schmidt greeted the world oblivious to his lack of natural leadership. The fact that he possessed neither the charm nor the poetic sensibility to draw the likes of Ronnie Thomas and David Warren under his control flew over his head like one of his father's dirt clods; and likewise, that on a playground where razor-tipped arrows had taken the place of cap pistols, it might not be a good idea to go around barking orders like some B-movie gangster. If I hadn't glimpsed the dark soul of this puppet's master, there's little doubt I would've pronounced Ricky's reputation as neighborhood pariah and ill-will magnet entirely justified. Had I not seen the motivation behind Mr. Schmidt gifting his son with professional-caliber archery equipment as anything but a subliminal message to go out and nail the sneaky bastards who'd ambushed him, I'd be hard-pressed not to label Ricky an incurable bore and a mammoth bully. But knowing as I did the depth of his need to please his father, compassion counseled that I cut the boy some slack.

For me, the hallmark of Ricky's obliviousness was how, when merrily turning the playground into a battlefield, he so blissfully ignored the fact that Dabbo and Ronnie would rather bury a dull practice arrow in his chest than tie their shoes. Because seeing him dead didn't mean enough that I wanted my pals to be sent off to reform school, I made it my business to keep an eye out for retaliatory signs among the Freedom Fighters.

One late-October Saturday, we gathered to play bows and arrows. Having gotten word that Ricky would be away on a father-son outing, we'd gone about organizing the game with crossed fingers. Communicating with handwritten notes passed in the hallway between classes—Dabbo alone had been filled in verbally, and this I'd done in a whisper—we were optimistic that our game of pretend might safely come to pass without Ricky being there to screw it up. But before we could get our bows strung and sort out who was pretending to be who, guess who came galloping up the sidewalk.

"Ya'll playin'?" Ricky called ahead.

"Was," Dabbo grunted.

"Dibs on fastest horse, quickest draw, and prettiest girl!" he shouted back.

The look of astonishment among the Freedom Fighters couldn't have been more pronounced had the Devil himself popped out of Mrs. Boyer's bushes and taken ownership of our souls. Ricky had broken the unspoken code of conduct governing fair play. Everyone knew that honoring first dibs was a universal law, even Ricky, and we'd sooner eat broccoli than contest a legitimate claim. However, playground rules clearly stated that the person calling dibs could reap only one special attribute. Ricky's claiming three of Roy Rogers's best qualities left only Zorro's swordsmanship, Lash Larue's expertise with a whip, Tonto's speech patterns, and Gabby Hayes's struggles with a headstrong Jeep named Nellybelle as the raw material from which to construct a character.

It's to Ricky's credit that he threw himself into games of pretend with wholehearted conviction. He alone rode a golden palomino with a hand-tooled saddle trimmed in Mexican silver, pearl-handled pistols adorning his hips. His hats were white, his boots polished. The minions playing supporting roles in his high-noon dramas were, at best, donkey-riding prospectors with virtually no prospects. But there was, as was often the case with my ex–new best friend, a glaring disconnect between the dreamer and the dream. As played by Ricky, archetypal heroes like Wyatt Earp, Roy Rogers, and the Lone Ranger came across as Snidely Whiplash wannabes. In spite of his exalted imaginings on the playground, the only role naturally suited to his boorish sensibility was archvillain.

So it was peeved desperadoes who spilled out into the grassy alley behind our house, Ricky harboring old grievances and the Freedom Fighters spoiling for another fight. I, too, would've been, but for practice arrows flying so close to human bodies. Ricky scarcely noticed that most of the close calls were his. For his safety, I kept the newly acquired razor-tip in my quiver.

But he was the one who initiated the re-enactment of his favorite scene from the cowboy movies: the bad guy emptying his revolver at the feet of some poor old sodbuster, who, lacking the will to defend his honor, dances like a fool. In contrast to the dandy who was Ricky's imaginary hero, Dabbo had in mind the infamous gunslinger turned into a simple farmer who was no longer looking for trouble but would, if provoked, rather die than let some tinhorn city slicker belittle him. By choosing Dabbo as his sap, Ricky had set the stage for a final showdown.

Ricky made the first move, growing right before my eyes to the height of six two. Decked out in a tailor-made city suit, a string tie, and a flat-brimmed beaver hat, his pencil-thin moustache neatly trimmed, he called Dabbo out into the streets of Dodge City. "Let's settle this thing man-to-man," he drawled. With a slight flare of his nostrils, Dabbo—in the humble wardrobe of a reformed outlaw trying to make a go of it with a pretty girl, a mule, and a plot of land—accepted the invitation. Ricky rested a razor-tipped arrow on the top of his bow's grip, pulled the string half taut, and pointed at Dabbo's feet, then snarled, "Dance, pardner." But this wasn't some gussied-up character actor pretending to call him out; it was Ricky Schmidt, intent on drawing real blood. So, too, was it Dabbo Buck, whose eyes flashed crimson as he hissed, "You can kiss my rosy red ass. I don't dance for nobody—'specially some Jerry son of a bitch like you."

Ricky let the arrow fly.

Following the arrow's slow-motion, downward trajectory, I noticed the three feather strips, white with brown flecks, that stabilized its rear end, and the arrowhead itself reminded me of one of Mr. Buck's triangle lead sinkers. Cutting these observations off, the arrow then sliced through Dabbo's jeans, flesh, and even a main artery before coming to rest in the muscle and bone of his lower left leg, sticking out of his britches like a clock hand pointing to two.

Dabbo screamed loud enough to alert his mother—two hundred feet away and inside her house—that he'd been mortally wounded. Trailing blood across the broken white shingles outside the garage, he hopped on one foot down the alley into Norvic Street, where the arrow worked its way out of his leg and fell onto the asphalt.

Neighborhood adults took little notice of our Tarzan yells as we jumped off the garage, and yawned at the panic-stricken screams of "Get off!" from the bottom of a ten-kid dog pile. Men walking home from the graveyard shift were immune to Margie Buck's hog calling, and late risers slept like logs through her husband's coaxing of his old pickup back to life at five-thirty. Breaking glass, busting shingles, bicycle collisions, and even my parents' knock-down-drag-outs were auditory non-events. Dabbo's wail, however, was recognized as a legitimate distress signal. Within seconds, screen doors were slamming shut behind a half dozen grown-ups racing alarmed into the street.

His mother and mine were the first to converge on him in Mr. Carnew's front yard. "Ricky shot me! He shot me!" Dabbo howled through the snot and tears covering his face like Vaseline. Margie ripped open the wet tear in his blue jeans to reveal the three-inch slice from which a two-foot stream of blood now spurted with the rhythm of her son's pounding heart.

My mother tore my T-shirt into strips for a tourniquet. Dabbo stuck his foot into the mop bucket his sister had been sent to retrieve from their house. By now a crowd had gathered around the scene, one or two of the adults unable to resist adding to the drama.

"You need to get that boy on down to the hospital 'fore he bleeds to death," Alley Jo Chenier blurted out with characteristic insensitivity.

"Shsst," Margie hissed. "What in the world's wrong with you? Why you wanna scare him like that? Somebody oughta shoot a arrow into that fat mouth of yours."

I was trying to blink away the image of my best friend dead when she and Dabbo and my mother sped off to the emergency room with his foot still in the bucket.

Crossing Norvic Street to await their return at home, I noticed Ricky skipping hurriedly away from the scene of the crime. I walked over to where his arrow rested in the middle of the street, picked it up, and called, "Hey, you forgot this."

This was the last time I remember seeing Ricky Schmidt. Not long afterward, his family moved away. And within a year or so, my partnership with Dabbo dissolved completely when I encountered the awkwardness of junior high and a whole new set of social concerns. Despite our best efforts, the two-year age difference between us became a chasm we simply couldn't cross.

PART THREE

Mrs. Boyer

Mrs. Boyer's property had a foreboding quality that scared every kid in the neighborhood. Jungle landscape and dense shadow obscured everything but the house's front entrance. My recollections of the turn-of-the-century furnishings crammed into her dingy living room put me in mind of a poor Miss Havisham. But it was long before any of us arrived on the scene that Mrs. Boyer's great expectations had turned to dark resignation. The atmosphere surrounding that household suggested only one thing to an otherwise curious nine-year-old: KEEP OUT.

More than any family in Jacinto City, the Boyers bore the heartbreak of World War II like a curse on the bloodline. By my mother's account, Mrs. Boyer's only son, an Air Force bombardier stationed in the north of England, met and married a girl from Coventry, and they had two daughters a year apart. Deeply in love and devoted to his family, it was said of Bruce Boyer that, in spite of all that was going on around him, a happier man was not to be found on British soil.

Near the end of the war, walking home from her job in a shirt factory, his wife was killed in one of the Luftwaffe's last air raids. Grief-stricken to the point of suicide, Mr. Boyer was given a medical discharge and brought the girls home to Norvic Street, where his mother took up the task of raising them.

The Bruce Boyer I knew was a wounded animal—whip-thin, his eyes as dark as poisoned pools, his head down and shoulders hunched forward. "That man looks like a question mark to me," my mother once said. Mr. Boyer made short work of any public outings. Along with Dabbo, I perceived danger in his sorrow and vowed to steer clear of the brooding ex-bombardier's flight path, though this was needless self-importance on our part, as he took no interest in anything outside himself. The demons eating his insides out held him spellbound, and the real world, if indeed it actually registered with him, seemed as much a private hell as his own heart's interior. He came and went, phantomlike, in an old Dodge panel truck.

Despite the residual shell shock hanging over their house like a nuclear winter, his daughters, Elaine and Jennifer, were adventurous spirits and quite accommodating to their nine-year-old neighbor. Thanks to them, during impromptu nurses-and-wounded-soldier games, I had occasion to feel pubescent hands travel the length and breadth of my growing body and was content to lie motionless in the cool dampness beneath the bushes next to their house while the girls took turns nursing me back to life with a thoroughness unmatched by the health professionals I've come across in my adult life. Free of charge, they allowed me to gaze upon their nakedness. And of course there were occasional forays into touching, once I learned to be still and allow the hormonal fruits of adolescent innocence to arrive at my door like fresh milk.

But my earliest Norvic Street memory is of the night their grandfather died, a few months after we moved in next door. At the time the Boyers were without electricity, the same on-again, off-again proposition in their household it would become in ours. The prolonged candle-lit deathwatch being held across the driveway was taking its toll on Mrs. Boyer. Given the nasty hand she'd been dealt by life's circumstances—the worst card now being her husband's impending death—it's no wonder that her first appearance at our door that evening in 1956 had such a lasting effect on me.

In this story, truth and fairness are overruled by first impressions. The image burned forever into my nearly six-year-old mind of a toothless hag's gnarly hands rap-rap-rapping on our screen door has been proven by time to be a distortion, but it must be an accurate account of what I saw. Death had made a house call to the wrong address, and I answered the door.

"Young man, are your parents home?"

No answer. I stood slack-jawed and frozen, watching the movement of her lips and hearing the words, yet words of my own would not present themselves.

"Young man, *are* your parents home?"

Her stern emphasis on the verb clearly demanded an answer, but the only response I could muster was none at all.

Then, for the third time: "Are your parents home?"

A simple enough question, had I not heard an implicit threat: *Look, you little prick, if you don't answer me I'm going to gouge your eyeballs loose and suck your brain out through the sockets.* In response, I finally peed down the front of my short pants, apparently a coded message: *Please don't kill me. I'm trying to cooperate, but right now only my water works.*

My mother's hand on my shoulder broke the stalemate.

Suddenly, my vocal cords issue a deep *"Whoaah!"* that gains volume and a machine-gun vibrato that matches my pounding feet as I beat a hasty retreat to the farthest corner of my bedroom. Beneath a pile of dirty clothes, I select a more pitiful intonation to alert my mother of my whereabouts, my heart pounding hard right up to my Adam's apple.

Undeterred by my cowardly lack of neighborliness, Mrs. Boyer came directly to the point. And my father, always effective when addressing someone else's woes, rose to the occasion. With a mechanic's caged lightbulb and an extension cord, he brought light from the wall socket in my room to the tiny bedroom where Old Man Boyer lay dying.

Calming me down was a long and tedious task: I attached myself to my mother's hip with vise-grip resolve as she made sweet iced tea and sandwiches for the family next door. Due to the fit I pitched about her crossing the line separating us from a house of death, she couldn't deliver these refreshments herself, and my father assumed the task of transporting them on a TV-dinner tray along the same line as the extension cord.

Calm enough now to be curious, I watched the drama unfolding across the driveway, where the bulb he'd hung cast a harsh yellow light into the four corners of the old man's bedroom, but sleep claimed me before Mr. Boyer stole quietly away that June night.

Later, my mother explained what it was I'd seen the night Mrs. Boyer sent me running for cover. "Son, her nerves were so tore up, she forgot to put her teeth in and do her hair up. She didn't even know all she had on was her housecoat when she come to the door. You're gonna have to go on over there and tell her you're sorry."

I approached Mrs. Boyer in her backyard a few days later with a composed apology. "I'm sorry you scared me so much the day Mr. Boyer died," I said, thinking that didn't sound quite right. "I didn't mean for you to scare me so much. Momma says I wasn't nice to you when you needed me to be, so I hope you won't be mad at me."

Mrs. Boyer and my mother would forge a peculiar friendship. Though they rarely spoke to each other, it was commonly believed among the neighborhood's gossip elite that they shared a bond no one else could understand. Except for the night her husband died, to my knowledge Mrs. Boyer never set foot in my parents' house again, which suited me fine. Although I eventually gained a measure of compassion for the poor woman's plight, ultimately I could see her only as the toothless hag who caused me to wet my pants.

.   .   .

In the spring of 1960, with a good deal of prompting from Mrs. Boyer, Dabbo and I decided to dig a vegetable garden. Two gardens, actually: one on either side of the chain-link fence separating our backyard from Mrs. Boyer's, Dabbo digging on her side, I on ours.

Under the watchful eye of this still-scary lady, we put shovels, rakes, and hoes to use, and by mid-afternoon two rows of gooey black soil—"east Texas gumbo," the locals called it—were eked out, mulched, and ready for planting.

Admiring our work, I remarked innocently to my mother, when she walked up to have a look, that I thought my row was prettier than Dabbo's.

"Is not," he said. Simultaneously, the hoe in his hand came down on the top of my head, splitting my scalp open.

All the sounds of a normal spring afternoon—chirpy chatter and the lazy traffic—silenced themselves, and Norvic Street suddenly seemed like a scene from that science-fiction movie *The Day the Earth Stood Still.*

My mother's eyes commanded me to remain upright and conscious until she got to me. I cast a glance in Dabbo's direction—an inquiry of sorts, to confirm if he'd actually just smashed me over the head with the sharp end of a garden hoe. And if so, why?

But his eyes were two television test patterns advertising the end of another broadcasting day; "The Star-Spangled Banner" had been played and the sign-off prayer delivered. No clues were forthcoming from my unpredictable little friend.

When my brain completed cross-referencing my reaction with Dabbo's and my mother's, it finally registered that the warm red sticky stuff on my left hand was my very own blood, and my scream could be heard in Beaumont. "He killed me with a brain concussion! He killed me with a brain concussion! Dabbo killed me with a brain concussion!"

He broke away and ran across the street, hiding under Mr. Carnew's house until long after I returned from the emergency room with seven stitches in my head.

Old Mrs. Boyer enjoyed bountiful snap beans, black-eyed peas, and okra that fall. Dabbo and I were back in stride long before the stitches were removed, and of course Elaine and Jennifer paid special attention to the treatment of my wounds.

Spit-Shine Charlie and Grandma Katie

As a boy my favorite place in the world was my grandmother's apron-covered lap. Her favorite place in the world was the tiny bedroom where she kept her Bible, a wicker rocking chair, and an old tube radio tuned to the hundred-thousand-watt radio station KXEG in Del Rio, Texas. Lost in the scent of her leather-covered Bible and the overheated transformers, we went places, met people, and saw things that would shape the remainder of our lives. Rocking on her lap and listening to a live Carter Family performance, I remember knowing for the first time that I was loved. In time I came to understand the nature of her love as being part of an even greater love, one that loved my grandmother for loving me.

One day I asked if she had anything to do with this God I'd been hearing about. Without pause or condescension she answered, "Why, yes, child, I do, but no more than you or your momma or a rank stranger on the street. Some say God's sittin' up in heaven mad as a hornet 'bout how we actin' down here, but I don't think he's mad at all. Ain't nobody mad coulda ever made somebody half as special as you." She was the enlightened enchantress of my childhood. I was, and still am, very much in love with Grandma Katie.

All these years later, the smell of burning leaves often transports me to the tiny front yard on Avenue P, where on an autumn day in 1954 my grandmother buried me up to the neck in freshly fallen post-oak leaves. Like every great adult playmate, she knew the value of repetition and, for my pleasure alone, spent the entire afternoon re-raking leaves in an attempt to create the perfect pile. More than just that, she created the perfect day. Then, when the daylight and my interest in being buried alive began to wane, she raked the pile high one last time. "Why, I do believe a fine young man like you should do the honors," she said, ceremoniously handing me a lit kitchen match.

From the blaze, sparks sprang like newborn shooting stars in reverse, defying gravity and rising far above our heads. A hoot owl on the telephone pole harrumphed his approval. Trees leaned in for a closer look. Houses kept a respectful distance. But the wind couldn't resist the urge to see what it could do, hence more sparks. The pyromaniac in me today can be traced to the moment Grandma Katie passed me that match.

Before long, our roaring fire gave way to a smoldering glow and, eventually, the pitch-black darkness of another star-studded witching hour. It was, after all, Halloween season, when the blurred edges of blue shadows, the coolness of day's end, and my encroaching bedtime normally put me in mind of ghosts and their attendant hobgoblins. Not on this evening. Backed by my grandmother's fierce innocence, the chains of my four-year-old imagination refused to be rattled. To be well loved is to be free of the evil lurking around the next darkened corner. Every child should know that feeling.

Later on, after I'd played in the bathtub until my fingers and toes were nearly purple as prunes, she read me my favorite Uncle Remus story—the one where Br'er Rabbit gets in a jam with the Tar Baby. I was fast asleep before B'rer Fox could outline, for the hapless Br'er Bear, his plan to snare Br'er Rabbit. My life since has been an ongoing search for the stillness that marked the end of that one perfect day.

By the age of eleven or so, I found that the simple comings and goings of day-to-day life on Norvic Street often sent me into prolonged periods of goose-bumped reverie. The perpetual motion of jet-black garbage men, gliding from the bumpers of slow-rolling sanitation trucks and tossing trash cans high over their heads, worked on me like a hypnotic drug. Watching crossing guards, meter readers, carhops, and even the lunch-line ladies at the elementary school could send me into a trance lasting from two seconds to five minutes.

The most reliable source of mundane enchantment around Jacinto City at the time was Spit-Shine Charlie, the humpbacked man who shined shoes at Blassingame's Barber Shop. Like my grandmother, he held me in thrall.

I fell into the habit of escaping the midsummer heat by sitting in that air-conditioned barbershop watching him shine shoes. Mr. Blassingame gave no indication he minded my loitering, and in fact made me feel welcome by allowing me to sweep up around the shop. Curly, the baldheaded second barber, called me Charlie's shadow, and my idol called me "lil potner." I was a member of the club.

Charlie's physical attributes lay somewhere between a dwarfish Louis Armstrong and Toulouse Lautrec. Arriving daily in a natty bowler and redolent with Violet talcum powder, he was nineteenth century through and through, and for all I knew he was well over a hundred years old.

As if in defiance of his thwarted stature, his eyes surveyed the room like enormous brown-and-yellow searchlights, his crippled body just along for the ride. His right leg was five inches shorter than his left, a defect remedied with a pair of black high-top lace-ups, one of them platformed to compensate for the shortfall. In place of his right shoulder blade, a hump the size of a bowling ball topped off his list of afflictions without hindering his disposition.

God's external gift to Charlie was his hands. He might've been five foot two, had he been able to stand up straight, but his hands belonged to someone who was six foot six. When he turned his long, graceful fore and middle fingers into a reverse *L* to put polish on a shoe, it was done with a maestro's touch. When I asked why he put the polish on with his bare fingers, his brown eyes twinkled like jaundiced stars. "I likes to puts da shinola on thisaway; thataway I gets a feel for what he need. A man's shoes be like a pretty gal; you gots to see whats they need fore you go puttin' a shine to 'em."

The finishing touch was the mainstay of Charlie's livelihood. It started with a maneuver he called the over-under and sideways-down, a trick that required the use of two brushes and blinding hand speed. To say he took a brush in each hand falls well short of the truth. In the hundred-plus times I watched, I can't recall seeing either hand ever touch a brush. Amid an appreciative chorus of oohs and aahs, he juggled, twirled, and flipped his brushes into the air while giving an old pair of shoes the first layer of a new shine.

This restoration was over when he whipped out his rag and started whistling "Chattanooga Choo Choo" or "Sweet Georgia Brown." Charlie had perfected a method that combined whistling, spitting on the toes, buffing in the shine, and yanking off the rag with a flick of his wrist that popped it like a firecracker, each element timed strategically with four-bar intervals. Charlie did with his hands what tap dancers do with their feet. With his song completed, he'd roll back on his stool and let the man examine the results for himself. When the customer beamed his satisfaction, Charlie carefully painted each heel and sole with black liquid polish. Beginning to end, the process took less than six minutes.

In a quiet afternoon lull, Charlie motioned for me to come closer. "Shine costs two bits," he said, nodding at his homemade kit, "but poppin' da rag is where I gets my tips. I might whistle a tune and pop my rag, but I cain't go lettin' myself think I shinin' better 'cause I's a cripple and rollin' on my stool down round his feet. Naw, suh, da good Lawd's on my side much as the next man's. It ain't no differnt if a man be black or white, rich or po'. If he ain't no good to hisself, ain't no good for nobody else. That's what I need my lil potner to remember one day when he thinks of Ole Shine dead an' gone."

Around age thirteen, I began drifting away from Charlie. As the sixties wore on, the barbershop became my least likely hangout. I dropped in from time to time, but a nervous interest in junior-high girls kept me from losing myself in Charlie's artistry. I had lost the innocence that he retained.

One slow Saturday morning, Curly came to the house on Norvic Street to tell me Charlie had passed away. "He nodded off on his stool like we all seen him do," he said, "only this time he didn't wake up." Allowing that he thought Charlie was "in a better place up yonder with two good legs, shinin' shoes and whistlin' up a storm," the bald barber adopted the deferential tone old men use when death claims one of their peers. "Seein's how he didn't have a family or next of kin, we thought you'd be the one who ought to have this." Tears crested but didn't break on Curly's lower eyelids as he handed me Spit-Shine Charlie's shoeshine kit. "It's what he would've wanted."

Within a year and a half of each other, Grandma Katie and Spit-Shine Charlie died. It should go without saying that I loved my mother and father with the fierceness inherent in both the bloodlines from which I sprang. It is, however, this common blood that for nearly two decades kept me from experiencing the love of my parents as anything but a primal instinct for survival, theirs and mine. With my grandmother and Charlie, though, I experienced love as something tangible between myself and another human being. In the gently powerful presence of these two exceptional souls, love was made easy for my understanding. Love was the source of their ability to mesmerize me so completely.

Their deaths triggered a prolonged period of muted loneliness that lasted until the birth of my children. And with the arrival of each of my daughters, the ability to love without expectation came bubbling slowly from the forgotten depths of who I was when I first crawled up in my grandmother's lap. Thanks to the abused wife of a sharecrop farmer, a crippled shoeshine man, and four little girls, I was able to emerge from the dark forest of an angry heart into the light of love that will forever exist between my parents and me.

LaQuita Freeman and the Kotex Kid

On a crisp November morning, the year Hurricane Carla reconfigured most of the southeast Texas coastline, I rode my bicycle to school, dreaming of what it would feel like to kiss LaQuita Freeman on the mouth. With the air bristling cool for the first time in six months, the world seemed freshly awakened from a long night's sleep. Mother Nature's lifting the lid on oppressive humidity came with a boost of optimism missing since Grandma Katie had died the previous April. A hint of autumn gave Norvic Street the feel of having made a turn for the better. Mental acuity was sharp, spirits were high, and flights of fancy, particularly those of falling in love, were making a comeback around the neighborhood.

LaQuita Freeman was out of my league and I knew it, not because she was rich—her father's absence left her mother as short of cash as a construction worker during the rainy season—but because she was beautiful and I was a moron. The sight of LaQuita strolling self-possessed down the hallway, sixth-grade notebook cradled in the crook of her arm, impervious to the hormonal hubbub stirred by her presence, made spellbound dunces of every would-be Prince Charming within spit-wad distance, yours truly most noticeably. Anglo-Spanish bloodlines rendered LaQuita Freeman the most compelling creature the Jacinto City Elementary School's student body had ever gawked at. The chances of my exchanging intimacies with such stunning beauty—being all frog and no prince—stood less than one in a hundred zillion.

The cool weather made the six-block ride to school on my bicycle a heightened-awareness meditation. Bike riding suited the natural fluidity of my eleven-year-old coordination, and few rode with more flair. I made it my habit to ride on the left side of the street, facing the oncoming traffic, more to maximize my ability to dodge what I saw coming than to minimize the odds of being run down from behind. Still, I couldn't have predicted seeing LaQuita.

Alternating between riding with no hands and steering with the blue and white streamers spewing from my handlebar grips, I was singing J. Frank Wilson's "Last Kiss" when Mrs. Freeman pulled up on the right in her lime-green Dodge Dart, catching me in the act of singing a stupid song and fantasizing about her daughter. The panic rising in my chest quickly subsided when something caught my eye. Sitting next to her mother, less than ten feet away from me, was the object of my obsession, pretty as a picture in a brand-new school dress.

Whether I can lay claim to what might be called a normal boyhood in the years leading up to 1961 is subject to debate. But in matters pertaining to LaQuita Freeman, apart from a brief stint spying on her from the tall weeds across the street from her house, I'd declare myself as normal as running water. Like any eleven-year-old boy, I'd sooner have danced naked in public than gaze into the dark olive eyes of Aphrodite's younger sister. Yet that's what I did. And to my surprise, a faint smile, slightly less noncommittal than the Mona Lisa's, appeared on the very lips I'd have drunk a gallon of Black Flag roach killer for the pleasure of a passing peck on.

Emboldened by this hint of promise, I began racing toward a future that included holding LaQuita's hand during the Saturday matinee at the Capitan Theater. Preening and pedaling, I kept my profile alongside their car. I was practically riding to school with the love of my life. "Who Put the Bomp (In the Bomp, Bomp, Bomp)" rocketed to number one on my internal hit parade. My Schwinn Jaguar roared like a '56 Chevy with glasspack mufflers. Considering the lack of influence that gravity had on the moment, I might as well have been hurling myself through space.

The cars belonging to teachers and other employees were always parked at an angle in front of the school building, front bumpers to the curb, and approaching school from the left-hand side of the street required me to skirt their rear bumpers. There was little room for error. Until that morning, I had little need of it.

Mr. Weiss, my sixth-grade teacher, owned a late-model Plymouth with vertical tail fins. There were two things about Mr. Weiss that everybody knew. One, he was the only Jew in Jacinto City. Two, he parked his supersized hot rod in the same slanted slot every morning, so normally I navigated around its protrusions with my built-in radar.

In the process of staging one last sidelong glance to lay the foundation for a later pledge of undying love, I decided on the move where I stand up on the pedals and steer with no hands. Bad idea. A second later I rammed the left-rear quarter panel of Mr. Weiss's white Batmobile. The impact sent me headfirst onto the pavement, where I left half the skin on the right side of my face on the pea-gravel blacktop.

LaQuita's mother was the first to reach me. She simply opened her door to where I lay listening to the sounds of a typical November morning. Not until a vision of LaQuita appeared above me like the Mexican ghost of Florence Nightingale did I feel the humiliating pain of crashing into Mr. Weiss's car.

The awkwardness of exchanging intimacies with my beloved under such unflattering circumstances was more than I could bear: I had no choice but to die in the vicinity of her open arms. So complete was my surrender, I think I actually drifted off into a dream in which I rode LaQuita home on the pump seat of my bicycle, its handlebar tassels a flying testament to my overall good fortune.

When I found myself back in the world, Mr. Vick, the head custodian, was directing curious onlookers to "stand back and give the boy some room." Before my defense system could realign itself, I spilled the beans to everyone in earshot. "I was ridin' along lookin' at LaQuita when I hit something."

The worst thing that could've happened just had. Debbie Twilley, the biggest blabbermouth in our class, heard my pitiful confession and sped off to spread the news that I'd totaled my bike, showing off for LaQuita.

Humiliation prolonged itself in every possible direction. My face flatly refused to heal. The dent in Mr. Weiss's fender was practically granted status as a historical landmark. And with me back on foot, taunts hurled by passing bicyclists—"Hey, lover boy, need a ride?"—were taken in grim stride as I turned inward, a marked man and a lovesick fool.

I can't remember how or when I was assigned the job of Kotex courier, the trauma of my first few solo purchases perhaps blocking the recall. Most likely it was the summer of 1960, a year and a half before the first flickers of sexual self-consciousness announced that something was fundamentally wrong about my mother's sending me out to buy her Kotex. As a boy of ten, I should've been spared the knowledge of packaging subtleties that differentiated one box of Kotex from another. No matter how violently or whimperingly I made my protest known, she refused to relinquish the ritual. Without fail, the arrival of her monthly curse brought me face-to-face with the dilemma of being seen holding a giant box of Kotex Supers in the checkout line.

"Honey," she'd say, "I need you to run down to the store and get me a box of Supers."

"Aw, Momma, don't make me go get you no Kotex. Somebody might see me."

"You ain't but eleven years old. Nobody's payin' attention to what you're buyin'."

"They do, too. I ain't goin'."

"If I get your daddy's belt, I reckon you'll go all right."

"You can use three belts, I still ain't goin'."

"One . . . two . . . three . . . four . . . five . . . six . . . seven . . ."

"Son of a bitch."

"Keep talking like that, and I'll wash your mouth out with soap. Now go on and git."

Blindfold and spin me in tight circles until I'm drunk as my favorite uncle, and I'll still know on which aisle the feminine napkins are to be found. Before taking the plunge into the sex-soaked world of Kotex possession, I make it my business to carefully gauge the activity on every other aisle in the grocery store. Knowing the whereabouts of potential unwanted encounters is crucial to a successful Kotex run.

By the Top Kick dog food—"three cans for a quarter"—I'll see Dennis Reed rounding the far corner, and he's not buying Kotex. I'll pretend to be considering the Austex Chili and the Miracle Whip and ketchup. When I'm satisfied the aisle is clear, to justify my aimless lingering I'll say aloud, should anybody be able to hear me, "In case Momma wants to send me back after a while, I better go make sure they got plenty of Dr Pepper."

On the canned-juice and soda-water aisle, an elderly lady I don't recognize is comparing the price of Del Monte prune juice to a lesser-known but equally effective brand while Orville, the middle-aged stock boy, unloads Coke twelve-packs from their wooden shipping crates. "Hey, Orville," I'll say, and continue making my sweep.

A box of Kotex Supers won't fit under my arm, behind my back, or down my pants. Hiding it beneath my winter coat works only up to a point: The moment of truth is at the checkout counter.

I know that misreading the ebb and flow of checkout traffic puts me at risk of getting trapped behind a housewife with a two-month supply of groceries some absentminded clerk is making a career of idly ringing up. Having already identified the slowpoke checkers, I'll keep my feet moving and an eye out for impending encounters. Experience will have taught me that to stand still is to invite discovery. Still, the simple fact remains that no matter how well I've laid the groundwork, a clean getaway comes down to pure luck.

The dreaded blue boxes of Kotex Supers are on the aisle with the Mr. Clean, squeeze mops, and aluminum foil. Once I've grabbed a box, I'll make a beeline for the checkout lane and avoid eye contact, especially with the clerk. The last thing I need is a dawdling conversation at the cash register. With luck, the box will make it into a sack even before I'm asked to pay. One kindhearted checker's sensitive enough to bag the box of Kotex before ringing it up, the lone bright spot in the Minimax staff; the rest are bovine in nature and impervious to the struggles of an eleven-year-old boy trying to buy feminine napkins without getting humiliated. Not until the purchase is out of sight will I be free to let down my guard, stroll over to the candy counter, and plop down a penny for a single pack of Dubble Bubble or a Red Hot Jawbreaker.

One particular run ended in such total disaster that my career as a Kotex courier was put to an abrupt end. I'd survived the bicycle crash of the previous fall, my face unscarred and my love for LaQuita Freeman still smoldering. Baseball season lay just around the corner, and I was beginning to regain my equilibrium. Then came the monthly trip to the Minimax.

I'd carefully gauged the comings and goings of every cart and customer in the store before making what I thought was a well-informed move toward an empty checkout lane. But it was my misfortune to round a blind corner and smack right into Mrs. Freeman's as-yet-empty shopping cart, where the box of Kotex landed like a turd in a punchbowl.

"My, but aren't you accident prone," Mrs. Freeman teased, her tone not at all friendly.

"It's my mother's," I apologized.

"Obviously," she sniffed, polite affectations no longer hiding a mean spirit. "You look like you've healed up pretty good," she said, a small pleasantry that did nothing to conceal her opinion of me as pathetic.

With the very hands I'd long dreamed of holding, LaQuita reached into the cart and fetched the Kotex box back into mine—a gift I had no choice but to accept. She averted her eyes, sparing me further shame. It was a kindness that caused an intense hatred for my mother to crest from deep down inside. I swore to myself on Grandma Katie's grave that I'd never ever buy Kotex again.

To be known as the dumb ass who crashed his bike into Mr. Weiss's Plymouth while ogling LaQuita Freeman was something I had learned to live with. The Kotex collision was far more complex. Although I knew she wasn't one to blab, I couldn't help feeling that every pair of eyes in the sixth grade saw me as the Kotex Kid, and soiled innocence no longer allowed me the luxury of fantasizing about my dark-skinned Valentine. Daydreams turned to nightmares in which I pictured her handing me the box of Kotex over and over again. At the end of the school year, when Mrs. Freeman removed her daughter to some faraway and undisclosed location, I found relief outweighed the sorrow of her vanishing.

I was destined to chalk up more than my share of adolescent misfortune, but never was anything as painful as having my unworthiness handed to me that day in the Minimax.

Tripod Throws a Punch

By the age of thirteen, Delbert Matheny was taller than most grown men. His were the raw physical materials of an old-time NFL down lineman. "Big-boned skinny" is how Freckles Joyce, the seventh-grade PE teacher and assistant football coach, framed his physical attributes the first day of class. And it was Coach Joyce who unwittingly saddled him with the nickname that echoed with ridicule in the hallways of Galena Park Junior High School. The first time he saw Delbert come naked out of the boys' shower, the affable coach howled loud enough to be heard in the girls' locker room, "I be got-dang, son, that's the longest tallywhacker I ever seen a boy drag through them doors. With a pecker like that, we might win some games around here. How 'bout it, Tripod, you coming out for football or not?" Recruiting Delbert Matheny to play football came to naught, but the Tripod moniker stuck.

If you show up for the first day of seventh grade standing six foot two, exuding befuddlement, with a schoolbook satchel in one hand and a Davy Crockett lunch box in the other, you might expect to be a marked young man. Factor in hand-me-down pants showcasing white shinbones and socks falling down around size-14 brogan clodhoppers, you just might expect the harsh light of adolescent exclusion to focus on you. Not Delbert. I doubt a more perplexed target of peer-group pressure existed in the fall of 1962. Short of becoming invisible, his chances of blending in were about as good as a Mongolian mud wrestler's.

I liked Delbert. We shared a common bond near the bottom rung of the economic ladder and even the same bus stop. Conversation didn't come naturally to him. In the four months we spent waiting for the morning bus, "I like the way you comb your hair" was his lone attempt at social banter. But he was an attentive listener, and we fell into an easy rapport. Each morning, I'd provide a rambling monologue on one of three topics—baseball cards, television shows, rock-and-roll songs—and he'd listen in rapt fascination. I was grateful for Delbert's friendship. His nodding approval made the transition to junior high a little less daunting.

By the third day of seventh grade, I was aware that danger lurked in the back of the bus with four junior members of the Jake City Rebels, Jacinto City's official greaser street gang. I knew instantly there was no chance a pack of ninth-grade wannabe Rebels itching to hone the craft of cool hatred could resist harassing smaller kids. Their backseat malevolence advertised itself with a smoldering luminescence. *Dangerous when bored* is how I saw it. Given that the bus ride to and from junior high school was only slightly less boring than *The Lawrence Welk Show,* I vowed to keep my distance. Anticipating where and how they'd strike became my number one priority.

High school compatriots wore black motorcycle jackets with "Jake City Rebels" stenciled in white across the back. The only prerequisites for membership were ducktails, a pompadour, and placing the musical merits of Gene Vincent and Eddie Cochran ahead of Elvis Presley's. Horseshoe taps and concealed switchblades were optional.

Jacky Kilgore, the Rebels' acknowledged leader, was my role model. The coolness with which he personified consummate danger while leading his gang of outsiders down nonbelligerent corridors of high-minded musicality inspired the notion that I, too, might someday ooze drop-dead cool and poetic sensitivity. During his brief reign—brief because Rebels were prone to scraping up cash for a mid-fifties hot rod and dropping out of school—knife fights reached an all-time low at Galena Park High School. Matters of manhood and whose girl somebody was got settled on the dance floor. It was common knowledge that during Jacky's rule, the Jake City Rebels bopped themselves to near legitimacy.

Occasionally his father and mine drank whiskey and played guitars together. In the early fifties, Jack Kilgore Sr. had served three of a five-year sentence for assault and battery. "I'm proof the Texas state correctional system works," I once heard him boast to my dad. "Ain't a damn thing I got better to do than work on cars and play this guitar. Huntsville can kiss my filthy white ass. I ain't ever goin' back to that motherfucker." Having the consummate Rebel's old man as my father's drinking buddy gave me a leg up in dealing with the dangerous minds of budding ninth-grade hoods stuck on a school bus with a bunch of seventh- and eighth-grade lame-os. I doubled my resolve to avoid drawing attention, figuring eye contact would come later in life.

It was a relief when they settled on Delbert as the focus of their hostility. The day Terry Holt, the junior ringleader, announced that come Friday he'd get off at our bus stop and "kick that sum-bitch Tripod's ass for lookin' at me wrong," I relaxed for the first time in weeks. Delbert's resignation was expressed with a clenched jaw and a blank stare.

When Friday arrived, Terry, his cronies, and a smattering of local riffraff got off when the bus pulled up in front of the vacant lot on the corner of Burman and Flint streets. Delbert, who could've crushed Terry with one hand, took the beating stoically. In my case, the instinct for survival took precedence over a guilty conscience. I watched from a distance, ashamed of my cowardice for not backing up my friend and at the same time relieved it wasn't me who was getting creamed.

In the coming weeks the remaining Rebels took turns getting off the bus at our stop and giving Delbert a sound beating. Once I took a chance and asked the driver to stop them. "I get paid to drive" was his reply. I took his answer as proof I'd done my best. Meanwhile, Delbert took his punishment quietly.

As the Friday fights grew in popularity, an unsettling realization began to emerge. The fights wouldn't end with the junior Rebels. Terry Holt would see to it that every boy within fifty pounds of Delbert's weight class would challenge Tripod or suffer the consequences. There was no escaping the brutal truth that I, too, would fight Delbert or face Terry's wrath.

Waiting for the bus became a silent affair. The seven a.m. cordiality Delbert and I shared vanished the day Terry set the Friday afternoon fights in motion. My friend's sunny disposition became the grim countenance of a wounded animal. A future featuring weekly butt whippings left little room for the Delbert of old. I was too numb with fear to lament our loss.

My time to enter the ring came the Friday before Christmas. On Tuesday Terry had cornered me in the cafeteria. "Friday you're fightin' Tripod, you got that? You chicken out and I'm gonna kick your ass all the way to Beaumont."

Having the inevitable spat in my face didn't legitimize the code of conduct I adopted to deal with my friend's ongoing predicament, but it did trigger the false notion that I had nothing to lose in a fistfight with Delbert. By my calculations, seven boys had gotten off the bus and he'd steadfastly refused to fight back. Given such pacifist tendencies, I thought it better to beat him up and apologize later than get beat up myself by Terry Holt.

When Friday came, Duke Fox and Larry Becker, junior Rebels, assumed the role of cornermen, and their prefight instruction on how to dismantle the gentle giant made me feel like the ultimate Judas. I saw myself for what I was: one more in a long line of Holt's bare-fisted puppets, chin down, dukes up, bobbing and weaving like some punch-drunk lightweight back in the ring after a long lay-off, an image I hated. The knots in my stomach were a sick testament to the absurdity of this warped rite of passage. I wanted to tell Terry to go fuck a duck. Instead, I made a serious tactical blunder.

If it wasn't my intention to look Delbert in the eye, it certainly was my downfall. The recognition that his only friend had become his latest adversary awakened something long dormant in him with a start, and a drastic shift in his body language announced his desire to put an end to this spectacle once and for all. For what was likely the first time in his life, he clenched his mammoth fist and threw a punch, a clean body shot that landed square in the middle of my solar plexus. The impact rendered my lungs twin whoopee cushions. Worse than being dropped with one punch in front of a capacity crowd that included Beverly Drake, Betty Jo Branch, and Pam Munselle was the mortifying suspicion I'd farted in the process. Mostly so I could ask Duke Fox if I had indeed cut one, I struggled for an agonized eternity to coax air back into my lungs.

The crowd unraveled, stunned and disbelieving. Delbert gathered his book satchel and lunch box and strode away in princely fashion. One blow had toppled Terry Holt's puppeteer empire like a house of cards.

Afterward, my mother's idle inquiries about my health were brushed aside truthfully. "I got a stomachache," I groaned, and pulled the bedroom door shut behind me.

That year, Christmas came with an ironic twist. A friend of my father's whom I didn't like gave me a pair of boxing gloves and a standing offer of free boxing lessons. It was another of Bill Broden's many attempts to ingratiate himself as some kind of uncle figure in my life.

The previous July, my mother was in the hospital with severe vertigo. One afternoon, Bill showed up at the front door with two tickets to see Don Drysdale pitch against the Houston Colt .45s that same night. Normally I'd have given my Mickey Mantle and Willie Mays trading cards to see Drysdale pitch, but the thought of going to the game with Bill struck me as less appealing than sucking on a dead dog's nose until its head caved in.

"Oh, sure he wants to go," my father volunteered on my behalf.

"Aw, I don't know," I said, hoping he'd sense my reticence. "We got a game tomorrow, and I gotta wash my uniform and all that."

"What'n the hell're you talkin' about?" he said. "It's Drysdale going against Nottebart."

"Then you can go in my place," I said, sensing a prearranged situation.

"You're goin' to the damn game or I'll wear your ass out," my father said.

So I went.

During the forty-five-minute drive to Colt Stadium, Bill made a big show of fishing a paper sack from under the seat of his Pontiac for long *glugs* of whiskey. "If you was to tell your daddy I been hittin' this mess takin' you to the game, he'd whip the shit outta me," he laughed, insinuating we were somehow partners in crime. "Reckon you'd blow the whistle on ole Bill if I was to give you a little sip?"

"Uh, no thanks," I replied, feigning indifference. "Tried it once, didn't much like it."

He drained the bottle en route, and after pulling into the gravel parking lot that in two years would become the site of the Houston Astrodome, he reached under the seat again and produced a snub-nosed pistol. "Just in case we run into trouble with the niggers," he said, laying the pistol on the edge of the seat, its nose pointing toward my left leg.

The idea of crazed Negroes leaping from behind a parked car, demanding our money or our lives, seemed less likely than Bill finding an excuse to use the pistol on an innocent baseball fan.

Ninety-nine out of a hundred African-Americans attending games at Colt Stadium in 1962 bought their tickets in the right-field bleachers, where a smattering of Caucasians drank their beer quietly and cheered sparingly for Pete Runnels, Walter Bond, Bob Aspromonte, and Turk Farrell. Not the blatant white-supremacist Bill Broden. His idea of integration was guzzling a pint of whiskey and a gallon of lukewarm beer and heckling whichever Alou brother was playing right field for the Dodgers that night. In a lenient court of public opinion, addressing Felipe Alou with "Hey, boy!" might have been fobbed off as drunken stupidity, but to invite every black man and woman within earshot to kiss his stinking white ass qualifies as unthinkable. I couldn't help visualizing the pistol in his khakis as anything but an errant spark in the vicinity of a ruptured gas main.

Most of the responses—along the lines of, "Hey, whitey, why don't you stick a sock in it"—went unnoticed. In response to whatever chiding did manage to register in his alcohol-soaked brain, the best he could muster was "I paid for these seats, and I'm by God sayin' any damn thing I want to." This he slurred with his back to the playing field and his head who knows where.

Whether Drysdale had good stuff that night I can't say. My souvenir images are the seething glares of the flagrantly offended. If I could've willed myself far away from Colt Stadium, the dark side of the moon wouldn't have been far enough from the action. It was the longest nine innings of my life.

Even worse than going to the game was sleeping on Bill Broden's fold-out couch. I wasn't so young that I hadn't noticed my father's appetite for trashy dalliance; he'd gone so far as to drag me to some chain-smoking barmaid's apartment under the guise of playing big brother to her six-year-old son. If packing me off to Colt Stadium with a paranoid, alcoholic, numbskull racist strained my paternal adulation, he shattered it by sentencing me to spend the night with the snoring bastard in a trash-heap trailer reeking of Siamese-cat piss so he could take advantage of my mother's hospitalization. As much as I hated Bill Broden, that night I hated him more.

My chilly acceptance of the boxing gloves embarrassed my father. What was mild anger led him to poor judgment and, in turn, ridicule. "I reckon the little sissy'd rather put on one of his momma's dresses than a pair of boxin' gloves," he said, thinking it would rile me into putting on the gloves.

But something else happened. I heard myself tell him this: "You're just like every other son-of-a-bitch bully in Jacinto City. You can stick them gloves up your ass."

His reflexes were lightning fast, and no sooner had the words left my mouth than his right hand landed flush against my left cheek, sending a swarm of cuckoo birds in orbit around my head, and my body to the floor.

Nearly knocking his twelve-year-old son out cold put my father in an awkward situation. Saving face in front of his boorish friend meant stifling the urge to scoop me off the floor to check for head trauma. Instead, the two of them headed for the nearest icehouse to drink the dull misery out of the remainder of the day.

Later that night, lying in bed, I heard the Studebaker grind to an asthmatic halt somewhere in the vicinity of the driveway. "Good mood," I called to my mother, who'd spent a long night biting her fingernails and chain-smoking Viceroys. I hopped from the bed geared up for a giddy homecoming. The effects alcohol had on my father's ability to park the car rarely, if ever, affected how he carried himself physically. I'd seen him vomit, heard him moan in his sleep, and marveled when he put a brave face on one of his blistering hangovers, but never had I witnessed him stumbling blind-drunk through the front door with one eye swollen shut, a busted lip, and splotches of blood decorating the front of his shirt. He was crooning "Under Your Spell Again" loud enough for the Bucks to join in singing harmony, if they'd happened to be in the mood. By his account of the evening, my mother and I gleaned that chasing whiskey with beer is counterproductive to settling a heated discussion on the subject of disciplining smart-mouthed boys. Judging by his good humor, he'd got the better of Bill in the brawl. "I finally woke up to his ass," he said, as if with this one statement he'd explained the mysteries of the cosmos.

Although he could never bring himself to say as much, I knew my father was sorry about punching me in the face. As for me, I was over it before I hit the floor. Letting Broden know what I thought about him and his boxing gloves was worth ten blows to the jaw.

When school resumed in early January, I was surprised at the lack of interest in my one-punch demise. The world I knew before Christmas break was now a weirdly different place. Terry Holt and the junior Rebels assumed their usual position in the back of the bus as if on sedatives; four lobotomies couldn't have produced a more marked change in their demeanor. As for Delbert, he didn't return to school and simply vanished from our midst. My curiosity about what became of him wasn't as strong as my desire to slip back into my invisible shell, and Delbert Matheny exited my life as enigmatically as he'd entered it four months before.

The first Friday afternoon in 1963, a seventh-grader named Tommy Hughey followed me off the bus. As my stop was six blocks past his, this struck me as odd. I liked Tommy, and his ability to remain invisible when the heartless barbs of teenage cruelty flew like poison darts was an inspiration. Though he was six months older than me, I had a four-inch height advantage. But when he took off his jacket and pronounced himself ready to fight, I nearly laughed out loud. "You gotta be kiddin' me," I said. "Did Terry Holt put you up to this?" Tommy seemed perplexed by the question, and it occurred to me that he was like my father's red Studebaker when the engine kept running after the ignition had been switched off. I had an inclination to cream the twerp on general principle, but instead told him to go home. "The fightin' stuff's over. I'm not gonna fight you or anybody else for the rest of my life."

I stood there remembering how Delbert hung on my every word those golden September mornings waiting for the bus. Tommy gathered his books and jacket, and as he trotted away called over his shoulder, "See ya on Monday."

Pawnshop Drums

In the late fifties, thinking he might pick up a little extra cash playing hillbilly music in east Houston's honky-tonks and ice-houses, my father cobbled together a sparse little musical outfit called J. W. Crowell and the Rhythmaires. In the beginning it was slow going, but in time his belief in the band proved stronger than the club owners' indifference, and business started to pick up.

The combo consisted of Elbert Smith, a harelipped harmony singer, on lead electric mandolin; Edward Lee Alexander on bass; and Bat Putnam, the "Blind Boy from Port Arthur," on drums. My father, as lead singer and rhythm-guitar player, used his knowledge of country music to create playlists suitable for white-trash dives like Cal's Corral and Red Bluff Sally's. Historically, the icehouses considered jukeboxes more user-friendly in the selling of cold beer, but dance-friendly icehouses like Cal's Corral, Duke's Highway 90, and Red Bluff Sally's were the exception. Bands were welcome to set up in the corner, tables were pushed aside, and those so inclined were encouraged to glide across the concrete floor until their feet hurt.

The financial arrangements were heavily in favor of the owners.

At first, a cigar box placed in front of the mike stand was the sole means by which the band got paid, and the stream of loose change and dollar bills destined for the "kitty" depended on the band-leader's ability to handle song requests and keep dancers on the floor. Whether it was a rare appearance at Cook's Hoedown or at some shit hole with only a neon beer sign advertising its existence, my father approached every performance as if he were hosting the Grand Ole Opry. He dutifully brought a brand of showmanship to the icehouses that, in the Rhythmaires' early going, flew as far over the heads of the lowbrow clientele as Shakespeare's sonnets would've.

Still, by the end of 1961 J. W. Crowell and the Rhythmaires were working semi-regularly at Cal's Corral and the Igloo. With a two-dollar cover charge on top of the kitty to split among band members, my father saw that his ship was coming in.

The rise in his musical stock irritated my mother. By default she'd inherited the job of collecting cover charges. Being torn between her wifely duties and God's will put her in an awful funk. "J. W. Crowell," she'd harp, "I can't believe you want to drag me in and out of the Devil's house just so I can take up money from ever' Tom, Dick, and Harry that walks through the door. And that's the sorriest bunch of women I ever seen, every one of 'em waitin' to spread their legs for you out in the parkin' lot."

"Aw, hell, Cauzette," he'd gripe back, "you ain't got a bit more sense than God give a mule. We runnin' a *biz-ness* here. You think I can trust somebody else to take up that money? What the hell's wrong with you?"

The Rhythmaires' increased activity didn't sit well with Bat Putnam either. Between cab fares—he was too proud to accept rides from his bandleader—and a fondness for whiskey (barrels of it, I've since been told), he wasn't seeing much cash prosperity. Preferring more convenient opportunities back home in Port Arthur, the blind musician bid J.W. and the boys a fond farewell.

In May of 1962, my father came home from work with a set of

pawnshop drums. Short of dragging pots and pans from under the kitchen sink, a more rudimentary drum kit would've been hard to find. A sparkly blue bass drum with an attached ride cymbal and a black-and-gray-striped snare drum on a stand were the extent of its working parts. But center stage in the living room, in spite of its poor quality, this contraption looked almost worthy of a Gene Krupa solo.

Springing it on his unsuspecting family, as my mother and I knew, gave him a temporary feeling of invincibility. Experience had taught us there was nothing to be gained by denying my father's craving for omnipotence. Somewhere along the way we'd made the choice to take at face value his wholehearted belief that he could perform the impossible if the two of us kept our mouths shut long enough for him to work out any kinks in his plan. As a result, we'd come to accept his refusal to explain his actions in advance as part of a deep-seated need for our blind loyalty. He would fill us in on the drums when he was good and ready.

As much as I'd like to think my father saw his only son as a prodigy, it was simple economics—not having to pay someone to replace Bat—that inspired him to invest eight dollars in the notion I could play drums.

"Come on over here," he said, between boasts to my mother about how using a kitchen chair as a drum stool further proved the limitlessness of his ingenuity, "I'm fixin' to show you something."

Pounding the bass-drum pedal with his right foot, producing the familiar wooden *thock* of a cross-stick rim shot with his left hand while riding the cymbal with the stick in his right, my father played a well-articulated shuffle that was very impressive.

"How'd you know how to do that?"

"I'm fixin' to teach you how."

"What, play drums?"

"Hell, yeah. They ain't nothin' to it."

By scooting the kitchen chair closer to the action, I found I could reach the bass-drum pedal with the tip of my toes, and within a short time I was playing a shuffle vaguely reminiscent of the one my father had demonstrated. By the end of the week, I was playing drums behind J. W. Crowell and the Rhythmaires at Red Bluff Sally's.

"Just watch my foot!" my father shouted before launching into the first song. "Match the bass drum to how I'm pattin' and every-thing'll be all right. If you get lost, stop and start over."

It was a long night. To conceal their embarrassment, Elbert and Edward Lee had matching ain't-he-something smiles smeared across their faces. The music itself was an endless succession of rhythmic train wrecks. As for Red Bluff Sally's hard-core regulars, my tendency to get the beat turned around did little to alter the ebb and flow of their dance-floor traffic. The kitty nearly filled up.

At night's end, several drunken women with big titties and bee-hive hair went to work pinching my cheek. Each had her own blend of cheap perfume, cigarettes, and stale beer. I had to agree with my mother that Red Bluff Sally's was ground zero for Podunk women. Considering the level of musicianship I'd put on display that evening, I found this cheek fondling wholly misplaced.

By the second weekend I'd worked out a few of the rough spots in my limited style. My starts weren't as slow to develop, nor were my stops as jarringly abrupt.

"I want you to watch how I keep 'em on the floor once I get 'em out there," my father said one night, driving us to a beer joint on Telephone Road called the Igloo. "Ain't nobody keeps 'em out there dancin' like ole J-Bo." I'd long before accepted the responsi-bility of diverting his predilection for braggadocio whenever I could without threatening his highly refined vanity. But in this particular case, his was a fair assessment. He did have a knack for keeping a dance floor full, and there were times when he'd string six or seven songs together without pause. His more inspired sequences some-times landed five or six dollar bills in the kitty before the sweat-soaked dancers repaired to their tables for cold beer and fresh cigarettes.

"Here's one by the late, great Hank Williams," he'd announce through the revved-up distortion that came with plugging a pawnshop microphone into an overloaded Gibson Falcon amplifier. There was implied immediacy in how he called a crowd back to attention that kept the focus on the business at hand. Four bars into "My Bucket's Got a Hole in It," the dancing clientele would dutifully have chugged their beers, stubbed out their smokes, and trooped back onto the dance floor by the first mandolin turnaround. Moon Mullican's "Pipeliner Blues" and George Jones's "White Lightning" would then follow in hot succession. This set up the all-important slow song.

"And now for a little belly-rubber," he'd say, lowering his voice to a more sexual register. "Here's one called 'May You Never Be Alone Like Me.' " My father knew how to set up and deliver a tearjerk ballad as well as any hillbilly singer in Nashville. If you didn't believe it, all you had to do was ask him.

It was during the belly-rubber that a honky-tonk's sexually charged undertones reared their horny little heads. While my father delivered heartfelt renditions of "(Now and Then There's) A Fool Such As I," "Slowly," "No One Will Ever Know," and "Cold Cold Heart," I saw every kind of skirt lifting, ass grabbing, ear licking, tongue sucking, and dry humping there is. Invariably, it was during the slow song that fights broke out—caused more often than not by some guy ramming a tongue down some other guy's best friend's drunk wife's throat.

At the first signs of violence, my father would drop whichever ballad he was rendering and break into a fast song, magically transforming the fight into a dance floor full of white-trash jitterbuggers doing the dirty bop. There were times when he seemed some kind of honky-tonk alchemist. His ability to turn bloodlusting drunks into dancing fools was a sight to behold, and that's when I was most proud of him.

The most vivid altercation happened to involve my mother—she and an unsavory barroom queen by the name of Nelda Glick. This particular night at Cal's Corral, Nelda chose to dance the slow songs all alone in a masturbatory reverie only two feet in front of my father while he came on to her like the honky-tonk gigolo he so often imagined himself to be. Soon after the thought crossed my mind that my mother wasn't going to allow this to go on much longer, I noticed her swimming toward the front through the dancers.

"I'm gonna teach y'all to act like heathens!" she hollered, grabbing a handful of Nelda's dyed black hair. Yanked without warning from her oversexed absorption, Nelda hit the sawdust-covered dance floor like a dropped medicine ball.

But she came up fighting. Quick as a cat, she buried her painted red claws in the side of my mother's neck—an unfair tactic, given that my mother had chewed off every fingernail she'd grown since 1930.

Dumbfounded, my father allowed the song he was crooning to unravel altogether. There would be no transformative fast song. From where I sat behind the drums, it was difficult to make out specific insults. Judging by the high-pitched wailing, territorial rights to his dickhead ardor were in hot dispute.

He made a feeble stab at re-establishing his control. "Dang if it don't look like the Wednesday night fights came a little late this week," he joked into the microphone. Two, maybe three, muted chuckles rose from the crowd, and I watched the back of his neck and ears turn as red as a new set of encyclopedias. This was the only time I ever saw his consummate showmanship falter.

Remembering the intensity with which my father could tear through ten straight fast songs evokes images of seeing Jerry Lee Lewis perform at the Magnolia Gardens Bandstand, the three-acre open-air dance hall and beer garden owned by the mayor of Channelview, Texas. Yet another oil-boom community built on a strip of marshland between the murky green waters of the San Jacinto River and the goopy brown chemical sludge of the ship channel, Channelview rivaled Jacinto City, Denver Harbor, the East End, and a few less-desirable municipalities around Beaumont and Port Arthur as southeast Texas's premier white-trash garden spot. Drunken brawls and the occasional gunfight added luster to the Magnolia Gardens' popularity. It was the most celebrated outdoor live-music venue in the region and perhaps the only stage in the world Bat Putnam would have considered coming out of retirement to play on. The rest of the band, myself not included, would gladly have volunteered for a group vasectomy in exchange for a half-hour set on that creaky old stage.

I loved Sunday afternoons there as much for the cheeseburgers and swimming as for the live music. To my father, the Magnolia Gardens represented something unattainable in his life, and he saw his inability to get a booking as proof that national stardom was beyond his reach. Although he'd rather get bit by a water moccasin than admit to despondency, his reluctance to acknowledge disappointment didn't prevent him from expressing petty jealousy. Those who knew him well were as intimately acquainted with his susceptibility to the green-eyed monster as with his penchant to brag. If by chance some up-and-coming local dance band swung into a Bob Wills tune, my mother and I automatically put some distance between ourselves and the self-proclaimed King of East Side Honky-Tonk Singers.

"I be got-damn," he'd bellow without regard for whoever might be listening. "I'd just as soon shit and fall back in it as listen at this bunch try and play. They sure as hell ain't no match for ole J-Bo and the boys. Come on, Cauzette, we goin' to the house."

And just like that, another pleasant outing by the river came to a premature end.

Jerry Lee Lewis's performance in the summer of 1958 was part of a package show that included Carl Perkins and featured Johnny Cash as the headliner. My father insisted we arrive two hours before showtime to claim a choice spot to watch from. Sun-bleached green and white canvas awnings lined both sides of the dance floor, sheltering a hundred or so picnic tables from the notoriously unpredictable weather. We took a third-row table, stage left and close to the dance floor.

As the crowd began to gather, so did an enormous bank of black thunderclouds on the horizon. It was well known in this neck of the woods that such thunderheads favored an ominous build-up to actual cloudbursts, so the general consensus among Gulf Coast natives was *Who gives a shit?*

By the time Carl Perkins finished his opening tune, the low-rolling rumble of approaching thunder was as loud as the doghouse bass blasting through the public-address system, but if the lanky performer was apprehensive about the threatening skies, he kept it well hidden. He led his band through "Honey Don't" and "All Mama's Children" with hepcat ease. Fittingly, it was his big hit "Blue Suede Shoes" that brought on the deluge.

At first, the crowd seemed unsure if the show would go on, what with the musicians being from out of town and all. It was raining, as my father was fond of saying, like a cow pissing on a flat rock. As if awaiting further instructions, Perkins and his band stopped playing but didn't leave the stage.

I asked my father if he thought the show might be called off. "Aw, hell," he scoffed, "this mess'll blow over in no time. Ain't no pissant sprinkle gonna shut this shit down." It was times like these, I had learned, that you could always count on his refusal to accept defeat as a source of comfort. His Don Quixote commitment to harebrained notions was one of the things I loved most about him. Whether the storm passed quickly or not, I knew his sentiments and the audience's would be the same. It would take more than the threat of electrocution to dampen the resolve of five hundred Scots-Irish wage slaves dead set on enjoying themselves.

When it became obvious that nobody intended to call a halt to the proceedings, everybody turned back to the stage. Carl Perkins responded with a rip-roaring reprise of "Blue Suede Shoes" and, inspired by the reaction, finished the song on one knee and playing an extended guitar solo behind his back, a leaky band-shell roof the only thing between him and death by lightning.

Not to be outdone, Jerry Lee Lewis shoved the Garden's weatherworn upright piano to the front edge of the stage. And from the moment he kicked into the boogie-woogie intro to "Whole Lotta Shakin' Goin' On," the place went wild. Ducktailed Jake City Rebels dived onto the dance floor, and poodle-skirted Connie Francis look-alikes ran on tiptoes through three inches of water to do the dirty bop with them. Lightning bolts exploded behind the concession stand and in the trees across the river. Nobody cared.

An Eddie Cochran clone tore off his shirt, fell to his knees, and started thrusting his pelvis skyward, both arms flailing wildly at his sides like high-pressure water hoses, his perfectly coifed ducktail sloshing in the water like a mop. When Jerry Lee lit into "Great Balls of Fire," I thought for a moment the Eddie Cochran guy might be having an epileptic fit, given how his eyeballs rolled back in their sockets like I'd seen my mother's do so many times. When I asked if she thought "somebody ought to do something," her dismissive glance suggested that everybody out there was crazy and deserved whatever happened.

Jerry Lee and the thunderstorm peaked simultaneously, and he showed complete disregard for the danger inherent in singing into a microphone less than two feet away from the downpour. In fact, he seemed to revel in the risk. Instinctively, and brilliantly, he incorporated into his performance the possibility that a gust of wind could put an end to his piano pounding forever. Five hundred waterlogged Texans took the bait and the Killer reeled us in.

There's no denying that Jerry Lee's brand of Pentecostal pyrotechnics rocked the ever-loving Jesus out of the Magnolia Gardens crowd that day. His determination to bend his audience's will paid off handsomely. Raw sexual energy and death-defying audacity is a disarming combination, and when the stacatto ending to "Great Balls of Fire" coincided with the end of the rainstorm, it was as if the hand of God itself had turned off the spigot. Striding to the lip of the stage, his arms spread wide, he crowed into the microphone, "Now you see what Jerry Lee Lewis can do." The crowd loved it but I didn't, his proclamation of victory reminding me too much of my father's megalomania.

The audience rained applause on him for two full minutes, and following the last splatter of handclaps came an eerie calm after the storm. The crowd milled around quietly, some soaked, some dry, as the cloudbank rumbled off to the east.

The sun burst through the remaining clouds just as Johnny Cash stepped onto the stage. I elbowed my mother and yelled above the welcoming applause, "Did you hear those voices?"

She looked at me as if I'd fallen out of a tree. "What voices?" She blew a gray funnel of Viceroy smoke out the far side of her mouth.

"All those angels' voices I just heard when the sun came out."

"What're you talkin' about?"

I was sorry I brought it up but sure was excited to see Johnny Cash step up to the microphone. Dressed in dark gray slacks and a white shirt open at the collar with the sleeves rolled up two turns, my grandfather's favorite new singer went into "Five Feet High and Rising," a song he'd written about the Mississippi River flood of 1937, his deep baritone booming over the public-address system. I was too young to recognize the conceptual brilliance of such an opening, but like the rest of the crowd I sensed that we were in for something special. Whereas Carl Perkins's and Jerry Lee Lewis's sets spread a sizeable portion of the audience across the length and breadth of the dance floor, Johnny Cash drew everybody closer, hanging on every word.

He took us on a tour of Depression-era America. We were shown flooded cotton fields and cabarets where dark-haired boys played flattop guitars. Freight trains rolled through the faraway night, filling the thoughts of a death-row inmate, whose mother had begged him not to take his guns to town, with visions of cigar smoke and fancy dining cars. Autumn leaves fell around sad memories of lost love and a blond, blue-eyed teenage queen who'd run off to Holly-wood only to find her true love was the boy next door who worked at the candy store. This was the kind of storytelling in which work-ing stiffs like my father could recognize where they'd come from. Johnny Cash spoke the language of common people with uncom-mon eloquence.

Snappy patter was beneath him. He said nothing. He didn't have to. His songs did the talking. Though not yet eight years old, I could tell that, in Jerry Lee's case, it was the music more than the man that was making those women dance nasty with Jake City Rebels. With Johnny Cash, it was the music *and* the man. Both women and men listened quietly, as if receiving instruction from on high. Stillness engulfed the Magnolia Gardens like never before. Lest I give the impression no one danced, let me tell you this: They danced, all right, just not with each other.

Johnny Cash brought his performance to its logical conclusion just as the sun began its plunge into the pine-forested expanse of Channelview's western horizon. It was one of those pink and gold southeast Texas sunsets when the last rays of the day probe the blue-gray heavens like Hollywood searchlights. Having graciously shared the spotlight, Johnny Cash and the setting sun bid the Mag-nolia Gardens good night.

The drive home had the feel of redemption. My parents seemed lighter, more talkative, than was usual. I myself was sifting through images of the candy store and the imminent return of my blond, blue-eyed teenage queen.

By now I hope it's clear that apart from his manhandling my mother, I idolized my father and had learned at an early age to view his fragile self-imaginings with bemused detachment. And it's safe to say I fostered some pretty flamboyant delusions of my own. One was the reason I was playing a shoddy set of drums in the sweltering heat of Cal's Corral in the first place. For me—and this is something my father could never grasp—it was the off chance that, should I measure up, I might receive the benediction of his approval.

.   .   .

Pondering the subtleties of my love for him early in life, I realize
there's no definitive answer to the lingering question of whether he
was an angel or an asshole. The thin line between his heartless
insensitivity and harmless self-absorption was never more finely
drawn than in 1962. Until then, more often than not, he was given
the benefit of the doubt. But on the Saturday night when my
mother nearly jerked Nelda Glick baldheaded, something else
began to surface. Watching my father struggle to regain his composure, it occurred to me that I was sick and tired of his big-time,
honky-tonk, singing-star act. It also occurred to me that falling on
his ass was just reward for the vulgarity of his little song and dance
with Nelda. Knowing he was more interested in saving face than in
my mother's health sent a flash of hatred through my body that,
had I not been paralyzed by the frenzy of her attack, might well
have caused me to bury a drumstick between his shoulder blades.
This, of course, I wouldn't do, but I didn't have to. The crowd
skewered him with dispassion.

I was proud of my mother for taking Nelda Glick down. That she
was knee-walking drunk did nothing to diminish the thrill of seeing
her stand up for herself. Her willingness to defend what was right-
fully hers showed signs of self-respect missing since the day, in the
middle of Hurricane Carla, she swore to kill my father if he ever hit
her again. Within her makeup was a seldom seen fuck-you attitude
that was a source of great comfort to me, and my anger at her for
withholding this comfort kept me from wanting to be as close to
her as to my father. Since neither father nor son was as forgiving of
her shortcomings as we were of his, a pattern had been established
whereby my love for her took a backseat to my need to please him.
But Nelda Glick changed all that.

A woman from a neutral corner helped my mother to the bathroom. But for a few scratches on her neck and a torn dress, she was
in pretty good shape. But when the adrenaline began to wane and

embarrassment set in, she could be heard bawling through the bathroom walls. Eventually the woman led her out to the parking lot, where she passed out in the backseat of our Studebaker.

The inclination to quit my post and go looking for her was held in check by my father's dogged determination to reclaim center stage. He intended to finish out the night. Within a few notes of "Why Baby Why," the burning question was whether Elbert, Edward Lee, and his little drummer boy could keep up with his frantic pace. I played the set out dutifully, my best ever as a Rhythmaire.

On the dark ride home, anger got hold of my tongue. I was surprised by how quickly "It's all your fault" went from something I was thinking to something I said aloud. When "If it wasn't for you thinkin' every woman in the world was in love with you, none of this shit woulda happened" poured from my mouth, there was the possibility that I'd just signed my own death warrant. Then came the kicker: "I hate you and I hate playing the drums like a damn idiot." As if to signal I'd gone too far, my mother moaned in the backseat.

My father ignored the tirade; but for the part about my hating the drums, he'd heard it all before. He drove home in silence, stopping once so my mother could vomit in a ditch.

This catfight brought her career as cover-charge lady to a halt, and that was the last night she ever assisted his quest for stardom. Moreover, at the same time, the Rhythmaires outgrew their child drummer. Without my mother around to babysit during breaks, I was an eleven-year-old impediment and only too happy to give up my seat in the rhythm section.

A series of drummers, nondescript and of no interest to me, filled my vacant slot. The Rhythmaires' cover charge reached the all-time high of three dollars a head in early 1963. Al Snider took over the lead-guitar work, leaving Elbert Smith free to concentrate more on singing duet harmony than playing lead mandolin. Ever the gentleman, Elbert took the demotion in quiet stride.

By late 1964, my father's dream of a honky-tonk career had all but run its course. Eventually, he and the Rhythmaires settled into a loose pattern of jam sessions at friends' houses around town, with an occasional paying job cropping up as late as 1966. Although she complained constantly about his drinking, this period was more to my mother's liking. She might not have cared for the wife of whichever friend of a friend was hosting a particular session, but to her way of thinking, a living room, converted garage, or some pea-gravel patio was a more fitting venue for her husband's music than any of Satan's lairs. That the music he loved was tailor-made for those very places didn't figure in her reasoning.

My father's passion for the honky-tonk spotlight waned quickly. Knowing how much he craved the attention, I couldn't shake the notion something wasn't adding up. For nearly thirty-four years, thanks to what must have been a blood-sworn pact never to reopen this chapter of their lives, both my parents left me to my own con-clusions. On the surface, the begrudging support my mother afforded my father when he voluntarily abandoned our house to the wrath of a Category 4 hurricane didn't extend to his musical ambi-tions. The pleasure she took, as often as possible, in pointing out that his pretending some piss-hole dive was the Grand Ole Opry made him look like a fool was impossible for me to ignore. I don't, of course, hold her responsible for his honky-tonk withdrawal, but I confess that for a prolonged period the onus was clearly on her.

It bears mentioning that the spotlight in eight out of ten ice-houses where the Rhythmaires set up to play consisted of nothing more than the 75-watt bulbs my father rigged into two large Camp-bell's Soup cans and hung from the ceiling with baling wire. Nonetheless, it never registered on the undisputed math champion of Kentucky that the resulting laser beams produced a less-flattering light source than a state trooper's flashlight. But he did seem gen-uinely grateful when I suggested he use rubber bands to strap green and red gels over the ends of his soup cans.

At the age of seventy-one my mother flatly stated she was afraid my father's love of music would take him away from her and that she used epilepsy to "keep him from runnin' off with other women." When I pointed out, sarcastically, that he would've had to been around when a seizure actually occurred for this to make sense, she stared blankly into the middle distance beyond the sliding-glass door of her ninth-floor assisted-living apartment, as if to give my father's ghost equal time to argue his side of the story. This version required her to remove her glasses and carefully wipe away a small flood of tears with her left thumb. "What you never knew about your daddy, son," she continued, glasses in hand, "is how much he hated not bein' there. He never got over it."

I doubted whether he hated having missed out on twenty-eight years of violent body-thrashing, jaw-clenching, mouth-frothing, tongue-swallowing epileptic seizures, but out of respect for her need to cut him some slack, I resisted saying so. This I did in spite of thinking she'd lost her mind. My choice to remain silent on this subject was rewarded with the realization that my mother had spent the six years since my father's death reframing the events of her life so her memories of the young man she'd fallen in love with held more sway than the poisoned images of what the middle years of their lives together would ultimately become. And with this gentle epiphany came the understanding that my tendency to state the obvious had outlived its usefulness. To blame her Pentecostal prig-gishness for the collapse of my father's musical aspirations wasn't only far too easy but also simply wrong. It undeservedly absolved him from his crimes while it laid at her feet his failure to define for himself what he wanted in life and how to get it.

Settling for the comfort of the ongoing jam sessions gave my father three things: one, a small but adoring audience, as grateful for his treasure trove of old songs as they might have been for Christ dying on the cross had they not been heathens to a man; two, the illusion of control over everyone and everything involved, his own family included; and three, the attention paid to the per-petual guest of honor. These jam sessions even provided his troubled marriage with a social context. Since he'd have sooner slit his throat than attend a tent revival, they gave my parents some place to go as a couple.

Of the twelve or so people in their circle, only Willie Hardin found a reason to enter our house on Norvic Street. It was early one weekday afternoon when Willie, part-time welder and full-time alcoholic, slagged off work to make a play for my mother. The near rape—he'd grabbed her hair and tried to stick his tongue down her throat—was for her more puzzling than troubling.

"Willie Hardin's the last man on earth I'd ever go with," she told me. "That man's a sot drunk. I can't believe he'd risk tanglin' with your daddy just to get me to go with him. It don't make one bit of sense. If I can push him off me that easy, there's no telling what your daddy woulda done to him."

My father denied it ever happened, and his refusal to admit that he might have been betrayed by one of his admirers was unwavering. It was easier for him to accuse my mother of lying or exaggerating than to accept that his omnipotence was an illusion. Nevertheless, from then on he rarely accepted invitations to lead the jam sessions.

The passing of his musical dream was sad to watch. For all his narcissism, there was a sweet innocence in the pleasure he drew from playing songs. And as his need for an adoring audience faded, I came to appreciate more fully his need for adoration plain and simple.

Inexplicable Behavior

A couple of years after the Buck family moved into the house across the street, my parents found themselves in a quandary over what to do about my obsession with Election Day yard signs springing up around town like so many proselytizing toadstools. This glut of placards—promoting the likes of A. J. "Burt" Holder, Mayor; W. M. "Pappy" Beck, Alderman; L. L. "Sleepy" Barge, Councilman at Large; and J. R. "Booger" Attenberry, Director of Parks and Recreation—had rekindled a criminal spark missing since I opened fire on their New Year's Eve party more than five years earlier. By late one afternoon, I'd swiped three dozen signs and planted them in our front yard.

An irate neighbor pounding on the door and demanding the return of his stolen property is how my father got wind of the political rally amassed on his lawn. Caught off guard and affecting indifference, he drawled, "You're welcome to it, if you can figure out which ones is yours."

No one hated situations beyond his control more than my father, and he'd sooner have his teeth pulled than admit he had no idea how thirty-six Election Day placards came to be standing in his front yard. The implications that placed his son in the criminal hot seat were even less bothersome to him than being seen as a man out of touch with what went on around his own home.

Volunteering guilt was pointless; before the door banged shut behind the first vigilante, he was on me like a bad paint job. "What in the name of Woodrow Wilson made you steal all them signs out yonder in the yard?"

"I didn't steal all of them."

"What'd you do?"

"I went up and asked."

"Aw, hell, son, don't lie to me. You already got both our asses in a crack. I want to know why you stuck all of them signs up in the yard."

Knowing that sniveling assessments of his inability to provide for his family was a surefire means of getting him off my back, I aimed low. "Because our house is ugly."

To explain my fascination with the subliminal use of down-home charm and good-ole-boy familiarity as tools of political seduction called for powers of articulation far beyond me. And since I possessed neither the skill nor the will to put in plain words my theory that the candidates were simply addressing the notion held dear by most residents of Jacinto City, that to be taken for a sucker was their God-given right, I let my gutless answer stand. Besides, why throw long-winded clarification at my father when half-truths worked just as well? He fired up a Pall Mall and lit into his wife for not keeping better tabs on my after-school activities.

Two sips into a half cup of my mother's instant coffee, Police Chief James L. "Jimmy" Daniels concluded his investigation. Seeing as how the old lawman had just spent a wad of taxpayers' money returning stolen placards to six persnickety citizens, I could've told my father that a rambling summation was the wrong way to go, but I doubt he would've listened.

"I don't think he meant nothing by it, Jimmy," he said, pleading my case in the same sucking-up style as the placards. "From now on, I'm gonna be on him like a duck on a June bug. You can bank on that."

Pushing the coffee cup aside as if this were his assessment of their parenting skills, the old officer summoned up all the gravity of thirty-plus years in law enforcement. "I expect I'll be leavin' this a family matter. I got no doubt y'all are gonna straighten all this out. J.W., me and you and the boy need to take us a ride in the squad car and see about stickin' a sign or two back up where they belong. Any left over, I'll take on back to the station."

Afterward, I took my mother's switch-whipping stoically.

Stealing yard signs was only the half of it. I'd also fallen into an involuntary habit of singing aloud in my fifth-grade classroom. The urge fed almost exclusively on the inopportune moment, written assignments being the worst. Something about the entire class engrossed in silent concentration brought out the oddball in me. If for no other reason than the consequent fall from social grace, you'd think my being shaken from a trance in the middle of a math test only to find that I'd been warbling some hackneyed anthem inspired by Election Day yard signs would've curbed the compulsion once and for all. Well, think again. Two days later, I'm crooning, "W. M. Pappy Beck, now there's a man you can't neglect / and for your councilman at large, don't forget ole Sleepy Barge," to the hybrid tune of "Davy Crockett" and "The Ballad of Jed Clampett."

The first time it happened, Mrs. Cain cited the rules of conduct in her classroom as including neither impromptu serenades nor "the egging on of fools with laughter." I went immediately to work on a disclaimer meant to separate me from the intentional rendering of such drivel, but Mrs. Cain's ill temper put me on notice that my audience allotment had been used up for the day. If there was a reason why I'd sung such a song, it was lost the moment I realized that the laughter of which the teacher spoke was at my expense. From then on I was as much a stranger to myself as I was to my teacher and peers. The second and third times I sang aloud in class, Mrs. Smith shoved my desk into the hallway and had me write "I will not sing in class" 250 and then 500 times. The fourth landed me in the vice principal's office.

Mr. Holcombe was as old as he was foreboding. On the wall behind his desk was a handmade illustration of his disciplinary credo: "If they can't sit down, they'll stand up straight." I, like every other student between the fourth and sixth grades, was well aware of the vice principal's legendary "Board of Education." Tales of its size, shape, and color flew like paper airplanes whenever one of our own fell prey to the wooden lash. There was also the unconfirmed rumor that—for the purpose of raising welts on deadbeat backsides—he'd drilled fifteen holes in the thing. It was my first time to brave the wrath of the paddle.

Mrs. Cain and I were ushered into his office by the school's inscrutable secretary, Miss Lyle. Tardy slips, unexcused absences, and disciplinary traffic were her domain. The first time I heard the word "spinster" used in conversation, it was in disparaging reference to her. When I asked my mother what Mr. Vick meant when he called Miss Lyle a "cold-hearted old spinster," I was told: "Some women like to work around children 'cause they don't like to go with men and can't have babies." I pressed for clarification on this bit of nebula but had to make do with her generic "You'll understand when you get a little older." Vis-à-vis her ongoing prediction that in the not too distant future I'd pluck out of thin air the meaning of no less than a hundred salacious words, well, there I was, a year older, the cold-hearted old spinster making a minor event out of announcing my case to the vice principal—"the fifth-grade singing problem" is, I believe, how she framed my transgression—and I'm no less confused as to why she liked to work around children.

Judging by Mrs. Cain's nervous fidgeting you'd have thought she'd been called on the carpet instead of me. No doubt she had it in her head that guilt by association was as good a reason as any for

Mr. Holcombe to take a dim view of her future prospects. And if frosty receptions were an indication of things to come, her instincts were spot-on, for it looked as if teacher and student would face the music as a duo. For the time it would take two people of average intelligence to decipher the meaning behind the sign above his desk, Mrs. Cain and I were ignored by Mr. Holcombe. Not until he was satisfied we had a grasp on the gravity of our situation did he bother acknowledging our presence.

The script called for him to deliver a prepared statement of some kind, I was sure of it. But he couldn't find the handle to haul it up. The teacher and I were soon to learn that clearing his throat was no easy task for the old disciplinarian. Several stabs into the ordeal, when it looked as if lodged debris would be the cause of his overdue retirement, we were obliged to read the shifting tides as a good omen—she more astutely than I. Where I saw a possible stay of execution, she saw a whopping career move. Aiding her faltering superior was her ticket out. Spouting a bunch of brown-nose crap about his disciplinary track record and my soon-to-be exemplary behavior, she bought the wobbly geezer a little time to regain his composure. Fresh off the hook, she made short work of disclosing the charges against me and fled the room.

A full six feet and four inches of antediluvian autocracy rose from its leather chair like the gray dawn of the Apocalypse, pulling from a hidden sheath the exact crimson Excalibur I'd foresworn never to lay eyes on. The courtly manner with which he cradled the artifact in the crook of his arm declared that he alone possessed the power to extract such magnificence from its magic stone. Honoring his wordless call to admire its candy-apple finish, custom-wrapped handle, and the gleaming white "Board of Education" stenciled across the paddle's sweet spot (no holes in this baby), I acknowledged, with a trembling, jujitsu bow, that indeed I'd never seen a more dazzling instrument of torture.

Recovered from his bout with laryngitis, Mr. Holcombe delivered the particulars of my sentencing with practiced formality. "You have left this office no other choice than to use the Board of Education. We have found it an effective tool in the stifling of disruptive behavior. You'll be back on an even keel in no time."

Three hard licks across my scrawny rear netted zilch. Two days later, I was back on the carpet—this time alone.

Dealing with me as a repeat offender confounded the vice principal. Involuntary disorders such as the one landing me back in his office didn't square with his concept of cause and effect. Had his faith in the paddle allowed the occasional need for a plan B, perhaps the once proud monocrat might have cracked my case. I felt kind of sorry for the guy. Gone was the sword-wielding Arthur of days past, and in his place was this watery-eyed old man with a catch in his throat. He hocked and hacked but couldn't clear a space in his vocal apparatus from which to address my inability to stop singing.

The summons to Mr. Holcombe's office rattled around our house for a couple of days before my father finally gathered the nerve to face the music. "Aw, hell, Cauzette," he grumbled, scowling, "I guess we're gonna have to go down to that schoolhouse tomorrow and see what he done." Being called in to discuss a disciplinary matter agitated him to no end. Believing that his method of discipline—that is, no method at all—was bound to come under scrutiny, he was close to eating his cigarettes when he trudged into Mr. Holcombe's office. Likewise, the thought of losing her job had my mother gnawing on the remains of her blood-tinged fingernails.

The principal, Mr. Wallace, who'd been ushered into the meeting by Miss Lyle, seated himself casually in the chair next to my father and started the ball rolling. "Your son has always been a model student here at Jacinto City Elementary." Mr. Holcombe nodded his head in oversized agreement. My father's eyes were the size of half dollars and he, too, nodded his head, though not in agreement. Okay, Mr. Big-Shot Principal, I've seen your jab, is the silent rejoinder I read behind his disconcerted expression. "Now come on and show me the sucker punch."

My mother voiced her solidarity with the inquisition. "Yes, he's always been a good boy. The Lord has his hand on—"

Switching his tone to worried concern, Mr. Wallace interrupted her and continued presenting the facts. "We've reached an impasse in our ability to persuade your son to refrain from singing in class."

As if invoking the name of her savior might disperse the approaching storm and play well with the judges, she muttered, "Jesus, sweet Jesus, thank you, Jesus."

My father's eyes narrowed to rattlesnake slits, and I readied myself for "What in the hell is a damn im-pass?" to come rolling off his tongue, but he held it in check.

Knowing he had my parents reeling, Mr. Wallace served up the gist of his agenda. "We think it would be in the boy's best interest if you were to seek professional help for his inability to control the urge to, uh, sing in class."

This was the low blow my father had been waiting for.

"You mean like a sy-ky-a-trist?" he asked tentatively. Then, ratcheting up a more challenging tone, he rephrased the question, "You want me to take him to a si-ky-a-trist just for singin' out loud? I never heard of such a thing."

"Traditional disciplinary methods have been of no consequence," Mr. Holcombe volunteered. "And with your son we have been un—"

This time it was my father who did the interrupting. "Now, y'all are educated men and I ain't. So y'all are gonna need to explain what the hell a traditional disciplinary method is."

"I gave the boy a pretty stiff licking with the Board of Education only to have him turn up in my office for the same infraction the very next day." Mr. Holcombe croaked, an obvious exaggeration during which I counted four more attempts to clear the debris from his throat. "Before that, on four different occasions, he'd been removed from class and made to write 'I will not sing in class' hundreds of times. I'm sure you can understand that I can't just paddle the boy every day. Unless you have a better idea, we can think of no other alternative than professional help."

"Y'all's traditional disciplinary methods, hmm?"

My mother and I exchanged knowing glances. The J. W. Crowell we knew and loved was about to play his cards.

"I can think of an alternative that ain't gonna cost me a nickel." In an instant, he had hold of my right ear and was marching me out of the office. Passing the old spinster's desk, he called over his shoulder, "Y'all ain't gonna have no more trouble with him singin' in class."

If ever I was in for a public beating, I figured it was then. But never one for predictability, my father cranked up the Studebaker and drove away in silence.

"What you fixin' to do, J.W.?" my mother asked.

Silence.

"You think he needs a psychiatrist?"

More silence.

Booger Attenberry, a friend of my father's since the two of them were second-string defensive backs for the Jacinto City Bears semi-pro football team, lived a block and a half from my school. Mr. Attenberry—only adults called him Booger—was running his campaign out of a spare bedroom to get elected Director of Parks and Recreation. Rumbling to a stop in front of his house, my mother and I were told to just wait in the car.

A few minutes later, my father was bounding down the steps with reams of paper tucked under each arm. Without expression, he pitched the bundles in the trunk and drove us home.

It was after a supper of grits and fried wieners that he finally spoke. "I'm fixin' to wake you up early in the mornin,' so you might as well go on and get in the bed."

I took the suggestion at face value.

The next morning was Saturday, and true to his word I was

awakened before dawn. "Get on outta that bed and start thinkin' up them songs you been singin.' We're fixin' to deliver some circulars."

Starting on Lane Street and working my way back home, I hand-delivered 750 "Elect J. R. 'Booger' Attenberry, Director of Parks and Recreation" flyers, each one rolled up and stuck in screen-door handles or folded and placed in mailboxes. Creeping along in the Studebaker, my father made sure I sang my heart out with every delivery.

His enthusiasm never sagged. "Come on, boy!" he'd shout from behind the wheel. "Sing that song. You call that singin'? I want you to reach down in there and sing like you do over at that school-house. Don't make me get outta this car."

Half a block into the exercise, I was cured. Singing my way past houses where Beverly Drake and Betty Jo Branch lived was enough to ensure I wouldn't sing so much as "Happy Birthday" even with a gun pointed at my head.

An hour and a half passed before he slackened the pressure. It was a clever mercy. But before I could find comfort in the reprieve, I'd be back warbling the remains of a repertoire in serious stages of decomposition. Eventually, he'd allow a few blocks to pass before cranking the humiliation up again.

The last straw came when I made a right-hand turn off Mercury Drive onto Munn Street. No sooner had it registered that this was the block where LaQuita Freeman lived than I found myself sprinting to the driver's-side door with what came out sounding like a prepared speech. "I think you're doing the right thing out here tryin' to break me from singin' in class and all. But you're gonna have to let me off singin' on this block."

He spit a Pall Mall shred off the end of his tongue to indicate he was listening.

"I'm never gonna sing in class again as long as I live. I don't even know why I did it in the first place. I hated them songs. I'll sing out loud on ever' block from the next one all the way to Market Street if you want me to, but not on this one. Don't try to make me do it, because I won't."

"All right, son," he said, squelching a smile. Shoving the Studebaker in low gear, he eased on up the street.

I delivered the last three or four hundred flyers in silence. My days of singing aloud in class, unconscious or otherwise, were history. Hell would sport icicles before I'd tune up again. And that's the truth if I never told it.

Shotzie Goes Deep

Near the end of a particularly rainy summer in 1960, my father signed on as weekend foreman for the Texas Ice and Fuel Company. As far back as the late forties, he'd driven a delivery route for the ice purveyors and had become one of the owner's drinking buddies. With his sights set on learning carpentry, he'd quit the ice business and gone to work for a slew of construction conglomerates, most notably Brown and Root. Through all this, their friendship lasted, and with it a source for extra cash when outdoor work turned spotty. His first assignment was overseeing the Sunday morning delivery to Jeppesen Stadium, the high school facility where for the first five years of their existence the brand-new Houston Oilers played every home game. On the same turf where six high school teams played their Thursday and Friday night schedule, the Oilers won the American Football League's first two championships and barely missed a third, losing by three points to the Dallas Texans in a rain-soaked triple overtime.

Icing down a 26,000-seat football stadium was a four-man enterprise. As boss of this operation, my father named me his helper, an act that resulted in his pulling the weight of two men. While I was pretending to make over-the-shoulder catches, he was hauling hundred-pound canvas bags full of crushed ice from the bed of a half-sized pickup built specifically for navigating the narrow ramps leading from the stadium's field level to the upper deck. In less time than it took his counterparts to finish their half of the undertaking, he single-handedly filled the metal chests lining every concession on ours.

One of the perks of his head-honcho status was that he and I worked the home-team side of the stadium exclusively. And there were two sizeable cherries sitting atop this good fortune: one, delivering two hundred pounds of crushed ice to the home team's dressing room, and the other, two free tickets in the end-zone bleachers.

We made it our habit to save the task of icing down the Oilers' locker room for last, which pact increased the chances of rubbing elbows with old-school warriors who'd take the field in the Oilers' trademark blue and white. One rainy Sunday I glimpsed Billy Cannon, the Heisman Trophy halfback whose receding hairline made him look older than my father, changing his cleats with a pair of pliers. And while my father was pouring ice in the Oilers' beer trough, George Blanda caught me staring at his massive jaw line. "Whatsa matter, kid?" he grumbled. "You never see a mug this ugly?" Mussing my cowlick with a Promethean throwing hand, the all-pro quarterback smiled. "I'm just kiddin', son. I'll tell you what, though. Playin' in this league, it doesn't hurt to be ugly."

I have a clear memory of a whip-thin Jim Norton, the team's punter and defensive back, clad in a jock strap and flip-flops, squirreling away a six-pack of Nehi grape soda in the bottom of the cooler. And Charlie "the Human Bowling Ball" Tolar, all five foot six and 210 pounds of him, sporting a beaver Stetson and bumming a smoke off the equipment manager. Orville Trask gave me half of his Hershey's bar, and crew-cut Charlie Hennigan, my favorite Oiler and the record holder for most pass receptions in a single season, patted me on the head and asked if I wanted to play on the team when I grew up. I wonder if he knew that I'd lingered near his locker for that extra twenty seconds in hopes he'd notice a ten-year-old boy who emulated his every move.

With our work completed, my dad and I climbed up to row 26, seats C and D, and settled into enjoying the pregame warm-ups, discussing the finer points of this or that player's possible contributions. My father was defense-minded and a big Mike Dukes fan. "If Dukes ain't hungover, we're fixin' to put a lid on Denver's runnin' game, betcha a buffalo nickel."

"Yeah, but if Hennigan and Groman don't haul 'em in—"

"We can't win if we don't stop the run."

"We can't win if we don't score points."

"I'd just as soon see us win seven to six as anything."

"How about fifty-five to nothin'?"

"Fifty-five to nothin'd do."

Before profit margins and spectator safety placed a retractable net between the place kicker and the cheap seats, extra points and field goals landed freely in the end-zone bleachers, where the ensuing tussle for a pigskin souvenir at times caused as much bloodshed as the game being played on the field.

One cold Sunday in December, my father got both his hands on a ball that was then sent flying by a wallop to the back of his head. To the hooligans who'd pummeled him from behind, he joked, "Boys, y'all reckon we oughta work together on the next one?" But to me he confided, "I shoulda had it, son. I dang sure shoulda had it."

Hey, J-Bo, didn't you practically put me inside the Oilers' huddle? Screw some Norman Rockwell version of a Boy Scout upbringing, the solidity of its camping trips and merit badges, and screw the guilt-tripping baby boomer who coined the candy-assed axiom "quality time." We've got two championships to dine out on forever.

. . .

In the Oilers' glory years—the bow-and-arrow fad of '61 notwith-standing—Billy Duncan, Dennis Reed, Marion Clark, Donnie Schott, Dabbo, and I could usually be found playing touch football, a thirty-five-yard strip of Norvic Street between Mrs. Boyd's drive-way and Mr. Carnew's water meter our field of play. "Two-below"—short for touching the ball carrier with two hands, below the belt—was the nexus of our existence. Oncoming traffic, parked cars, garbage cans, tree branches, and approaching darkness were as much a part of the action as buttonhooks, quick outs, and the stop and go.

Nine out of ten contests pitted Marion, Dennis, and "Dunk" (Billy Duncan) against Dabbo, Donnie, and me. Donnie Schott, whom we affectionately nicknamed "Shotzie" or, depending on the situation, "Shotz-Mo-Dilly-Ack," suffered from a violent strain of cerebral palsy. In the parlance of the times, he was a total spastic. Flailing arms, spidery legs, misshapen speech—Shotzie didn't so much talk as bray loudly—and the grandfather of all protruding chests drew attention away from his soulful blue eyes. Together with these afflictions, his close resemblance to a blond Elvis Presley, circa 1954, seemed a cruel joke. Life wasn't remotely fair for this sensitive soul.

His parents, whom I saw but once, and then from a distance, constructed small living quarters in the back of their garage, where their son, it seemed to his gridiron-crazed cohorts, lived in exile. Cot, sink, commode, desk, chair, and transistor radio gave it the feel of a jail cell. But for his inclusion in our continuing run of fun and games, it seemed that Donnie Schott lived a life void of human interaction.

In the early days Dunk, the oldest and most gifted athlete on the block, instinctively picked Shotzie to play on his team. His own nat-ural size and speed, offset by Shotzie's disadvantages, made the games more evenly matched. But once I'd nursed our spastic friend through the first of countless epileptic seizures, it was a given that he and I belonged on the same team.

As the unofficial captain and play caller for our trio, I was glad to have him. He was loyal and, in spite of his pretzeled body, a determined defender. Plus, I had the sneaking suspicion that, sooner or later, he was bound to contribute something on offense.

It took him most of the '62 season to get the hang of hiking the ball. Even then, his accuracy was so sporadic that my chances of hitting Dabbo with a pass while he was still open were, at best, one in five. And what if, God forbid, one of his flubbed hikes was the cause of our team giving up six points? Time to get out the earplugs, because an agitated Shotz-Mo-Dilly-Ack was prone to repeating some seriously deafening blather. After a bad snap, he'd start ranting about me wanting to kick him off the team, until I was forced to yell louder than him, "Shut up and hike the damn ball, Shotzie. You know I'm not gonna kick you off the stupid team."

By the start of the '63 season, Shotzie was hiking and blocking well enough that I started drawing up plays with him in mind. Spread over the first half of the season, a sideline pass here and a lateral there—most of them dropped—revealed a weakness in Dunk's game plan. He and the boys weren't bothering to defend Shotzie, an oversight that gave me the idea for a onetime shot at hitting him with a long bomb.

In a game nearing the end of the season, behind by six with darkness descending, we had the ball even with Mrs. Boyer's rear tire, twenty-five yards from the goal line. "Dabbo, line up left, next to the Packard, and come around for a fake reverse," I said in a low voice, tracing his movements on the asphalt. "Dunk and Dennis'll follow you and Marion'll rush me. Shotzie, hike it on two and go long. I'm gonna hit you deep."

Before barking the signals, I sneaked a glance at Dabbo, who with his fingers crossed behind his back looked every bit the designated receiver. Dunk noticed this and inched closer to the line of scrimmage. Dennis, too, cheated a step in Dabbo's direction. Marion lined up to the right of Shotzie, arms dangling, head tilted forward, body bent slightly in the middle, like a long-distance runner awaiting a starting gun.

"Ready-down-set, hut one, hut two." For perhaps the third time in three years, Shotzie hiked a perfect spiral. As predicted, Dunk and Dennis shadowed Dabbo while Marion slid past Shotzie's brush block and came tearing after me.

I looked up and saw my intended receiver lurching down the middle of the street like some overgrown mantis. Faking the reverse to Dabbo and freezing Dunk and Dennis in their tracks, I lobbed a wobbling pass that landed lazily in Shotzie's open arms. For a split-second he stood admiring the ball as if it were a treasure fallen from the sky.

"Run, Shotzie!" Dabbo and I yelled in unison. "Run!"

And run he did.

By the time he reached Mrs. Boyd's driveway, our teammate had a head of steam the likes of which his twisted body had never attained. Remembering his touchdown, I can still see the scoliosis letting go of his spine as he charged through the Kilroy Street inter-section. Dabbo and I lit out after him immediately, Dunk, Marion, and Dennis throwing off their dejection and joining in the chase. A third of the way into the next block and still fifty yards behind him, I heard Dunk marvel, "Look at him go. He looks like Crazy Legs Hirsch."

When Shotzie turned left onto Mercury Drive, Dabbo, Dunk, and I ran home to get our bicycles. When we caught up with him, halfway through the Munn Street intersection, he was bellowing, "Rodney hit me deep! Rodney hit me deep!" in rhythm with his stride. "Whoa, Mo-Dilly-Ack!" I called after him. "You tied the game! Time to back it on off!" But Shotzie kept on chugging and bellowing. Only Dunk's motioning for the ball changed the cadence of his chant, and then only for a beat. "No, it's mine!" he bawled, wrapping his arms more tightly around the ball.

And so we rode silently alongside our galloping friend through two more intersections before he collapsed breathless in a vacant lot, seven and a half blocks beyond the goal line.

Letting our bikes fall in the grass, we sat cross-legged while Shotzie sobbed from the pit of his soul. He cried as though wrenching the tears from the very marrow of his elongated bones. When he began to convulse, shuddering like a puppy with distemper, Dabbo and Dunk were moved to dredge unspoken mercies from some shared bottomless quarry, and not until his heart lay parched did I even think of lifting his head from my lap.

By the time we'd resurrected our friend and set out walking him home, it was dark. Pushing our bikes and quietly commemorating his catch, we found a tranquil stride that delivered the four of us back to the Schott residence.

We stood watching that day's hero move listlessly up the driveway, the sodium luminescence of the corner streetlamp lighting his path. "Hey, Shotz-Mo," Dunk called after him, tossing a left-handed spiral that flew past his hands and bounced with a hollow thud off his protruding breastbone, "you hold the ball till tomorrow," and Shotzie retrieved the errant pigskin and disappeared into the black canvas of his family's backyard.

It wasn't for lack of trying that Shotzie's catch stands as his lone shining moment on the asphalt gridiron. In the aftermath of his touchdown we periodically ran the same play, but never successfully. And though he never gave less than an all-out effort, pay dirt came but once to my spastic teammate.

In the weeks that followed, no less than twenty times before the start of a new game, he'd bray for me to hit him deep, that he was on my team. It was as if his memory of hiking the ball to me exclusively for three years had somehow got lost on his marathon run. Reassurances were a waste of breath. If we were lucky, a soothing "Yes, you're on my team, Shotz-Mo" would halt his barrage for a full ten seconds. A couple of times I lost patience and shouted, "Shotzie, when are you gonna get it through your thick skull that you're *always* on my team!" But no sooner had these words dissolved into nothingness than he was back ranting his standard theme. "Hit me deep, I'm on your team."

Only the opening kickoff on a new game of two-below silenced Shotzie's need to make known his preference to play on my team.

PART FOUR

From Love's First Fever to Her Plague

Around the time of the Kennedy assassination, my parents' slugfests shifted into high gear. By then I'd reached the age where duty required that I protect my mother, with fists if need be, and throwing my body between my father's blind rage and her need to wear its markings had become a matter of less consequence than, say, stepping barefoot on a smoldering cigarette. One particularly bloody fracas—starting as an ordinary Saturday morning grocery run and ending up a front-yard melee—left my mother nursing a broken arm and my father with six stitches over his eye. According to her, the break occurred when she, with a sack of groceries in the crook of each arm, got shoved to the ground. When I caught up with the action, he was dragging her down the sidewalk, trailing canned goods and sandwich fixings in their wake, a dozen eggs and a jar of Miracle Whip lying cracked in the driveway.

It was as if I'd sprinted onto the set of some preposterous sitcom. A handsome nutcase with a twelve-pack of Cokes dangling from his free hand is hauling his wife off to God knows where, caveman-style, and she's cursing their ill-mannered new neighbor, who's ignoring her tongue-lashing and idly slathering soapsuds across the hood of his Pontiac. I was surprised to hear her aim "pencil-dick idiot" at Clayton Poole but thrilled she could verbally castrate a guy like that, showing some fortitude and presaging a kind of breakthrough.

Realizing that my mother was drawing strength from her predicament, I held off jumping into the fray and was soon glad I had, for in the next instant, she made a move that would ultimately redefine her marriage. Denouncing Mr. Poole as a worthless sack of shit, she managed to scramble to her feet, pull a Coke loose, and coldcock my father with the blunt end of the bottle, and as quick as that their battle was over. As for the war: A scattering of skirmishes were yet to be waged, one minor dustup coming as late as the summer of '66, but from that day on the fire of their inferno was dwindling out.

I'd never been more proud of my mother than I was at that moment. My father gave the impression that he, too, was pleased, that he knew he'd been bested and chosen to be magnanimous in defeat. Neither one of them knew what protocol followed a haymaker of that caliber, and they more or less milled around next to the street until it was clear their injuries necessitated crawling into the car and speeding off to the hospital.

The calm after this storm, like the one at Magnolia Gardens, was very much to my liking, and I went about gathering up the scattered groceries at a leisurely pace. Eventually, I wandered indoors, pried the cap off a warm Coke, and drained its spewing sweetness in one long gulp.

My mother's triumphant recount of the emergency-room scene went like this: "Son, I wish you coulda seen your daddy at that hospital. There I was with my arm as crooked as a snake, and him just a-bleedin'. That doctor was tryin' to figure out what in the name of Pete happened to us, and your daddy's tellin' him about how we got in a bad car wreck. The nurse kept on lookin' at me like she knew that was a big bunch of malarkey, so I went on and told 'em he was lyin' out his butt. I told the doctor he was tryin' to strangle me to death, so I busted his head open with a Coke bottle. Your daddy turned whiter than a bed sheet. If he'd a jumped up and finished the job on me right there, it woulda been worth it just to see the look on his face. He didn't say one word all the way back to the house."

The turbulence threatening their marriage and my own club-footed tromp through post-pubescence mirrored the Norvic Street house's steady decline. When sections of the roof started caving in, my father's halfhearted attempt to patch the holes with plywood and canvas succeeded only in causing the rotted studs to crumble into damp dust. A month later, the roofing material was strewn across the yard like bombsite debris. Without asking, the Langston kids hauled away the scraps and built a fort in their backyard.

The grace with which I'd once navigated the streets, sidewalks, and alleys of Jacinto City vanished overnight. Where once I'd ridden my bicycle "hands free" and thrown touchdown passes to Dabbo Buck, I was now shaving the sparse hairs on my upper lip and licking the stubble until it looked like a ripe plum. There was also the problem of what to do with a constantly engorged penis.

I can pinpoint the beginning of my downward spiral to the day the seventh-grade algebra teacher reassigned me to the slow learners' class. Until then, I'd spent a full month sitting across the aisle from Kathy Wallace, a doe-eyed Rapunzel at whose innocent expense I'd been concocting pathetic fairy tales in which she was a beautiful maiden and me her charming prince—that kind of stuff. It had actually been going pretty well. Twice she'd said hello as we passed in the hallway, each time turning my brain to Jell-O. Validation of the dream-girl variety was hard to come by, and I wasn't prepared to resume the burden of an insignificant existence. But the class demotion put me so far out of step with my peers that a year and a half dragged by before I could regard myself as anything but irrelevant.

On the bus one morning, not long before the math teacher made my learning disabilities public knowledge, Linda Graham assessed my romantic potential point-blank: "You're kind of cute," she stated flatly from the seat in back of mine, "but everybody thinks you're on free lunches." Historically, this was correct; I *had* been on the free-lunch program in the third and fifth grade, but things were supposedly different now that my father was pulling down three bucks an hour as a carpenter on a building site. But then along comes the rainiest summer in years, and only nine full working days in August kept my mother from paying off the few items of back-to-school clothing she'd put on layaway, so I entered the seventh grade garbed in sixth-grade fashions *and* back on free lunches.

Not until Linda's casual rebuff did I realize that the pretty girls saw me as a poverty case. Protest was useless, as first impressions of early teens aren't often changed. Instead of railing against the social structures rendering me unworthy of attention, or informing the teacher that I'd dedicate heart, mind, body, and soul to unlocking the secrets of algebra's every nuance if it meant keeping my seat in her classroom, I gathered my books and skulked out the door, feeling the warm glow that came from sitting next to Kathy Wallace drain from my body like blood from a knife wound.

At the end of ten months of darkness, Sheila Williams entered my life wearing a bathing suit, with a thumb and forefinger casually realigning its snug fit and tracing the exact curve of the most exquisite rear end ever bestowed on a fourteen-year-old girl. It was, of course, love at first sight.

It the mind-numbing wake of my first ejaculation—self-engendered in the Gulf gas station's men's room—an imaginary Sheila appeared lovesick and naked in a series of dream encounters wherein I was the author of her soul's deepest longings. And in my fantasies, when the eruptions came, they didn't land onto the splotch-stained page 3 of the *Houston Post*'s sports section I'd kept hidden under the bed ever since discovering love's addictive throb, but into the velvety triangle made evocatively intimate by her swimwear.

However, my obsession was no secret. One day an ultra-cool

ninth-grader stopped me outside the lunchroom. "I know you," he said. "You're the guy that goes around singing 'Sheila' to yourself all the time." Tommy Roe's "Sheila" was a big hit around Houston at the time. "Shit, man, everybody's in love with her. Get in line." A few days later, he and another ultra-cool ninth-grader squared off behind the gymnasium, intending to duke it out to prove who stood the best chance of going steady with my "girlfriend." I was one of maybe ten or twelve students on hand for the showdown.

When the fists flew, for reasons beyond my knowing—perhaps the gut-wrenching hopelessness I shared with these warriors, of being madly in love with the teen goddess of all time—I stepped between them. "All right, let's break it up!" I shouted in as officious a baritone as my squeaky tenor could muster, just as a vicious right hand sailed past its target and smashed into my left eye. The next thing I knew, a boy from the track team was helping me find the bus. At home, my mother made an ice pack out of a dishrag and advised me to mind my own business, and my father offered to "clean both their daddies' plows" if I said the word. I thanked him for the gesture and trudged off to my room. For a fortnight I wore the multicolored shiner—blue, black, green, and yellow—that identified me as the fool who broke up the Sheila Williams brawl.

Early in 1964, I retreated into my bedroom with a pawnshop record player and transistor radio, and the music in my sanctuary was, if not the only thing that existed, certainly the only one that mattered. Strumming my Green Stamps tennis racket, I performed "She's Not There" and "World Without Love" to an audience consisting of *ten thousand* Sheila Williamses.

Six months later, when I sang "Help Me, Rhonda," it wasn't along with the Beach Boys but to Rhonda Sisler. Whereas Sheila was sex-soaked and unattainable, Rhonda was willowy, whip-smart, and accessible. Without knowing it, she inspired me to trade my cheap racket for a Merseybeat band of my own, and I began practicing guitar with a purpose. Winning the eighth-grade talent contest and Miss Sisler's affection became my singular goal. Believing as I did that the only way to get a girl was with a guitar, David Warren started showing up after school with an electric guitar, grinning and grateful for my mother's who-gives-a-shit attitude about rock and roll. A few months later, boasting a repertoire of the simplest Ray Charles, Animals, Beatles, and Rolling Stones songs, we considered ourselves primed for the local stage. With Jake Harper on drums and Chris Bechtold, David, and I strumming guitars, the Rolling Tones were ready to rock.

The band's first public appearance, at the Green's Bayou Teen Canteen, was a meandering affair, and our shouting matches over what key and in what order the six-song set would be presented were far more memorable than the music itself. The moments of cohesion we'd achieved during three rehearsals were absent when the curtain went up. After the concert's merciful conclusion, Chris, Jake, and David chatted with newly converted fans like seasoned superstars while I chose instead to sulk.

The Rolling Tones broke up three days later, ostensibly due to the piss-poor quality of my pawnshop guitar and amplifier, but most likely it was my attitude. I'd already decided that these losers were holding me back.

I entered the talent contest solo. Plunking away on my father's beat-up acoustic guitar, I got through "Can't Buy Me Love" and placed third. Emboldened by my success, I attended the celebration hosted by the winner, a chatty tap dancer whose mother, I soon learned, had herself hoofed it to a first-place finish in a similar contest two decades earlier. The upside: Rhonda Sisler would be there.

Thanks to a delegation of blowhard ninth-graders who were boring her stiff with tales of their basketball exploits, I slipped into the gathering unnoticed. Remaining so was my next objective. Accepting congratulations from Duchess Ledbetter and Cyril Easley on the third-place finish was a good start; like me, they were strictly bottom-tier personalities and unlikely to draw much attention. Staging a phony conversation with a science geek everybody called Ray-Gun was even better; as long as we stayed huddled in a corner, nobody would ever guess I was turning the party into a Rhonda Sisler surveillance maneuver. Incidentally, the consensus among my ex-bandmates was that the high point in the talent contest had been when the science geek—sporting a white lab coat and affecting every cliché in the amateur illusionist's handbook—demonstrated an "experiment" in which, by rigging an electric-train transformer to an extension cord, he infused a ten-penny nail with great magnetic powers. Halfway through the act, the junior Rebels in the audience let him have it from all sides, which outburst sent Mrs. Gann, the junior high vice principal, scurrying up and down the aisles in a useless attempt to silence their taunting. But no sooner had she squelched one set of hecklers than another delegation broke out in some hard-to-reach section of the auditorium. All this went on longer than it might have if "Old Eagle Beak"—Mrs. Gann's nickname since time immemorial—hadn't threatened the entire student body with two weeks in detention, an overreaction that resulted in the science geek's finishing his routine to a nasty chorus of boos meant instead to lambaste her. After the eighth-grade Mr. Wizard's effusive final bow, old Mr. Tatum, the dyspeptic janitor, sauntered onstage, broom and dustpan in hand, and swept up the pile of paper clips and safety pins that had fallen to the floor so Miss Win Another For Mother could dance unimpeded into the history books. Just for the record, my disgruntled musician pals had it right: Ray-Gun's performance was by far the most memorable of the competition and deserved the top prize.

It wasn't until I enlisted the services of our hostess's mother that Operation Rhonda ran into trouble. At first, her prattling fit my needs perfectly. By feigning agreement with such pronouncements as "Tap will outlast rock and roll, by golly" and "I'm just sorry the war ended before I was old enough to go over there and dance for the boys," I was able, via stolen glances, to memorize my new dream girl's lanky figure. But when her observations about "doilies" and "throw rugs" and "matching end tables" started scrambling the secret fantasies I purportedly was sponging from my beloved's subconscious mind, I knew we'd lost something as a team and was a breath shy of thanking her for allowing me into her lovely home when "converted garage" smashed through my skull like a drunk driver. And that's when Rhonda Sisler caught me staring.

I averted my gaze but she refused to accept the cowardice. "I saw you looking at me," she scolded playfully, crossing the room with an economy of stride that rendered the floor her own private conveyor belt. "I'm Rhonda Sisler," she said, beaming, insisting with a carefree toss of her head that I admire her honey-colored tresses. Then came a smile that would dazzle even the blind.

By now I'd forgotten how to breathe.

"I liked seeing you up on stage," she said, sounding sincere. "You're a good singer." She allowed that because I was in the eighth grade and she the ninth, we could never "go out"—using her fingers, she placed quotation marks around the phrase—but since we were both artists, it would be all right if, once in a while, I walked her to class. And if I ever wanted to *talk*—God, did I ever—I should give her a call. The A-bomb thus dropped, she slipped back into the party's mainstream without disclosing her phone number, leaving me too dumbstruck to call out for it.

The opportunity to walk Rhonda Sisler to class presented itself only once. In the time it took to navigate the hallway from Mrs. Witt's science class to Mr. Cassius's art class—about fifty yards—she shared in detail her dream of moving to France and becoming a well-known artist. This was a vision of the future so far beyond me that, feeling the need to match her farsightedness with some forethought of my own, I spat out the first unexamined thought that sprang to mind. "Oh, that's all right," I blurted. "You can stay right here and do that."

I knew immediately that this was irrevocably stupid, but before I could dream up a do-over she nailed me: "Of all the boys in this school, I thought you'd understand me," she said *very* seriously.

I tried retracing my steps, but the path was closed. She had moved to Paris without me.

And so I came to understand—too late—that golden girls were as susceptible to isolation as tongue-tied boys with learning disorders. When every other pretty girl cared only about potential football stars, why Rhonda had her sights set on art and music and dual citizenship was, given the time and the place, almost incomprehensible. In fact, against a backdrop of oil refineries, chemical plants, paper mills, salvage yards, and beer joints, how she knew such things even existed was a bigger mystery to me then than tetrahedral triangles are now. Yet as I kept slogging through adolescence, I came to revere this force of nature as a symbol of possibility. Though years away from knowing who I was, thanks to her I finally knew what I wanted. I wanted out.

One rainy Saturday afternoon in March, I hesitated before answering a knock on the door. Since recent visitors over, say, the last fifty-two months numbered in the single digits, greeting callers had become a forgotten propriety around our sodden little abode. Company was a rare thing indeed, and I took a minute to rifle through my store of worst-case scenarios before calling out, "Who is it?"

On the porch were Jerry and Jeanette Hosch, both of whom I'd known since our mothers had hired on as janitors at Jacinto City Elementary School. Although they'd moved away the summer before seventh grade and I hadn't thought of them since, I knew a leaking roof wouldn't faze them in the least and invited them in without hesitation.

Jerry came straight to the point. The rock-and-roll band they were putting together in a little rice-farm township some thirty miles northeast of Jacinto City needed a guitar player and singer. Even out there in the sticks, paying jobs were plentiful enough for every band member to make, three weekends out of four, ten or twelve bucks. He and his sister had agreed that I was about as close to a Beatle as they could hope to get and sure would appreciate it if I'd think about joining up.

When I announced that I was leaving home to start a band, my father was working on the engine of his latest used-car disaster, a baby-blue and white '57 Ford whose previous owner had most likely relied almost exclusively on public transportation. Dragging his upper body from beneath the hood, he made a quick study of the middle distance a foot above my head and said, "Tell 'em you write your own songs, son." Nodding his satisfaction with the pith of this advice, he peered back into the mouth of this $175 lemon, then issued a barrage of expletives that I took as a sign of approval.

My mother's response was no less typical. "Go ahead, son," she said, pointing to some numinous elsewhere beyond our screen door. "There ain't a day goes by that I don't wish I'd've told Mama to let the Devil take the hindmost and gone on to that school. If this shit round here don't kill us when it falls down, me and him might catch up with you out yonder."

To find Crosby, Texas, one had to travel east on Interstate 10 and turn north on Farm to Market Road 2100 and then, heading away from the Lynchburg Ferry and the San Jacinto Battlegrounds, pass through the townships of Highlands—so named for its location on the banks above the river—and Barrett Station, an ex-slave settlement dating back to the Emancipation Proclamation, before reaching the Highway 90 intersection and the outskirts of your destination. Beyond the fairgrounds, rodeo arena, and antiquated water tower lay the town center, where Glover's Burgerland, Hechler's Department Store, the post office, Stasney's Feed Store, Swanson's Drug & Appliances, Prescott's Esso, and Jay's Grocery huddled alongside the Southern Pacific Railroad tracks as living proof that wars, tornadoes, and economic depression couldn't break the will of this turn-of-the-century whistle-stop.

North of the tracks, another ten-mile stretch of road cut across the irrigation ditches, rice fields, and cattle farms lining Lake Houston's eastern shores. Clarence and Flora Mae Hosch maintained a two-acre outpost half a mile from the Farm to Market Roads 1960 and 2100 junction, and I arrived there on a Friday less than a week after the surprise invitation to join the band. On Monday morning I enrolled in the tenth grade at Crosby High School.

After the murk and misery of junior high, to be fifteen going on sixteen and a big-shot member of the Arbitrators—a name we'd plucked from the *A*'s in the dictionary—and hauling down a little spending money and answering to nobody was a mighty potent cocktail.

Jerry owned a '63 Chevy, in which the band, guitars, amplifiers, and drum kit fit snugly. Crammed in that car like sardines, Ronnie Joe Falk, Jeanette, Jerry, Ronnie Hechler (the band manager), and yours truly traveled to small towns like Huffman, Humble, Barbers Hill, Dayton, Highlands, and Baytown for paying engagements. Hechler even had cards printed up:

The English Sound	The Surf Beat
THE ARBITRATORS	
Rhythm and Blues	Country, If You Want It

I soon adopted the habit of skipping school in favor of sleeping late and spending idle afternoons drinking beer and smoking cigarettes with Jerry and Bernie Wilson, high school dropouts and my new role models. When the principal called me into his office to discuss my eight absences in the first month, I made up a big lie about there being no such thing as an unexcused absence at Galena Park High School, to which perjury I tacked on the assurance that one phone call would validate my claim. He ignored this bluff and forthwith delivered a three-pronged sermon on the perils of negative influences, Jerry Hosch's well-known disdain for authority, and the importance of getting off on the right foot. When he'd finished reading aloud the state laws pertaining to truancy, I was given a mimeographed copy of the student handbook and abruptly dismissed. Final score: Mr. Prohazcka, fifty-six; cocky new rock-and-roll star, zero.

During the years that our mothers scrubbed floors, Jeanette and I had been trusted after school to walk the two blocks to her house where, under the not-so-watchful eye of her older sister, we were left to do pretty much as we pleased—climbing fences, throwing rocks, shooting marbles, making mayonnaise sandwiches, watching *Adventures of Superman,* and snooping around for her big brother's dirty magazines. Come four-fifteen, my mother would call from the sidewalk that it was time to go, and we'd walk the five blocks home.

Out of the blue, Robbie Green started spewing nonsense about this after-school arrangement. A well-known mama's boy, Robbie was a full head taller than his peers, his protruding lower lip quivered when he spoke, and his father was rumored to have skipped town with his wife's inheritance. And among the more gossipy women, Mrs. Green herself, being tall and beautiful and without a man, was suspected of being up to no good. I'd been inside their house twice and the nattering about her didn't wash. True, it was a strange household, but whose wasn't? If Robbie and I had gotten on better, I'd have hung around his place on a regular basis, since they had an air conditioner in the living room window. But according to Robbie, what Jeanette and I were up to was "too weird," and he threatened to "set the record straight." Why being looked after by her sister was at all weird and what record needed straightening was never elaborated on. And then, on the third day, he declared I could "no longer run from the truth" and began babbling about unwanted children and Jeanette saving herself for her wedding night and me being long gone once I'd gotten what I wanted—the kind of spiel that is usually delivered by some uptight grown-up.

By the fourth day, Jeanette had had enough. "If you don't quit mouthin' off at us," she warned him, "I'm gonna teach you a lesson."

Instead of heeding her tone, Robbie made some deprecating remark about her mother's hairstyle that wasn't, as I recall, too far off the mark; Flora Mae wore a cult-religion bouffant piled so high on her head that even my mother made jokes about it looking like a two-story bird's nest.

Jeanette responded by throwing a solid punch that opened a gash in Robbie's lower lip, and for a long moment he stood there examining the blood on the tips of his fingers and making sure it was his by tasting a drop or two.

Then, despite being two feet shorter, Jeanette wrestled the poor fool to the ground and made good on her promise as a crowd of students cheered her on. Over and over again, Robbie yelled for somebody to get her off him, loud enough to be heard back in his mother's house, but no one volunteered.

"Me and J.W. figured we might as well move on out here to be close to the boy," my mother told Flora Mae. I was hiding behind Jerry's bedroom door and sneaking looks out the window at my father, who sat behind the wheel of a four-year-old Ford pickup. "We got no intentions of ruinin' what he's got goin' on with his band and all," she continued. "We just wanted to let y'all know we're here—in case he wants to come back home."

In the nine months since I'd seen my parents, something in me had changed. I no longer cared if they killed each other, or if the house they'd rented across the street from Ronnie Joe Falk's was a step down from the one they'd just had repossessed. It was an eighty-year-old farmhouse whose land had turned into Crosby's only neighborhood, and an indoor toilet and a back bedroom had been added on sometime later. Whereas the original foundation was stacked quarry rock, the addition rested on a thin slab of concrete and was caulked to the exterior wall, and to access the main part of the house one had to climb the rickety back steps and pass through a kitchen the size of a broom closet. Due to these renovations the back door had been repositioned near the far end of a windowless wall facing the driveway, so the freedom I had cherished living with the Hosch family continued unabated. In fact, the yearlong crime spree Ronnie Joe and I went on resulted directly from the placement of that door.

A typical evening's burglary started with the two of us pushing one of our parents' cars halfway down the block before cranking it up for a late-night joyride. If breaking and entering was our fantasy, stealing tools out of some old farmer's barn was our reality. We did manage to pry into the high school gym and steal all the varsity football team's game jerseys. Matching player and number, we spent the rest of the night flinging each jersey into the corresponding yard, including Ronnie Joe's, and got up early the next morning to drive around admiring our handiwork.

Our most spectacular act of delinquency came on the night Ronnie Joe climbed the water tower. Belonging to the class of '65, he intended to burn the canvas "Seniors '64" banner that some daredevil had hung from the metal walkway circling the tank. He climbed the tower's exposed ladder, tied eighty feet of gasoline-soaked rags to the sign, and climbed back down. I then lit the dangling fuse with a kitchen match, and the two of us watched the blue-edged flame traveling upward as fast as the adrenaline charging through our bloodstreams. A whoosh and a ball of flames pronounced our mission complete, and from the Falks' back porch, three blocks away, we lingered for a few minutes in its waning glow before heading off to bed.

The next day, a handful of students and Saturday shoppers were milling around the tower's base, where kitchen matches were strewn over the ground like leftover party favors. Such was the attitude toward criminal investigation around Crosby that I overheard the sheriff say, "There ain't no need in worryin' about who done this, since they ain't nothin' else up yonder to burn down."

Only once did Ronnie Joe and I get into real trouble. Out on the far south side of Houston, he'd tried to make a U-turn and gotten his mother's Ford stuck in a ditch. The road was desolate, as most in that neck of the woods were, and the prospect of a long walk hung over our heads like a burned-out lightbulb. Flagging down the first set of headlights was an equally daunting proposition, for most of the people traveling there at that hour were lost, stupid, or dangerous. Or, like my partner and me, all three.

Before we could muster the courage to set off on foot, a two-toned '55 Chevrolet station wagon pulled up alongside. "What're y'all boys doin' out here this time of night?" a menacing-looking man asked through the passenger-side window, the driver hidden from view in the dark interior.

"Hey there, neighbor," Ronnie Joe called out, his hollow tone of voice betraying his attempt at friendly confidence.

"I ain't nobody's neighbor," the man replied, flashing a smile that looked more like a blood-stained dagger. "You anybody's neighbor?" he asked the unseen driver, mocking Ronnie Joe's fake chirpiness.

"Naw, I ain't nobody's fuckin' neighbor," the driver said, my imagination conjuring from his voice a drunk Robert Mitchum.

"Y'all got any money in them pockets?" the first man demanded.

"I got a little," I said, as evenly as possible.

"I got some, too," Ronnie Joe chimed in, "and we wouldn't mind givin' it up if it'll get us outta this ditch."

The ratcheting sound of the emergency brake being engaged echoed off a colony of white oil-storage tanks some fifty yards off in the darkness, breaking the audio stalemate. Enchanted by the rhythm of the station wagon's idling engine, I was staring at the exhaust pipe, thinking of how it reminded me of an old dog panting on a hot day and wondering if it might accompany the sound of my own dying breath.

The driver's door creaked open and a tall, skinny man of indeterminate age—he could've been twenty-five or fifty-five—stepped out into the light. He wore sunglasses across the top of his sandy-colored, slicked-down hair, faded Levi's that hung impossibly off his hips, motorcycle boots, and no shirt. Jailhouse tattoos covered his upper torso, and I zeroed in on "Blood and Money" scrawled above his heart. The passenger stayed seated. "Give me all of it," the driver said, lighting a Camel. Ronnie Joe and I coughed up sixteen dollars total.

In the back of the station wagon was an assortment of burglary equipment, including a hand-operated come-along. The tall, skinny man fastened the wench to a trailer hitch welded to the car's chassis and the grappling hook to the Ford's front bumper and jimmied Mrs. Falk's car out of the ditch by hand, then put away the come-along and wiped his hands on an oily rag. "I reckon y'all think you was up to somethin' out here this evenin'. This here's our territory. I catch y'all back out this way, I'm gonna kill the both of ya."

Safe inside his mother's car, Ronnie Joe and I sat collecting our senses for a moment. The driver put the station wagon in reverse and backed up alongside us. The passenger flashed his tobacco-and-blood-stained smile one last time and laid a snub-nosed revolver across his right shoulder. "If y'all ain't hard of hearin', Ole Slick over here won't have to go puttin' nobody out of his misery."

Late in 1966 the Arbitrators disbanded. Jerry and Ronnie Joe enlisted in the Army; Ronnie Hechler joined the family business; while Jeanette and I went straight, she as a cheerleader and me as a second-string quarterback. Had I known that by trading in the brooding-outsider persona for a more mainstream likability I'd experience a succession of intimate firsts with a quietly adventurous girl of Czechoslovakian lineage, I would've splashed the cologne on sooner. I'd never had a real girlfriend before and she was perfect in every respect, and I sometimes suspected everything was right in my world.

Senior year, my parents found a decent house to rent, and I graduated somewhere in the middle of a class of forty-three. For eight months of the fifteen that I commuted to Lee College in Baytown, I attempted to pass the courses required for a degree in political science or marine biology or English literature; I could never decide which.

In the summer and fall of '69, my father and I built a three-bedroom house on a two-acre tract of swampland adjacent to an irrigation ditch north of Crosby. The neighborhood—assuming this mud hole and stand of pine trees qualified as such—was called Gum Gully. If a more unwilling participant in this venture was imaginable, I doubt my father could've dug him up with a steam shovel. And if arguments built houses, we'd have knocked this one out in no time.

From the beginning, his quest to complete the basic construction before Christmas was beset by obstacles far more troublesome than my general disinterest. Too much rain, not enough daylight, and the ebb and flow of out-of-pocket financing kept him in a state of perpetual anxiety for nine months.

My job description fell somewhere between unpaid laborer and unskilled craftsman. Suggesting that my mother was a more suitable partner, sympathetic to his cause and happy to do what I wasn't, was a waste of breath. In his mind's eye, the building of what he'd come to call "your mama's house" had father and son written all over it.

My mind and body were in two places that summer. The Czech girlfriend had taken her leave, and I'd fallen under the spell of a red-haired twenty-eight-year-old, an ex-collegiate swimmer who taught nutrition at the college. Our acquaintance was made the night I experienced the effects of marijuana for the first time. I spent the evening plastered to a beanbag chair, listening to her extol the virtues of some guy I'd never heard of named Che Guevara while scorning Richard Nixon as a criminally insane warmonger who'd sold his shell of a soul to the military-industrial complex for a shot at immortality. The invitation to drop by her apartment the next day—she hosted a Sunday afternoon discussion group of some kind—put me in mind of Rhonda Sisler, and I wasn't about to blow it a second time.

Degas nude prints, scarf-draped lighting, fresh-cut flowers, beaded doorways, a carved rosewood letterbox full of marijuana, and a component stereo system gave Renata's garage apartment a feeling of warm existentialism. Pine-board-and-cinder-block shelves lined an entire wall, stuffed with books on astrology and Buddhism. Hardcover translations of Leo Tolstoy and paperback Khalil Gibrans could be found between *A Guide to the Macrobiotic Diet* and the Kinsey Reports. I scanned two or three pages of a handful of these and made a mental note to go back and read the ones I'd heard of, and maybe some others. The books, marijuana, record collection, and a well-stocked refrigerator were openly available to an assortment of misplaced characters who, like me, had nothing better to do than take advantage of her progressive lifestyle.

I didn't share my exotic new mentor's enthusiasm for the self-aggrandizing prognosticators who hung around her place quoting Karl Marx and Joseph Stalin. One guy in particular, always spouting off about the day when a single worldwide government and the *Communist Manifesto* would reign supreme, bored the hell out of me. But as long as there was a remote chance that, if I paid attention to them, Renata might renege on her refusal to have sex with me on the grounds of emotional and physical incompatibility, I considered each and every one a direct descendant of Nostradamus. Even after she confided in me about Monica, a soon-to-be-divorced lifeguard from Deer Park, I held fast to the notion that my new friend would swear off "girls" in favor of me.

One moonlit evening in July, Renata, Monica, and I spread a blanket in the commons across the street from Renata's apartment and proceeded to get thoroughly stoned on white wine and Thai-stick joints rolled in strawberry-flavored papers. Scattered around the park were similar parties listening to the news reports on transistor radios and, as if hoping to glimpse an astronaut walking on the moon's surface, gazing at the sky in wide-eyed wonderment. In the middle of Renata's rambling discourse on the subject of team sports and individual effort, which somehow pertained to the lunar landing, the thought popped into my head that my father's determination to build a house was no less focused than NASA's fixation with landing a man up there.

"My dad's like the government when he gets a wild hair to do something," I said aloud, though not intending to interrupt her monologue. A dew-drenched quiet fell on our picnic, and then Renata commenced a tutorial on "the alpha aspects of the father-and-son archetype."

"It's a trait I'm sure you've inherited," she said, referring to his single-mindedness. "In your case, if the path doesn't lead to pussy, you're not the least bit interested. Put yourself in his shoes. Unless he offers up the vestal virgins as an incentive, he's stuck with a cretin for a helper. It's too bad you can't appreciate that the opportunity to build a house with your father is nothing less than a divine rite of passage." She loved the word "divine" in both sound and meaning. "Isn't it interesting that the father's instinct for the survival of the family and the son's instinct for the survival of the species are so often at cross purposes? If I didn't like women, I'd be drawn to the father. A young man would think nothing of fucking you in a garbage dump. With an older man, at least there's the possibility of clean sheets."

That night I drove home thinking my father's project was right up there with the Holy Grail, and for a week, maybe two, my work reflected this epiphany. When he commented on the shift in attitude, I was ready with the quip, "If they can put a man on the moon, we can build a dad-gum house." Failing to notice the reconciliation happening under her nose, my mother rejected the moon-landing analogy. "Aw, shit, son," she scoffed. "They got them astronauts locked in a television station around here somewhere."

This was also the summer I spent doing grunt work for a crew of alcoholic sandblasters who'd landed a contract to renovate the interiors of ten storage tanks belonging to the Shell Oil Company. Eight hours inside one of those, pushing a wheelbarrow and shoveling sludge out through its lone portal, put me in the mood to go somewhere and get drunk with my coworkers. Instead I'd head for Gum Gully and argue nonstop with my father about how to build a house, though I really had no concept of the end product.

It's hard to say whether my workmanship was marred more by indolence or ineptitude. In either case, it was rare that I completed a task without my father yelling something like: "God almighty, son, you're slower'n a prison sentence" or "Shit, son, if there's a thought goes through that head of yours 'bout anything but poontang, I'll be damned if I know what it is." At best, the odds of my fetching whichever tool he'd called for on the first try were about one in seven.

Early one evening, I came perilously close to severing my mother's arm with a Skilsaw. She was holding the end of a piece of two-by-eight siding I was cutting to my father's specifications. When I finished the cut, the board collapsed between us and she toppled into the saw's path, the blade skimming her left arm and leaving a long red welt similar to those she used to raise on my legs with a chinaberry switch. Another sixteenth of an inch and the teeth would have ripped her arm off. My father scrambled down from atop the ladder where he'd been watching this near disaster unfold, grabbed the still zinging saw out of my hand, yanked the cord unplugged, and flung the tool into the woods behind the house. "If y'all don't wake up," he declared, lighting the first of several rapid-fire Pall Malls, "I'm gonna pour high-test over every inch of this shit and burn the whole mess down." A half hour passed before I was sent in search of the saw.

Following a plan that called for finishing the interior at a pace dictated by available funds, my parents moved into their shell of a house on the twenty-first of December. I have a clear memory of spending the long, hungover day after Christmas stapling strips of asbestos insulation to the roof's underside and the attic floor, after which I wolfed down a tuna fish sandwich and collapsed, unwashed, into bed. Three feet from where I slept was a tall stack of the toxic wadding destined for the living room walls. An even sharper recollection is of my father as seen and heard through the still-naked wall studs at five-thirty in the morning, hugging the commode and retching up five-inch strands of nicotine-stained phlegm. Pointing out that I'd give up cigarettes if all I had to look forward to each morning were these predawn puke-fests garnered the comeback: "If you don't like it, you can kiss my miserable ass." Meanwhile, my mother was frying eggs and bacon on a butane camping stove and listening to the early-bird gospel hour on a transistor radio.

While I was stuck helping my father, the lifeguard was moving her belongings into Renata's apartment. When I turned up after a monthlong absence, Renata greeted me no less affectionately than in the past, but I also sensed a disconnection. Monica appeared her usual self, distrustful of me and overly possessive of her girlfriend, yet even with her, things didn't seem the same. Nevertheless, by the beginning of the spring semester I was sleeping four nights out of seven on their sofa. And when this grew tiresome for everyone involved, I was invited to find another couch. Although I'd known for months that Monica was sick of watching me follow her girlfriend around like a lost puppy, this ultimatum blindsided me. Since it was easier to blame it on my rival than admit to wearing out my welcome, I focused all my embarrassment on Monica. I'd never called anybody a fake lesbian before, nor had I ever been accused of having my head so far up my ass that I couldn't spell the word, but once the slander got rolling not even the professorial Renata could get a word in edgewise.

Monica eventually pronounced our name-calling childish and stomped out of the apartment, leaving her partner the job of negotiating a final truce. I can't say that "a mutual decision" or "we can still be friends" came as any real surprise. But "Monica's never done this and I'm afraid I'll lose her" struck me as the truest thing Renata had ever said to me, and on some primal level I already knew that our student-teacher liaison had run its natural course. I might have taken to heart her heads-up that in the future it might be a good idea if I tried to work on my all-or-nothing intensity, which at times was so downright suffocating that any girl interested in getting close to me would first need an oxygen mask. But some things you just have to learn for yourself.

I was sitting on the couch with my parents and watching *The Glen Campbell Goodtime Hour* when a voice inside my head offered this bit of sour advice: *Tonight's as good a night as any to end this shit sandwich of a life you've got going on here. The 20-gauge will do the job just fine.*

Was this the same voice that advised me to relax and enjoy the scenery while drowning in the Brazos River, a voice I associated with viable alternatives to hopeless situations—if not the voice of God, certainly a prescient authority acting on behalf of a long-dead relative, preferably Grandma Katie? Or was it my own? I couldn't decide. No doubt there were some similar speech patterns, but that voice sure as hell didn't sound like me. I spent a sizeable chunk of nonlinear time considering whether Paw Jim or Sol T had hijacked the afterlife's public-address system and was wreaking his brand of havoc from the other side. Summarily nixing the possibility that marijuana was causing my brain to malfunction—I'd snuck out behind the garage to smoke some potent grass just before the television show came on—I went on weighing the pros of blowing my head off against the cons of continuing down the road to nowhere.

Just before Glen Campbell announced the John Hartford banjo segment, another voice—the old Tonto-like one familiar from days gone by—offered this pearl of high-toned wisdom: *In order for your life to begin, this has to end.* Now I was really confused. Did "this" mean my miserable existence out here in Podunk, Texas, or was it some cosmic insinuation that I didn't know my ass from turnip greens? And for that matter, would it be too much to ask that whoever was filling my head with this crap just come out and say he's pissed off at me for smoking dope behind the garage?

Thankfully, I met a girl who kept my mind from going bonkers. And for a while, she was the answer to every dream that never came true for me. A near-Mensa IQ did nothing to quell Matty Jackson's appetite for carnal delicacies; if anything, it heightened her desires. A case could be made that intelligence as fierce as Matty's was animal instinct functioning at its most primal level, citing as evidence the claw marks and bite bruises I was soon wearing like Boy Scout merit badges.

By now you'll have noticed that my tendency to fall for the girl who was either unattainable or my superior, or both, was truly an Achilles' heel. Years later, a psychiatrist suggested my preference for the exceptional female stemmed from my hatred of my mother's nonexistent self-esteem, that I'd inherited her sense of shame and was perpetuating my own lack of self-worth by failing upward, sexually. In my case, she believed, chasing the beautiful or smart or inaccessible girl was—and this is where she lost me—the exact opposite of an Oedipal complex. According to her, my driving desire was to kill my mother and make love to my father. And on top of that, as long as I continued showing up at her office trying to entice her into having sex with me, our sessions were useless. She offered to refer me to one of her male colleagues, and I wondered aloud if she'd lost track of my reason for seeking out her services in the first place, that I was hoping she'd cure my fear of dying in California's next big earthquake. She hadn't, but I got the drift that she wanted off my case. I declined the referral.

Matty Jackson accepted my proposal and an inexpensive ring as proof of my good intentions. Her father, a blue-collar ramrod at one of the southside refineries, slapped me on the back, shook my hand, and welcomed me to the family. I liked the guy a lot. Her mother made southern fried chicken and broccoli with hollandaise sauce to commemorate the occasion, and her brother gave me the

Band's album with "Up on Cripple Creek" and "The Night They Drove Old Dixie Down" on it. Good people.

I never informed my parents of the upcoming wedding. Despite Matty's intelligence, she failed, as did I, to detect the layers of delusion at work in my psyche. As long as the fires of passion were raging out of control, love was real. That's all either of us needed to know.

At some point it was decided that her plan to attend Stephen F. Austin State University was sound. I'd tag along and enroll in classes, and the wedding would sort itself out in due course.

But attending classes didn't figure much in my days that crisp fall of 1970. Afternoons spent with any of the coeds fond of visiting the fifty-dollars-a-month digs my new best friend Donivan Cowart and I shared off campus were far more appealing. The counterculture's sexual revolution was just then reaching its zenith in northeast Texas, and the so-called doors of perception being flung open by pot and the occasional tab of LSD were ours to walk through at our own pace, or so we imagined.

My fiancée had so admirably thrown herself into the rigors of college that excluding weekends and the occasional hour after homework—that golden hour before the dorm mother informed any couples out there French-kissing and finger-fucking in the shadows that curfew was in ten minutes—I was free to follow my urges.

For a while, I managed to keep this freedom and my engagement two separate issues. In defense of my twenty-year-old self, I can say only that I was probably living more in the moment than at any other time in my life, save riding my bicycle, stealing fishing lures, and perhaps chasing after the Mosquito Dope Truck. That I'd become a lousy husband-to-be and a shit-heel to boot never occurred to me. And then I met Annie McGuane.

Once she entered the picture, I vowed to become a different man. Nothing less than my very best was good enough for this new Aphrodite, so before our first date I broke things off with Matty.

Why I thought it was a good idea to gush to her about how deeply I'd fallen for Annie is anybody's guess. Apparently the new me was just as self-absorbed as the old.

Had my vision not been so clouded, I would've seen signs of trouble from the beginning. Practically from our first pizza Annie was desperately trying to avoid becoming engulfed by my intensity. My pledge to make her happy or die trying was so over the top that I all but gagged the poor girl on her own beauty. When she was unable to meet my cravings with desires of her own, I'd complain bitterly or pout until she was forced, out of self-defense, to surrender to my will. She blamed her need to keep a safe distance between her true feelings and my twenty-year-old passion on a strict Catholic upbringing and, for a while, I was happy to accept that her ambivalence might be rooted in religion. But still I couldn't shake the sneaking suspicion she was saving herself for someone more substantial.

It was obvious Annie intended to make the most of her life, starting with college. She went to class, studied, made good grades, and spoke assuredly of her future as a speech therapist. I, on the other hand, was determined to become a dropout. And I never stopped to consider that, from her point of view, sitting around playing guitar and toying with the idea I could write songs seemed more an avoidance of reality than a respectable career path. So I internalized the feeling of being misunderstood and went on trying to make her love me, as pathetic as that was.

The death knell sounded on my college career when I found work playing bass guitar five nights a week behind a middle-of-the-road lounge singer at the Holiday Inn. Short of building chicken coops—a job Donivan and I held briefly the following summer—playing four sets a night and drinking for an hour or two after closing was as uncollegiate a lifestyle as there was in Nacogdoches. Newly flush, Donivan and I moved into a bigger house in a swankier neighborhood, and a couple nights a week my girlfriend would be waiting up when I got home from playing "Help Me

Make It Through the Night" and Three Dog Night's "Joy to the World" until I wanted to vomit. Still, life wasn't that bad.

When it came to winning Annie's trust I was my own worst enemy. She wasn't above smoking the occasional joint if conditions were conducive to enjoying a break from her studies. But I went at it like a viper. During Christmas break, while she was away visiting her family in Dallas, Donivan and I went on a search for weed that led us to a biker den somewhere on the outskirts of Lufkin. We were told before entering the compound not to speak until spoken to, but my friend couldn't restrain himself from saying, "This crew would have to clean up their act to join the Hell's Angels," and our furtive middleman advised him that such commentary would get our balls shot off.

"The things we do to get high," Donivan sneered.

"I'm warning you, man," our guide hissed, his chin an inch off Donivan's nose. "These cats ain't who you wanna mess with."

Before selling us a lid of street dope, the head dealer insisted that to prove we weren't narcs we had to smoke some of his private stash. Appearing on cue was a tall black guy in Army fatigues and holding a 12-gauge shotgun. After locking his mouth around the bowl of a Sherlock Holmes pipe, he started blowing a heavy stream of blue smoke out the end of the shotgun's single barrel. "Go on," the head guy goaded. "Show us what you boys are made out of."

Thinking my life depended on how well I handled this killer dope, I wrapped my lips around the shotgun barrel and inhaled as if it were a two-dollar joint. The result of this bravura was a coughing seizure so intense my body seemed to be turning itself inside out, the spasms coming in waves. And the more I coughed, the less it amused the dealer. Donivan tried pouring beer down my throat but couldn't find a gap in the convulsing. Early in the ordeal I felt a pop in my lower abdomen, and later discovered an unsightly bulge of internal organs on the right side of my pelvis. The coughing fit had given me a hernia. It was a ghastly sight, and my first thought was *Oh, shit. Annie's going to think I'm a freak.*

Who could blame a goal-oriented girl for starting to rethink a relationship with a guy who'd do such a thing? I tried passing off the hernia as an out-of-the-blue accident that, left untreated, would provide a guaranteed draft deferment, but I could tell she wasn't buying it. From then on I could sense her growing more distant by the day.

During a period of receptivity to what little charm I could muster with half of my intestines bulging out from behind my lower abdominal wall, Annie invited me to meet her family in Dallas. I'd been feeling so low that I jumped at the chance to make a positive impression, though had I taken the time to think it through, surely I would've known that my inability to account for the lack of direction in my life might cause her father to dislike me instantly.

"What's your major?" he asked.

"Poly sci," I lied.

"Oh, and what do you plan to do with your degree?"

"I thought I might run for mayor of Nacogdoches or something. Sorry, sir, that was a joke."

"I see. Annie's only told me a little about your background, but I think it's safe to say you don't have a serious attitude about your education. I came up the hard way. My success in box-tape sales is the result of dedication and hard work. I'm very serious about education, especially my daughter's."

"Yes, sir, you're right. I've been thinking lately I need to buckle down and start making something of myself. I've got this job playing music five nights a week, but I'm not all that sure where that's gonna go. And I've been thinking that to make a life for me and Annie I need to figure a few things out before I can figure out what it is I really want to do."

"A life for you and Annie?"

"Well, sir, I figure you can tell I'm crazy about your daughter."

Mr. McGuane looked as if he'd just caught me crawling through his back window in the dead of night. The forced cordiality was long gone, and from that moment on the battle lines were drawn.

Mrs. McGuane was the source of Annie's exceptional dark beauty. Her Spanish ancestry filled the house with the aura of fine breeding, and she made me think her kindness toward me wasn't attached to some misplaced sense of duty. What she lacked in approval she made up for in decency.

Annie's siblings greeted me with a mixture of yawns and giggles, her younger brother's brooding disinterest oddly as comforting as her little sister's instant crush. But it was her middle sister whom I overheard say: "If you're happy, I'm happy for you, but good luck getting this guy past Daddy."

I spent a restless night on the couch and limped home to Nacogdoches the next morning.

Back at school, Annie and I continued on as semi-compatible lovers, she dropping hints of transferring to the University of Arkansas and me floating the notion that we should get a place of our own. When at semester's end she was summoned to spend the summer at the family retreat near Hot Springs, Arkansas, most self-respecting boyfriends would've seen her giddy relief as a sign the end was near. But by then my central nervous system could hardly be trusted and I was far enough around the bend to think our time apart would lead to a sexed-up reconciliation and a wedding.

By the end of June, phone service between Hot Springs and Nacogdoches was in such a state that "I love you" and "I know you do" and "Do you really?" and "It's not that simple" and "Why isn't it?" and "It just isn't, but I've gotta go," punctuated with deeper and longer pauses passed for intimate conversation.

The invitation to visit the McGuanes' lake house over July Fourth arrived like the opening line to one of the Dylan Thomas poems my tweed-encrusted and Scotch-soaked snob of an English-lit professor had always raved about. When you're coming off a steady diet for six weeks of three- and four-word utterances, the difference between "Daddy said it would be all right if you come for the Fourth" and "Light breaks where no sun shines" is hardly perceptible; ditto "Maybe we'll get a chance to talk" and "When, like a running grave, time tracks you down."

It's possible that Annie's summons knocked me unconscious. One minute I was on the phone in the kitchen, and the next, Donivan was lowering the flame on his fried-hamburger-and-white-rice casserole and poking me in the arm with his beloved spatula. "Hey, lover boy," he called from somewhere outside the whiteout occupying my skull, "you need me to go get you some smelling salts?" If my laconic friend was postponing his culinary tasks in order to snatch me from a sleepwalker's peril, you can bet money I was out on my feet.

The Fourth of July fell on Sunday, and I'd translated two nights off from the Lufkin Holiday Inn into forty-eight lingering hours to spend pressuring Annie for sex. With half the Ozark foothills as my base of operation, there was no chance Christmas wasn't coming early that year. At ten-thirty sharp, a friend rang the bar phone with the phony, prearranged "news" that my parents had been in a head-on collision down around Crosby. So, six songs short of finishing the third of four sets on Saturday, I sped north on State Highway 59, and got to Arkansas in time to board the McGuanes' speedboat for a morning round of waterskiing.

Mr. McGuane was never more the proud patriarch than when piloting his customized boat and nitpicking about his children's flawless ski technique. Under his watchful tutelage, all but Annie put on single-ski exhibitions the likes of which only the residents of pristine Lake Ouachita had ever seen. Had I been naked, with my hernia on full display, I couldn't have felt more out of place. I knew why Annie was hesitant to exhibit her waterskiing skills, as did her father, and it galled him to no end to watch his pride and joy coddle a loser. I wanted to yell at her to go on and turn the freaking somersault if that would make her old man happy, but could muster only a few weak shouts of false encouragement for her to come on and show us her stuff.

Mr. McGuane made a big deal out of how he couldn't wait to see what I could do on a ski. Before we left the dock, I'd lied about knowing how to ski slalom. Now I was hiding behind the hernia and blaming the strain of getting up on one ski for my nonparticipation. When he offered a lesson on standing takeoffs right off the dock, I mumbled some blurry excuse about the doctor advising me to go easy on the sports and tried to change the subject.

"How'd you get the hernia?" he asked.

"Climbing a ladder," I lied, "with two seventy-five-pound bundles of roofing shingles on my shoulder."

He seemed so impressed by my working knowledge of the roofing trade that, with this first inkling of approval, I saw a willingness to forgive and forget. *So what if this kid will never be a doctor or a lawyer? I see the makings of a man behind that muddled exterior.*

I was in the process of dredging up more evidence that I really was a man's man when Annie's youngest sister took a nasty spill. And before I could put images of ceiling joists and hundred-pound bags of crushed ice into any usable context, he was whipping the boat around and encouraging the kid to try it again.

Toward the end of the session, in spite of his concern that there wasn't enough gas in the tank to pull a conventional skier once or twice around the lake, I got up on two skis. Mrs. McGuane made a small show of appreciation when I crossed the wake, but her enthusiasm smacked of too little, too late. A lowly bass player from East Houston or Crosby or wherever it was had no place in a family as fine as this.

By the way, I got up on one ski for the first time on my fiftieth birthday, and it was one of my most personally satisfying moments. After twenty-five failed attempts I stayed up for a glorious half hour as a friend pulled me across the glassy, late-afternoon waters of a lake in Tennessee. Toward the end of my run, I no longer could contain myself, and shouted: "James McGuane, wherever you are, check this shit out, pal!"

Begging Annie to sneak off for an out-of-doors quickie produced a half-winced, exasperated "Not now!" She was even ignoring the secret body language we'd perfected to get through occasions such as this—a nod-and-sigh foreplay that conveyed a longing so deep that our wrists might have been being slit. If this didn't tell me that Cupid had dropped the anvil, nothing possibly could.

It rained all night and the next day as well. Unless you fancied lying about how you'd gotten drenched—which I did and Annie didn't—the opportunity to get off by ourselves was nonexistent. And so I decided that stomping off in the deluge—à la my parents during Hurricane Carla—was a good way to get back at her for denying me the pleasures I'd driven so far, and so fast, to enjoy. After lunch, I faked remembering an early band rehearsal the following morning, thanked the McGuanes for their hospitality, and dashed for the car. The plan for Annie to run after me, begging me please not to go, didn't materialize.

Once I was back in Nacogdoches, her letters started arriving from Hot Springs, the first of which I took the liberty of reading as an apology, the second as a reminiscence of our early courtship, and the third as an impassioned plea to stay strong until she worked a few things out in her head. That I turned these casual reports of fun in the sun and day trips to the flea market into remorse-filled accounts of lonely days and empty nights says more about my grip on reality than her inability to make a clean break.

Revived nonetheless, I wrote back, describing past triumphs and future fantasies in great detail, as well as smoking pot and skinny-dipping at the Blue Hole, a spring-fed quarry thirty miles off campus and a favorite destination for the drug-crazed and sex-starved. I also made the mistake of reliving on paper the night, not long after the Fourth, when Donivan and I each took a purple tab of LSD. By luck of the draw, only mine contained any hallucinogens. After he complained sorely about getting ripped off and went to bed, I spent a harrowing night touring the inner and outer galaxies all by myself. The next day, Donivan reckoned I'd gotten his dose on top of my own, but by then it didn't matter. I'd found peace wandering through the pine thickets in back of the house, and that night I crawled inside my sleeping bag beside a singing little creek and slept for sixteen hours. Two years later I began to recognize my mind once again as my own.

The next communiqué came via pay phone from Dallas. "He read your letters," Annie cried. "He knows everything about us. Everything! He says I can't come back to Nacogdoches. He's moving me to Fayetteville."

"Hold it right there," I cried back. "He can't do that. I won't allow it. I'm coming to get you."

"No. No, you can't. You don't understand, he's mad enough to kill you."

"I don't care. Pack a suitcase, I'm coming."

By mid-afternoon I was knocking on the McGuanes' front door, and Annie answered with her father standing a few steps behind her.

"You got your stuff?"

She tilted her head back and slightly to the left—a motion meant for me to acknowledge him, so I ignored it.

Thinking sweet talk would dissolve her reticence, I laid it on thick. "Come on, baby, grab your stuff and let's get out of here. We've got everything we need. We've got each other. That's all that counts. We're meant to be together; you know that as well as me, so let's go."

"Please, don't make this any harder than it is," she pleaded quietly, painfully, with such a gut-wrenching sweetness that I could only surrender my will to the secrets of her heart. For the first time since chance brought us together, I knew Annie McGuane had strong feelings for me, and I knew, too, that I had to let her go.

Her father took two steps in my direction, the first a challenge, the second a dare. Which set me to thinking: *I'll be damned if I'm giving in to some son of a bitch who thinks he can stick his nose in my business. Why doesn't he leave us alone to kiss and cry and say good-bye? A couple of promises never to forget each other wouldn't hurt anybody,*

and they sure would help me out. But he wants to get up in my face?
Fuck him and the horse he rode in on.

Strapping the gloves on was the last thing I wanted to do. I'd rather have held her hand for half an hour and died of natural causes or, at the very least, given her the satisfaction of knowing that I knew she'd made up her own mind about our future.

But no, this man was calling me out. Staring him dead in the eye, I asked his daughter the question to which we both knew the answer: "Who's it gonna be, him or me?"

"It's over," she said, casting her almond eyes gently downward. "I hope you find somebody who can make you happy."

Then James McGuane shut the door in my face.

Earlier that spring, I was standing next to the lounge singer when he told the Holiday Inn's regional club manager, "You can kiss my west Texas ass adios, mu-fuckin'-chacho. I've sung my last song in this gin hole."

I liked the guy but didn't wait for the dust to settle before piping up to the boss that by hiring a trio with Donivan on bass, Joe Smith on drums, and myself on electric guitar, his worries would be over. And thus, at five hundred a week, plus half price on drinks, the Greenville Three was born.

All went well until our audience started drifting in. The clientele we attracted, mostly hippies and underage college kids, were more interested in our music than ordering drinks, and this sent the manager flying into fits of rage. Two Saturday nights a month he'd work himself into a hydrophobic frenzy after closing and stomp around yelling about profit margins and how hard it was to sell booze to traveling salesmen in a bar full of long-haired freaks. By his fourth or fifth Chivas Regal, we'd have gotten the axe. But come Tuesday, around lunchtime, lacking suitable replacement, he'd hire us back. This pattern went on well into the summer.

Donivan and I began scarfing amphetamines—he to get through playing "Joy to the World" and "Help Me Make It Through the Night" at least ten times a night, I to get over losing Annie. At the end of a five-day stretch at the Longview Holiday Inn, we settled a hefty bar tab and announced a permanent hiatus. Donivan and I popped a couple of black mollies, bid Joe Smith the fondest of farewells, and roared off into the night, speed-rapping and chain-smoking, heading south. Stinking of nicotine and wired to the gills, we landed on the front porch of Donivan's mother's house in the southeast Texas oil community of Daisetta, and Mrs. Cowart made a huge breakfast of bacon, eggs, biscuits, and gravy, but neither of us could take the first bite.

I left my friend in his mother's care and made the thirty-five-mile drive to the house on Gum Gulley. En route, I stopped off to see an old doctor friend of Renata's who I knew to prescribe downers.

That first week back at home, I slept. The second I spent moping around the house listening to Neil Young, never getting past "Cinnamon Girl" and "Round & Round (It Won't Be Long)," listening to each song over and over. As soon as one finished, I'd drop the needle on the other. Just before my mother reached the point of yanking her hair out, she yelled, "Son, don't you have anything else to do but listen to that alley cat in heat?" And, when I obligingly switched to Leonard Cohen: "I never thought I'd say this, but I like hearin' the one that sings through his nose better than the one that sounds like the world's comin' to an end. Why don't you get you some Chuck Wagon Gang or Tennessee Ernie Ford to listen to? That kind of music might bring you out of whatever it is that's got you so far down in the dumps." Somewhere in the latter part of the second week, I hit my father up for a job.

On the third Sunday, I dialed an old phone number from memory. As luck would have it, Renata answered the phone and I later found her exactly where she said she'd be: sunbathing in the park. She fussed that I looked terribly undernourished and pronounced the tuna-and-pasta salad back in her refrigerator the natural cure for all that ailed me.

"Where's Monica?"

"Upstairs."

"Is she gonna be all right with this?"

"Of course she'll be."

At first Monica eyed me no less suspiciously than when we were last in each other's company. "Be nice," Renata cooed. "Our old friend has returned. Nothing besides food and conversation is fit for the occasion."

While the three of us polished off several bottles of sauvignon blanc, I recounted the story of Annie McGuane, hernia included. Monica so warmed to this account that she invited me to spend the night on their couch, but I begged off with thanks, blaming work in the morning and hugged her tight as she hugged me back.

"Come here, you," Renata gushed, holding me close while I cried on her shoulder. "You gonna be all right?"

"Yeah, I'm fine."

I drove on to the Dome Shadows nightclub on the west side of Houston, and from there it's by providence alone that I made it back to Gum Gulley without riveting a vehicular manslaughter conviction to my permanent record. I don't know how many downers I swallowed that night—I'd guess four, maybe five—but whatever the amount, my father couldn't shake me awake at five-thirty the next morning. And in light of my recent despair, who could blame him for hauling me to the North Shore emergency room. The polite reason given for those three days in the hospital was observation.

On the second day, a shrink dropped by to discuss the incident, but until I sensed he was tiptoeing around the subject of suicide, I was in no mood to talk.

"I wasn't trying to kill myself, if that's what you're driving at."

"How would *you* define the incident?"

"I don't know. Too many reds on top of too much wine and vodka gimlets, I guess."

"Is this something you've done before?"

"What, take too many downers? No."

"But what if your parents found your prescription for secobarbital?"

"I'd say they'd probably be pretty upset."

"Do you use other drugs?"

"Like grass and such?"

"I mean drugs of any kind."

"I hate downers. I only got those to come down off too much speed. I hate speed, too."

"Then why do you take these drugs?"

"Who knows? I only like grass. The rest of it messes with my head. I don't even like beer."

"Then let me put it to you this way. Can you think of any good reason you would take a dangerous amount of barbiturates with alcohol?"

"I just wanted the hurtin' to stop."

"What hurting is that?"

"My whole life."

"And did it?"

"I don't know."

I broke down and told the Annie McGuane story for the second time in thirty-six hours, this time going back to Matty Jackson.

"Do you have feelings of remorse over how you treated this Matty?" he asked when I finished the story.

"Yes, sir."

"And would it be safe to say you think you deserved what happened with the young woman from Dallas?"

"No, sir, I love her with all my heart. And I always will."

I talked to this doctor for more than an hour and never knew his name. He said he was torn between reporting the incident as an accidental overdose due to depression or a lame attempt at suicide.

I told him that if I'd really meant to kill myself, I would've put more into it. He then prescribed an antidepressant that I stopped taking the day I left the hospital. His parting advice? To forget about girls for a while.

My roommate during this incarceration was a burly guy who'd fallen off a second-story balcony. I never learned his name or the extent of his injuries, but I knew he planned to sue some dipshit motherfucker named Rafe Blanton the minute he got out of the friggin' hospital. Somehow he'd gotten wind of my story, and on the last night of my recuperation he spoke directly to me for the first time.

"Listen up over there," he said, for once dropping the subject of Rafe Blanton. "I don't give a good goddamn how you wound up in here. Personally, I think you're a limp-dick pussy who I'd rather wipe my ass on than take a look at. But what I need to know is the number of that doctor who wrote you that script for fucking reds."

My parents were drained of their color for months. My mother lost twenty pounds she didn't have to spare, and my father went through cartons of Pall Malls like gumdrops. I could practically hear eggshells crunching whenever they walked into a room with me in it. The funny thing is, I felt calm inside, even oddly restored. Overdosing on barbiturates caused a shift in my perception. The pain of losing Annie was no less prevalent, but I knew it would pass. And, that it probably wouldn't be anytime soon, no longer seemed impossible to bear.

PART FIVE

Transition

Isometimes wonder how my father might've reacted had he known—on the day we saw Johnny Cash, Jerry Lee Lewis, and Carl Perkins at the Magnolia Gardens Bandstand—that twenty-three years later I'd produce a live recording of those same three artists. Doubtless the man I idolized would've seized the microphone and gloated to the audience that his son was some kind of wunderkind they'd damn well better watch out for in the future. Then again, since it was only through songs that he was ever truly comfortable expressing the dark places in his heart, there's no reason to think he wouldn't have taken it as just another sign that even back then—he was almost thirty-five the day we heard them play—such glories had already passed him by. For that reason I often wish I'd told him how, in the early seventies, when I first found myself sitting in on late-night Nashville song-swapping sessions with, among others, Guy Clark, Townes Van Zandt, and Mickey Newbury, I hung on to my seat in the circle only by trotting out the old folk ballads I'd heard him sing as far back as I could remember. Thanks to my father, I knew all the words to "The Great Speckled Bird," "May I Sleep in Your Barn Tonight, Mister?," "Put My Little Shoes Away," and "The Rosewood Casket" and could sing them pretty convincingly, which musical currency purchased me enough time in the presence of these master songwriters to absorb something of their craft. Luckily, I was a fairly quick study and in a year or two turned out a handful of songs that Emmylou Harris was interested in recording, and at her invitation I moved out to Southern California and joined the band she was putting together.

While working with Emmylou, I met Rosanne Cash, who thought it would be a good idea if I were to produce her debut album for Columbia Records. The pairing clicked personally as well as professionally, and before long we were married. I brought to the relationship a twenty-two-month-old daughter, Hannah, whose custody I'd been granted in an amicable divorce nine months before. A little over a year after the birth of our first child, Caitlin, Rosanne was again pregnant—this time with Chelsea—and her misgivings about raising children in Los Angeles led to our packing up and moving back to Nashville, where she had family and I had good friends. The youngest of our brood, Carrie, was born seven years later.

As the seventies were closing down, I was beginning to suspect my nearly decade-long need to put as much distance as possible between me and the past had outlived its usefulness, and that the five years I'd spent avoiding my parents, and Gum Gully, like the plague had more to do with finding comfort inside my own skin than escaping our family history. The cause of this slow dawning was my own fatherhood, and for the first time in my life I started shifting my focus away from what had gone on before and onto what was coming to pass. My reward? To witness a growing bond between my children and their grandparents that put me in mind of the ties I once shared with Spit-Shine Charlie and Grandma Katie. And also to finally realize that life's basic impulse—given half a chance, even in death—is to heal itself. By the late eighties, my attitude toward old wounds and subsequent anger had changed entirely for the better.

But to return briefly to Magnolia Gardens and to my speculations about my father's likely response to the career I ended up having, I can honestly say that not until long after I'd had a gold record and made numerous appearances at the Grand Ole Opry did it ever occur to me that my professional life was in fact the one he'd always dreamed of for himself. The two of us never spoke of such things, for that would've meant acknowledging his disappointments. No, I was only too happy to hold up my end of an agreed-upon forgetfulness that allowed him to feel proud of me without speaking a word of it in my presence. I always knew, of course, that he was back in Texas singing my praises to anybody who'd listen, and even more loudly to those who couldn't have cared less.

Late in September of 1979, my father and I went to the Houston Astrodome to watch his beloved Astros play baseball. Through a friend in the music business, I'd landed a pair of dream tickets—seventh row behind home plate—and flown in to celebrate the team's first winning season in almost a decade. The last such father-son outing that either of us could remember, save for our foray into house building, was an Oilers game in 1963. In the nine years since I'd left home, there were long stretches when we'd had very little contact, and I was hoping this ballgame would begin a new chapter in our lives.

As the evening progressed, I became increasingly aware that my childhood hero was in a poor state of health. Besides the astonishing number of cigarettes he was lighting, one off the other, his skin seemed stretched taut across a bloated bloodstream badly in need of a high-pressure escape valve. Dark blue capillaries lined his reddened cheeks like a city map, and his breathing alternated between a rasp and a perforated wheeze. All of this was made even worse by a dye job that rendered his wavy hair a more unnatural shade of blue-black than Nelda Glick had sported in her snuff-queen heyday.

Adopting an obsequious tone, I put forth a lenient question that

I'd much rather have posed as a screaming wake-up call. "Don't you think maybe you should cut back on the cigarettes, Dad?"

"I have," he said, failing to register my desperate worry.

"Really? How much were you smoking before?"

"More than I do now."

By the end of the eighth inning we'd seen enough baseball and, like the other ten thousand Astros fans trying to get a jump on the traffic, headed for the exits. Standing up to leave, I counted sixteen Pall Mall butts stamped out beneath his seat.

The next morning I made a point of informing my mother that, if something wasn't done, her husband was headed for a heart attack, a stroke, or both, to which she replied: "He's got a lot on his mind."

"What does that have to do with his heart blowing a freaking gasket?" I snapped, thinking my testiness might convey a sense of urgency. "We need to get him to see a doctor as soon as possible."

"I told him he needs to," she fired back, "but when did J. W. Crowell ever listen to a word I say? Besides, a while back this angel come down to tell me the Lord has a plan for your daddy, and I believe it. Not long after that, he walked in and told me he wanted to turn his life over to the Lord. I like to've broke down and cried. You know how long I been waitin' for him to accept Jesus? You can try to get him to go to the doctor, and I pray he listens to you, but as long as he keeps goin' to church, I ain't arguin' with him."

Thus did I learn that my father had been—as they say—saved. And though I doubted the day would ever come when he'd acknowledge a power greater than his own ego, I was sincerely happy for my mother. If anyone deserved to tame the lion, it was Cauzette. Yet I couldn't help wondering what the hell would become of Ole J-Bo?

Saturday afternoon, I found him sitting in his favorite lawn chair, smoking. He'd been there awhile, waiting for me to come out and admire his one and only addition to the house we'd built together. This was the situation I'd been hoping for.

"Nice side porch, Dad. Looks like you get both morning *and* afternoon shade."

"Me and an ole boy from over in Humble built it in one weekend. Cost me a hundred and twenty dollars, countin' what I paid him. Got all the materials off a cost-plus job over at Exxon."

"Any way I can get you to see a doctor about that shortness of breath?"

"I been studyin' about buying a Winnebago so me and your mama could drive around some on the weekends, maybe take off in it when I retire. Nah, I don't need to see no doctor."

Rationalizing that it would do my parents more good than it would do me harm, I invited myself to join them on Sunday morning. Upon reaching their church, the first thing I noticed was how much Pentecostalism had changed since I'd last witnessed it. Lone-wolf sermonizers like Brother Pemberton and Brother Modest, who in their day ran the show according to their own particular interpretation of the Scriptures, had been supplanted by a his-and-her parsonage that was sorely lacking in religious theatricality. My immediate impression was that the gender-blurring seventies had completely neutered the concept of hellfire and brimstone. Within this new model, you got some pussy-whipped Adam preaching all this middle-of-the-road stuff while his disapproving Eve assumed the role of the official first lady—and if, by chance, she played the organ, so much the better.

The Assembly of God in Crosby, Texas, was home to thirty or forty regulars, all of whom, I gathered, preferred its redbrick simplicity to the more imposing Baptist or socially acceptable Methodist branches in town. The preacher, a pudgy mid-forties sort of fellow whose name I never caught, but whose guacamole-colored leisure suit and brown superwide tie I'll never forget, stood behind the pulpit, smiling beatifically on his flock and exuding reverential certainty. Five steps to his left, looking every ounce like a begirdled Queen Bee, sat Sister So-and-So in a straight-back chair. To her left was an old Lowrey parlor organ she'd no doubt dragged from one church to another for twenty-plus years. My instant dislike for this woman had more to do with the chain I imagined she'd tied to her husband's genitalia—fond of giving it a sudden yank whenever the question of who was boss came up for review—than her hidebound personality.

My father sat in another straight-back chair five steps to the preacher's right where, on cue, he picked up his guitar and, to get the ball rolling, sang "The Old Rugged Cross" with way too much vibrato for my taste. In his prime he never would've subjected a honky-tonk to such soppiness. In this new incarnation, however, he was pouring it on like a huckster. It was as if he'd been told that, in church music, his natural instincts were a detriment. But from where I sat, the vibrato served only to turn a damn good singer into a poor man's Don Ho.

When he finished singing, the preacher nodded his high-handed approval and excused my father to join his family in the pew. Watching the once-proud Casanova climb down from that Christian stage to cross a room filled with pious silence filled me with both sadness and anger. Surrender didn't look good on him. Missing his cocky arrogance and hating seeing him so sanitized, I found myself wishing he'd jump up and bark, "Cauzette, this shit's for the birds; me and the boy's goin' to the house." Then I'd have the old J-Bo back.

Brother What's-His-Name's strong suit was detecting apathy, but he was also highly sensitive to insolence. It was his congregation's misfortune that on this particular Sunday I'd walked through the doors brimming with both. And since I knew that any Pentecostal Bible-thumper worth his salt was loath to suffer any dissidents—especially one visiting from California whose name occasionally appeared in the newspaper—I braced myself for a showdown.

Having a smart-ass near-celebrity in the pews threw this fellow right off his game. His rhythm was knotted and his necktie too tight. The congregation sensed his discomfort, and I could feel their resentment mounting. The difference between their God and mine, I realized, was a matter of semantics, but because I held the

Queen Bee mostly responsible for my father's emasculation, I decided to play the uppity outsider and challenge their leader's supremacy indirectly.

Brother What's-His-Name had no ability to create a sense of impending doom among his followers, and none of Brother Pemberton's flair for snatching a flock of lost sheep out of the Devil's flaming inferno. But then, who did? I will concede that he preached a decent sermon, quoting the Bible in all the scripted slots and rebuking the pitfalls of contemporary life, putting in pedestrian terms the evils of television as opposed to the word of the Old Testament God. But there was no outlandish context that placed the congregation in mortal danger. Whatever was going on inside my mother's brain that made her settle for such low-stakes salvation, I didn't like it. In 1959, she'd have stomped out denouncing the unremarkable reverend as unfit to pass the offering plate around.

Mercifully, he ceased his oration and signaled for Sister So-and-So to tear into a version of "Just as I Am." It's to their credit that they made short work of getting the folks out of their seats and onto their knees. Judging by the rush to the altar, I concluded that the congregants were standing eagerly behind their pastor in a time of need. If my parents were torn between joining their friends or siding with me, neither showed it; they were among the first to bolt from the pews, while I adamantly stayed put.

Maybe twenty minutes into being the lone salvation holdout, I noticed that some of the faithful had forgotten themselves. Besides the twenty-odd dutiful penitents whose numb knees and aching backs had resulted from our clash of egos, I saw an old man wind his pocket watch in between waving his hands high over his head in holy rapture. An attractive middle-aged woman seemed to be fondling the breasts of a very attractive teenage girl, both of them apparently grateful the preacher and I were at loggerheads. Best of all was watching Sister So-and-So work up a sweat behind the organ while throwing me hard glares I interpreted as telling me to get my skinny, stuck-up California ass down to the frigging altar so the righteous among us could go home and eat some fried chicken and potato salad.

At around the thirty-minute mark Brother What's-His-Name called it quits. I liked the guy then. He knew when he'd been beat. I give him credit for taking a run at breaking me down, but out of respect for the predecessors I'd known this just wasn't possible.

Three months later, he and Sister So-And-So were replaced by thirtysomething hot shots—a his-and-her extension of Pentecostal Christianity's newly acquired business savvy—and my father was summarily dismissed as the church's regular performer. According to the cunning new first lady, they were taking their Assembly of God in a more contemporary direction. In other words, old-timey gospel music ate too far into potential profits to suit these two up-and-comers. Religion was undergoing a face-lift, and throwbacks like Brother and Sister Crowell could only impede progress. Evangelicalism was the new order of the day.

My mother was openly indignant. "I told Miss Priss that she and that husband of hers was gonna learn that what goes over the Devil's back ends up under his foot," she reported during one of our regular Tuesday night telephone conversations. "I told that new minister he might wanna walk a mile in his own shoes before he goes knockin' somebody else out of theirs." My father framed the sacking more quietly, saying only that he didn't see how a good old gospel song could stand in the way of prosperity.

The demotion sent my parents in search of a church that would appreciate his song selections and beat-up guitar, and in a forgotten neck of the woods not far from Gum Gulley they found a meager flock of sinners who, following the leadership of Brother and Sister Looney, welcomed the ex-honky-tonk bandleader and his wife with open arms. In return, my parents found a pair of late-in-life running buddies. With the Looneys now their constant companions, they entered a six-month period that my mother would later refer to as the happiest days of her life.

EPILOGUE

One Monday morning, just after dawn, the phone rang by my bedside. The night before, I'd gotten back to Nashville from three weeks in England, and my jet-lagged brain wouldn't or couldn't put into context where I was or what the caller was asking me to do. I picked up on "You need to get down here as soon as you can!" at the end of a loud whooshing noise, most likely an early morning garbage truck on busy Franklin Road, and I wondered where down here might be. "Your daddy probably won't last till you get here." . . . Well, that should've been the tip-off, but it wasn't. I identified my own mother's voice only by determining that the urgency of the words didn't fit the serenity of the delivery. No one else would be reluctant to disturb my rest with the news that my father was dying.

"What's going on?" Rosanne asked, with the familiar grogginess of a sleep-deprived woman who'd just been awakened after settling back into bed following the three a.m. breast-feeding of our six-month-old daughter. I was leaning over the bathroom sink and splashing water on my face. "Dad's not going to last the day," I said to her reflection in the mirror.

I climbed halfway up the hidden staircase leading from the bathroom to my third-floor office, sat down on the steps, closed my eyes, and said (telepathically, I suppose), *Hang on until I get there, Dad. I'm on my way.*

Rosanne, baby Carrie, my cousin Larry, and I were on the first plane to Houston—Larry booking the flights and arranging for a car and driver to deliver us to the community hospital north of Baytown where my father lay dying.

I assessed the situation in the intensive-care unit as just short of too little, too late. My father was in a coma, the ventilator stuffed down his throat keeping him alive. The doctor pointed to his blue lower legs and feet as telltale proof that the life support was beginning to fail. "Your mother has said she would rather you make the key decisions from here on out," he confided to me. "As soon as you've made your peace, I'll advise you of the options."

My mother wore the glazed look of the sedated. It also appeared that she hadn't slept through the night in months. Her own doctor was hovering in the wings and dispensing drugs. I know this because I overheard him saying, "Do you need something to tide you over?" with a chin gesture I knew all too well from my days of buying cocaine and marijuana from dope dealers back in Los Angeles.

I motioned for her to follow me to the chapel down the hall. "What's he giving you?"

"Who?"

"That doctor."

"You mean Doctor Fritts?"

"Yeah, that guy."

"Just somethin' for my nerves."

"Listen, Mom, it's none of my business what you do. But it's clear to me that Dad's getting ready to die in there. You can be present when he goes, or you can be whacked out and miss the whole thing. It's up to you. That doctor isn't doing you any favors by keeping you blotted out like this. I'm about to send him packing."

"Be nice to him, son. He's been good to me while your daddy's been sick."

"I'll bet he has."

When politely told his services were no longer required, the doctor argued, with all due respect, that I didn't know what I was doing, that pulling her off the meds cold turkey could be life threatening. "We're in a hospital," I said nastily. "I'll take my chances." He countered this with "So you're willing to gamble with your mother's life?" I assured him I was indeed willing to roll those dice, and that I had her permission to run a check on his billing records, a lie that prompted his sulking exit.

Once the pill pusher was banished, I leaned in close to my father's right ear, hoping the medical staff couldn't hear my thirty-eight years of hero worship distilled down to a few mumbling sentences. Sensing as much, they quickly left the room. "Go ahead, Dad," I said. "It's all right if you want to slip on out of here. You've been a good father to me. I love you. And don't worry, I'll look after Mom." I backed away so Rosanne and Larry could say their good-byes, but they already had.

His body shuddered, a leg gave a jerk, the temperature in the room shot up a degree, an alarm went off somewhere behind the life-support equipment, the medical team hustled back into the room, and my father came back to life. The doctor flashed a penlight in his eyes, checked his pulse, and stepped back, shaking his head. "This is a miracle," he said. "What's left of your father's heart is beating again. I've never seen anything like it. I was two seconds from advising you to disconnect the life support when his vitals came back. Can I speak to you in the hallway?"

Out there, apparently having changed his mind again, he recommended pulling the plug and moving my father to a private suite where, with help from the nursing staff, we could spend the time he had left however we liked.

For the next four days and nights my mother made herself as comfortable in the sitting room as a person coming off Valium possibly could be. There was a sofa bed and enough furniture in there to accommodate a revolving cast of well-wishers and supportive church folk, whom my garrulous cousin Dee thought could help Sister Crowell through this troubled time by babysitting our little Carrie, who seemed happy to provide some distraction.

Determined that my father should die peacefully, I taped a MEDICAL STAFF ONLY sign to his door, and Dee enforced my decree that only my mother, Rosanne, and Larry were allowed to enter the bedroom without my permission.

A nurse showed me how to operate an apparatus designed to siphon off the fluids filling my father's lungs—his heart being too weak to pump blood away from his chest cavity—and this became a chore I very much looked forward to. Every third hour, I'd rig up the contraption and we'd harvest another pint of the red liquid; then I'd hoist the container in the air and ridicule its contents for supposing it had the power to drown my partner. "Not on my watch," I'd declare, a boast that produced a faint, wordless smile from my father.

On the second day we found our rhythm. If I needed sleep, I crawled in bed beside him. And when I was hungry, food would appear. We even watched an inning or two of an Astros game on television. That night I woke with a start from a restless nap. The window was open and the curtains swayed gently, courtesy of a moonlit breeze. He was awake.

"Who's that girl you used to sing for?" he asked.

The girl was Emmylou, whom he knew well. He and my mother had visited her house on several occasions.

"She wants me to move that pile of dirt out yonder by the street," he said, pointing out the window.

I teased him for getting his jobs mixed up with mine, but soon found that decoding snippets of the fantastic reality he'd hauled back from some dreamworld was one more thing to look forward to.

Later, after he'd drifted off again, I found myself watching scenes from our shared past that were being projected, in no particular order, onto a memory screen behind my eyes. We're on the beach in Galveston when I'm five years old, and he's teaching me to dance. We're doing the toe-to-heel bop in the hard-packed sand, with the car doors flung open and "Hearts Made of Stone" blasting from the dashboard radio. . . . I'm thirteen and mired in a batting slump, my average dropping to a dismal .238. Before the game, he takes me to the ballpark and throws two hours of batting practice. That night I go four for four, with two home runs, and finish the season batting .375. . . . I flash forward to a sub-zero, full-moon three a.m. in Nashville. We've finished assembling a Christmas extravaganza for my three little daughters and decide that a brisk walk in a foot of snow is just the ticket to a few hours of sound sleep before the first of countless happy squeals. I insist on trading my insulated boots for the senior Santa's Tony Lamas, but midway through the trek I'm halted by cramping feet. His boots are too small. Bracing each other, we stand one-legged and swap boots again, then lose balance, topple to the ground, and lie there laughing in the frozen snow. I'm thirty-five, he's sixty-two. . . . There he is, a second-string defensive back for the semi-pro Jacinto City Bears, pulling his blue jersey with a silvery-white 29 sewed on both sides over his leather shoulder pads. He's thirty-six, and I'm both his proud son and the team's waterboy. . . . I see him walking barefoot down a red-dirt road with a stringer of crappies in one hand and our cane poles in the other. He's drunk on moonshine and singing "There's More Pretty Girls Than One." I join him singing, knowing that, like me, he can't wait to get back to Grandma Iola's farmhouse and start bragging about what great fishermen we are. . . . In an empty field beyond the railroad tracks, we're running after a kite he'd made from balsa wood and grocery sacks. The wind's too strong and the string has snapped, so our giant flying cobra hangs limp in the air, its tail-first plummet destined to end in the middle of six-lane Interstate 10. . . . I'm pacing the dressing room of some showcase club in Dallas, waiting to go onstage when word that he's had a massive heart attack arrives in the pinball fashion reserved for news of the real world when you're on tour in 1980. One cousin calls another cousin in Nashville, who calls my wife in California, who calls my booking agent, who gives her the number of the Dallas promoter, who doesn't believe she's who she says she is, so he has my tour manager call her back, and she notifies him that my father's not expected to live through the night, at which point he informs me—two minutes before I go onstage— that he has bad news. And the next day, when my father's heart quits a second time, my mother and I are standing in Baytown General Hospital's cafeteria line, optimistically discussing the merits of Jell-O over banana pudding for recovering heart patients. And back in intensive care, we're told the attack destroyed 60 percent of his heart, words that test our ability to process cold, hard data. Acting on the advice of a physician I know, we have him airlifted to Ben Taub Hospital in Houston and into the care of a Dr. Cauthren, an all-star cardiologist whom Dad admiringly calls Dr. Cottridge. . . . Then there's the digital Casio watch I gave him to help monitor the good doctor's prescribed walking regimen, to which he adheres with Olympian dedication. It's a watch he loves to show off to friends and strangers alike. . . . There are memories of walks we take on the north side of Kauai, in New York City, our last on Radnor Lake in Nashville on Christmas Day, 1988. We're a hilly half-mile from the car when his shoulders droop and he stops midstride. "I can't do it anymore, son," he says, moving in a long, slow stagger to the parking lot, me carrying him the last two hundred feet. . . . Later that same night, we find him in the pitch-dark nursery, cradling two-week-old Carrie in his arms, rocking his granddaughter in the old wicker rocking chair at the beginning of her life and at the end of his.

"You see them two Spanish girls standin' at the foot of the bed?" he asked, late on the third night.

Not wanting to challenge or deny his version of reality, I said that I did.

"They want me to go with 'em through that door up yonder," he said, motioning toward the corner of the room.

"I can see them, Dad, but I can't make out what they're saying."

"Time for me to go."

"Go where?"

"Through that door with 'em."

"Are you ready to go?"

"Not yet."

"When?"

"After a while."

"Are you afraid, Dad?"

"Naw."

I made a point of mentioning the Spanish girls every so often, and according to my father, they never left the end of his bed.

Earlier that day, I'd allowed my mother's least-favorite brother to pay his final respects and regretted it the minute Uncle Porter stomped into the room with horseshoe taps on the heels of his cowboy boots. I nearly had a heart attack myself when he whacked my father on the back in greeting. Ignoring the blood spilling down both sides of his mouth, a direct result of the blow, he then lit into a rambling prayer identifying my father as a lowly sinner he thought Saint Peter ought to go on and let through heaven's pearly gates on account of all that being behind him now. While Larry escorted Uncle Porter to the parking lot, I seethed and swore that no one else would be allowed into the room.

Dawn broke ominously on the last morning. My father woke up looking hideous and grew more appallingly so as the day progressed. His skin turned the color of cigarette ash, his eyes bulged, and his head swelled to what seemed like twice its normal size. His condition seemed to mirror every ounce of self-loathing I'd managed to accrue in thirty-eight years of living, and an overwhelming desire to kill him screamed through every pore in my body. Horrified at the thought of harming a dying man, I asked Larry and Rosanne if they could understand what I was feeling. Larry said he wasn't sure, only that Uncle J didn't look too good to him. "He's burning off the past, Rodney," Rosanne said quietly.

Her gentle wisdom stilled the storm inside me, but the urge to knock his head off soon came roaring back on a wave of anger larger than I could contain. Just then, a voice in my head—the same last-ditch counselor who'd told me to go with the flow when I was drowning in the Brazos—said, *Call Brother Looney.*

This suggestion made me realize that my determination to keep people away from my father had more to do with me not wanting religion to cast a lowbrow pall over his death than with what he might want. Turns out I was the one who was ignorant and prejudiced. It was an embarrassing, even shocking, revelation.

Forty minutes later, Brother Looney entered the room, took my father's left hand, and looked deep into his eyes. I cried at the beauty of the moment, one that I'd had every intention of preventing. Rosanne and Larry cried, too, as one must when compassion opens your heart. Elegantly and simply, the country preacher said, "Go to God, J." Then he took a respectful step back and bowed his head. *His* prayer was said silently through tears.

With his friend in the circle, my father was finally free to die. I was humbled by how quickly the hideousness gave way to astounding beauty. My father was a nineteen-year-old boy again. I called my mother and everyone else in to see it. Sister Looney, Dee, Sister Ballard, and people I'd never met, those who'd been keeping a vigil with my mother, said soft good-byes and quietly rotated out of the room. My mother was the last.

"You gonna be all right?" he asked her, as gently as he might have that long-ago night when he stepped in to defend her honor at the Roy Acuff concert.

"Yes, baby, I will," she replied.

Half an hour later, his last three breaths came like a set of waves off the ocean. The pause between the first and second was so unusually long that I thought he'd surely breathed his last. The pause between the next and his final was a full forty seconds, an absolute eternity when you're trying to pinpoint the exact moment when a life is over. And then his life *was* over. One day short of nine years after his heart quit for the first time, my father was gone.

In the minutes that followed, his eyes shined a shade of sparkling blue deeper than I could've imagined. His skin seemed sculpted from marble ten grades finer than Michelangelo's *David*. The peace settling over the room was so intense that everyone cried at the joy of knowing such serenity. I found it hard to close his eyes, not because of the finality of this act but because I couldn't bring myself to alter something so beautiful.

My mother and her friends were shown in. "Your daddy looks like he did the day I married him," she told me in a long embrace. "He may be gone but he'll never be forgotten."

All was a heavenly glow until the funeral director arrived stinking of highballs. Three sheets to the wind was six short of where this guy hung. Luckily, his assistant was sober, so I informed the undertaker that once he was in a cab headed home, I'd release my father's body to his assistant, whom I made promise he wouldn't let his boss touch my father until he was sober. I wrote all this out on a sheet of paper, which both he and I signed. Doubtless it wouldn't have been binding in a court of law, but I took the assistant's word as truth.

The funeral wasn't without its comedic moments. Aunt Nadine showed everybody her girdle when she screamed, "Don't go without me, J.W.!" and tried to climb inside the casket. I calmed her down with reassurances that we all knew how heartbroken she was that her brother had died. She went sniffling back to her seat but was soon up and at it again. This time I told her that she made an excellent grieving sister, the best I'd ever seen, and, satisfied she'd grabbed her share of the spotlight, she settled down and let the preacher have his say. Brother Looney gave a short, respectful eulogy, and we laid my father to rest in the shade of tall pines and sycamores.

I arrived back at the house on Gum Gully ahead of everyone else to find Uncle Porter loading my father's hunting rifles into the trunk of his car. The backseat was filled with his clothes.

"What are you doing with all Dad's stuff?" I asked, more amused than angered by his audacity.

"He won't be needin' none of this where he's going."

The Browning 20-gauge automatic was a gift from my father on my twelfth birthday and I wanted it. The bolt-action .270-caliber deer rifle had been promised to Brother Looney. Feeling charitable, I gave Uncle Porter the Ithaca 16-gauge pump and the single-shot .22 that I used to break up the New Year's Eve party in 1955.

My mother lived alone in the house on Gum Gulley for five years, an amazing achievement given that she'd never learned to drive. The driving lessons I arranged in Nashville six weeks after the funeral didn't pan out, not after an informal practice session instigated by my well-intentioned wife when Mom launched a minivan off a dangerously steep cul-de-sac.

"My right foot just froze all the way down," my mother explained, when I arrived on the scene. "I couldn't get it to unstick and we flew headfirst over that bank into the top of them trees, with the motor still runnin'. It like to have scared Rosanne to death."

"You know how your mother keeps telling you she'll never learn to drive?" Rosanne said, laughing. "You should listen to her."

Nerves were Mom's familiar excuse for never climbing back in the driver's seat. But she soon developed a stable of church friends and well-intended young women who clamored for the right to drive "Miss Cozy"—the pet name she picked up early in widowhood—anywhere she wanted to go.

She claimed never to know loneliness. "I don't mean to speak bad about your daddy," she said, "but I feel freer than I ever have. I miss him all the time, but I wouldn't trade these last few years for nothin'."

When the phone rang early on her seventieth birthday, I was a year and a half into the shared-custody arrangement that Rosanne and I had concocted during our selfishly amicable and thoroughly modern divorce. Meanwhile, our daughters were having trouble adjusting to this revolving-door policy that kept them shuttling between private schools in New York City and Nashville. Their grandmother saw the need for a stabilizing influence in all of our lives.

"You know what I want for my birthday?" she asked. But before I could issue the usual reminder that FedEx would arrive with her presents by ten a.m., she provided the answer to her question: "I want to move to Nashville and help you with the girls."

I then made the mistake of thinking she'd be happy in an assisted-living facility. My mother hated it. "The women in this hell-hole are all in competition for three old men who can't remember their own name," she fumed the first time I paid a visit. "I never seen so many nasty women in my life. Did you know they have a morgue in the basement?" She claimed her neighbors were simply too grumpy to get along with and vowed to get out of there before their irritability started rubbing off on her.

She'd spent many happy weekends in the house I'd bought over-looking Radnor Lake. Still, she turned down my invitation to move in with me and the girls on the grounds that she wanted the free-dom to leave whenever she felt like it. Instead, she found an apart-ment and, at an old-school Assembly of God out on Nashville's western edge, another set of Sisters who were delighted to ferry their frisky new friend anyplace in the city. Her congregation took up a collection and bought an easy chair to make Miss Cozy com-fortable during the long, drawn-out Sunday morning sermons while the rest of them made do with straight-back wooden benches. With a church and friends and her grandchildren nearby, Cauzette blossomed yet again.

Over the next four years I jettisoned the traveling musician's lifestyle and the nanny and housekeeper I'd been paying to fulfill my own responsibilities. In the bargain, my mother and I grew very close. We had dinner twice a week at my house or a restaurant near her apartment—I couldn't brave eating at her place—and we shared the exaltation and misery that accompany a house full of teenage girls.

In these years I was also approaching a marriage. My mother adored Claudia, and I learned to laugh when she'd brush me off in favor of spending time with my girlfriend. I also came to understand that their relationship was healing something inside them both that they alone could comprehend.

My daughters, too, grew close to their grandmother, and she to them. By her insistence, Miss Cozy was known to them only as Nana Zeke. "I swear on Nana Zeke's soul" became their blood oath. It still is.

Aping Mae West, she once sprung a bright red bathing suit on her granddaughters, prompting squeals of delight. "Please, Nana Zeke, don't ever take it off, *please*!" The occasion was white-water rafting in Tennessee. And later, on the same vacation, in the same red bathing suit, she was tossed in the Florida surf for six straight days, along with my daughters, in giggling unison. "Anybody can stand up in the ocean, Nana Zeke," one of them announced, "but Crowell girls like to roll around in it."

"I learned how to make do with the short end of the stick bein' married to your daddy all those years," she said one evening over bologna-and-cheese sandwiches at my house. "I never was mad at him for thinkin' the world revolved around him. That's just the way he was. But if anybody ever tried to tell his and my life stories, J.W.'s would take up a whole encyclopedia. Mine might take up half a funny book. All I ever done was love you and your girls and your daddy and Tex Edward and Momma. . . . I guess that's not really the short end of any stick, is it? But I'll tell you this: Where I'm goin' to be with Tex Edward, son, there ain't any stick at all."

"What do you mean," I asked, " 'going to be with Tex Edward'?"

"Oh, he comes to see me just about every day now," she said, as if my long-dead brother lived in an apartment two doors down.

"It's as real as you and me sittin' here talkin'. I've held him in my arms. He's about four years old and has beautiful curly black hair. He needs me now more than you do. I'm gettin' ready to go be with him."

Ever since she'd moved into the house on Gum Gully, my mother had become something of an authority on dead friends and relatives, and my father and I rarely gave more than a passing thought to her assertions that from time to time she visited unseen worlds where she held lucid conversations with family members and strangers alike. Whether these occurrences were genuine or imagined seemed beside the point: They were real to her, and that was good enough for us. But this Tex Edward business was different. Until then, in fact, she'd claimed there was a protective veil between the two of them that neither was allowed to cross. But now her reports of these daily visits seemed so vivid, the details so specific, that I myself started having visions of a beautiful boy with curly black hair, though I knew these imaginings were the product of my lifelong wish to have a big brother. Nevertheless, I was taking her claims as seriously as she was.

Claudia and I were married on what would have been my parents' fifty-sixth wedding anniversary. After the ceremony, my mother took my face in her hands, as she often did when she had something important to say. "I need you to listen to me now, Rodney. My work here is done. I don't need to worry about you anymore. I love Claudia like she's my own daughter. God sent her to me the same way he sent her to you. I know she'll take care of you. I'm not goin' to be around that much longer now. I've got other things to go do."

I wanted to say something flip, but she held my face tight in her hands. "I said listen to me, son," she continued, summoning more gravity than I'd ever heard. "I'm not goin' to be around much longer."

Five weeks later, she made good on her word.

The phone rang at seven a.m. "I'm havin' a heart attack," she said, with no more urgency than if she was commenting on the weather. "I need you to come drive me to the hospital." So casual was her request that had she not tacked on, "You better get on over here in a hurry," I might've gone for a walk around the lake before moseying across town to her apartment. Instead, I raced there.

I was bewildered by the call. Just the day before, dressed as Madonna circa *Desperately Seeking Susan*—torn fishnets, miniskirt, red lipstick, and a polka-dot bow tied around her head—she'd appeared in a big-budget music video that Claudia was making. During the shoot, she'd kept the cast and crew in tears of hilarity by speculating on her new career as a television pitchperson. How a heart overflowing with happiness on one day could be malfunctioning the next was hard to comprehend.

"She's adamant about being taken to Baptist Hospital," I told Claudia on my car phone.

"Don't you dare take her to Baptist," she said. "They'll kill her. I promise you they will kill your mother. Take her to St. Thomas— they have the best cardiac care in Tennessee."

Mom wouldn't hear of going to St. Thomas. I was told that she was her own boss and I could either take her where she wanted to go or buzz off. So I took her to Baptist.

"It's a mild attack located in an area on the back side of her heart," the attending physician said. "I can give her an IV of thinner to help the blood flow past the blockage, or I can order up a simple angioplasty to get her stabilized."

That it was a mild heart attack should've been welcome news, but listening to this fine young doctor's deliberations on the pros and cons of each procedure made me anxious. I was beginning to think he was going to flip a coin instead of making up his mind. I had him walk me through each procedure again, hoping the better decision might seem obvious, but it wasn't. He then assured me that both procedures were routine and in either case the side effects would be minimal. I still felt ill at ease, yet talked myself out of demanding a second opinion. "It's your decision," I said, and he chose to thin her blood.

I went home for dinner but couldn't stop worrying, so I called the hospital. "She's resting comfortably," a voice lilted over the phone, and I used that as an excuse to call an end to a difficult day. I figured it would be best to get some sleep and head back over in the morning.

I'd just turned off the reading lamp when the phone rang and a woman informed me there had been a change in Mrs. Crowell's status. I didn't get what she meant by status and asked for a clarification, and she carefully explained that it would be best if I came to the ICU as quickly as possible.

We jumped in the car and sped off, with Claudia driving and me struggling to make sense of the news and fearing the worst. "This feels all wrong," I confided to her.

"Yes," she said, "I know."

The doctor was pacing the hallway outside intensive care, his indecisive manner now replaced by well-rehearsed professionalism. It wasn't what he said so much as how he was saying it that made me regard him as warily as I would a used-car salesman. I can honestly say I would've rather heard "Mr. Crowell, your mother's had a really bad reaction to the blood thinner" instead of "Complications have arisen as a result of things we're not sure of yet." Perhaps I'm being dismissive of his good intentions, but it seems to me now that "Your mother's probably not going to make it" would have been not only more accurate but also a more compassionate assessment than "We're watching her closely." But then I didn't have the prospect of a malpractice suit hanging over *my* head like a moldy cheese.

When I realized he was trying to cover his ass, I eased up on the guy. Given what had transpired, I'm sure that he, too, was wishing I'd taken her to St. Thomas. "You can relax," I said truthfully. "I have no intention of hitting you with malpractice. Just tell us where we stand."

"Not so good. It's a hemorrhagic stroke and most of the brain is involved. Whether the Coumadin caused the hemorrhaging, I can't say. It's rare, but there are cases where that's happened. She's in a coma. With this much damage to the brain, her bodily functions will start to fail. It could be an hour. It could be six. By the way, did you know your mother had a stroke in uteri? The CAT scan picked up dried blood from before she was born. It looks as if she was predisposed to hemorrhage."

Caitlin walked in as I was telling the doctor to pull the life support, winced at the sight of her Nana Zeke, and leaned her head against my chest. It was a slow Sunday night in intensive care. The lone nurse on duty wore the countenance of a loving soul who'd spent more than her share of late shifts witnessing family gatherings such as ours. With her kind permission, we had the run of the place.

The three of us climbed into the bed with my mother—Claudia by her right ear, Caitlin her left, and me at her feet. We sang "What a Friend We Have in Jesus," "Amazing Grace," "The Old Rugged Cross," and "I'll Fly Away" a cappella. We poured packages of salted peanuts in cans of Coke—something she'd always done—and drank to her health. Caitlin brushed her hair, and we each took turns thanking her for the difference she'd made in our lives. It was a lovefest fit for the Queen of England.

Claudia caused the big send-off's first dip in energy. One minute she was laughing about something Miss Cozy had said or done, and the next her eyes were fluttering like cartoon window shades. Caitlin and I traded shrugs and waited. "She wants me to speak for her," Claudia said almost apologetically. My wife is the recognized psychic around our house. Lost papers, misplaced car keys, and which pile of dirty laundry a favorite item of clothing is buried in are among her specialties. Channeling the spirit of her nearly dead mother-in-law, however, was beyond her usual range. But knowing that their relationship involved modes of communication only they could understand, I waited to hear what the two of them had to say as one.

"Cozy says, 'Be of comfort, my sweet babies, for I am happy!' "

Claudia had barely finished delivering this parting hallelujah when my mother's heart rate shot sky-high while her blood pressure took a nosedive. A few seconds later, a flat digital line and a lifeless body were all that was left to show for her long, uphill battle.

Whereas the moments after my father's death were marked by profound beauty and involuntary serenity, in my mother's case it wouldn't have seemed out of place if Claudia or Caitlin or I had said, "Catch ya later, Zeke, we're going out for Chinese food." Clairvoyant high jinks notwithstanding, my mother's passing was just that casual. We thanked the nurse for her kindness, collected Miss Cozy's belongings, and arrived home just after dawn.

As was the case with my daughters' births, my parents' deaths were unique to their personalities. Being a sensualist, a backwoods dramatist, and a lover of the limelight, my father made a big production of coming back from the dead to enjoy four more days as the center of attention. To show his appreciation, he left us a stunning reminder of the magnificent creature we knew and loved so well. My mother, on the other hand, having never been comfortable in the physical world, put in a brief cameo at her going-away party and split the scene posthaste. In keeping with the flinty wisdom and wry humor that defined the last years of her life, Miss Cozy's passing was a testament to her belief that once the spirit is gone, the physical remains amount to nothing more than a discarded piece of clothing.

That said, my mother's death was just as awe-inspiring as his. Knowing that she was the mastermind of her own exit strategy— and I'm as sure of this as I am that the sun will rise tomorrow—was deeply comforting. It was a display of willfulness that I often dreamed of as a boy when she made herself a volunteer doormat for my father's muddy boots. One of the gifts of orphanhood was my certainty that they'd both outgrown or, more accurately, outlived their childhood conditioning. Another was my conviction that in the end she was a wise and powerful woman, and he a kind and gentle man.

The next day, Claudia, Caitlin, and I commandeered a freezing private room in the morgue's basement where, with the funeral director's permission, I watched my wife and daughter bathe and moisturize my mother's skin, paint her fingernails and toes, curl and comb her hair, apply makeup, and dress her body in the blue negligee she'd picked out for the occasion. With only a thin sheet between her modesty and my nervous hands, I made my lone contribution to the project by helping the girls shove her into the girdle she'd insisted on wearing beneath the negligee. Occasionally, the funeral director would appear, ask if we needed anything and, shaking his head, hurriedly disappear back up the stairs.

With twenty or so close friends and relatives in attendance, the private wake was a riot. It's a tradition in the Crowell family that, on holidays and special occasions, after eating, we go around the dinner table and everyone says a few words—most times, more than a few—about what that particular event means to them personally. My daughters decided that a standing circle around the coffin was the only fitting send-off for Nana Zeke. What the girls didn't know I knew was that later on they planned to hold a big gossip session when they'd speculate about what their grandmother would've made of the speeches given in her honor. Since I was given the job of seeing that everyone gathered around the casket understood that they were being invited to say as much or as little as they wished about what Cauzette meant to their lives, I perhaps should've told them that they were surrounded by a pack of she wolves and had best be careful with their words. But I'll admit that my daughters' collective sense of wicked humor is to me a complete joy.

As a courtesy to my mother, I invited her pastor and his wife and informed the preacher that, once everyone in the circle had spoken, the ceremony was his to finalize however he saw fit. As luck would have it, my crazy cousin Charles—who was as well known for his drunken yarns as he was for the ubiquitous nonfiltered Camel cigarettes dangling from his lower lip eighteen hours a day, and who'd recently discovered the truth and beauty of Alcoholics Anonymous *and* the Lord, both on the heels of a nasty hangover—would be last to speak before the preacher took over. I could see the pissing contest coming before we'd gotten halfway around the circle.

Charles was more talkative sober than he ever was drunk, when by his own admission he could "out-blabber Fibber McGee." He eulogized, philosophized, moralized, politicized, itemized, criticized, and spoke longingly of the perils and pitfalls of "drankin' likker" before delivering a half-hour monologue on the redemptive power of Jesus Christ, his personal savior. Then he started in on Aunt Cauzette.

His fans in the circle were squirming to keep from howling with delight. A few, namely my daughters and Larry, egged him on with "A-*men*" and "You tell 'em, brother." Those who didn't know him were either aghast or in awe of his audacity. He took ten times as long getting his piece said as the rest of the speakers combined.

To borrow a phrase from Charles, the poor preacher didn't know whether to shit or go blind. He did, however, grasp instinctively that in the wake of such gale-force testifying, he was pretty much in a bind. He made a brief comparison of heaven to the house Solomon built in the Book of Chronicles, in which the Israelites would never be made servants and instead would be captains of the army and homemakers of the highest order, which theology invited Cousin Charles to hold forth on ivory thrones and golden footstools and lions lined up on both sides of marble steps and something about ten thousand horses and whether or not old Solomon and the Queen of Sheba had something going on the side and the fact that drinking wine out of golden vessels was just as bad as chugging it from the bottle and—

"Now hold on a minute, friend," the preacher said irritably.

"Solomon's mansion was a fulfillment of the prophecies. He ruled over all of Israel for forty prosperous years and was buried in the city of David. Kings and queens alike came to pay their—"

"And then along comes that no-account boy of his," Charles hastened to say, "ole Reboham or whatever his name was, the one that drove the whole blamed mess into the ground."

I hated interrupting the debate but knew it was time to quell Charles. I thanked everyone for coming and asked the preacher for a closing prayer. He obliged with a meat-and-potatoes farewell to Sister Cozy and bolted for the door. I can't say I blamed him.

My daughters were ecstatic because they were sure Nana Zeke would've loved seeing Cousin Charles mess everything up. I was secretly thrilled that he'd gotten out of hand but had some doubts as to whether my mother would have enjoyed him hogging the preacher's airtime. Since we'd run an hour and twenty minutes over the schedule, I tipped the funeral staff generously and called it a day.

"I could hear Cozy's voice as clear as if it were mine," Claudia said quietly that night. It was three a.m. and she and I were lying in bed, unable to sleep. "She said she wanted me to speak for her. I asked her if she needed to use my body the way Patrick Swayze used Whoopi Goldberg's in that ghost movie with Demi Moore. She said, 'No, silly, I just want you to tell 'em somethin'.' Then she added, 'You better make it quick because I'm outta here.' I almost didn't say anything because I was afraid you'd think I'd completely lost my mind. It was her, though, I know it was. No one can tell me it wasn't."

A few days later, closing down my mother's apartment, Claudia and I found letters addressed to every member of the family, the text of each ending with "Be of comfort, my sweet baby, for I am happy."

Her body was shipped back to Texas and laid to rest next to the boy she married.

I grieved over the loss of my mother much longer than I had for my father. Early in the second year of a general melancholy, I began to make peace with the possibility that this sorrow would never go away. Out of that reconciliation came the notion that the most fitting tribute to my mother, and indeed my father, would be to put the sadness to better use.

The impulse to try to sculpt a narrative out of my family's history started when I remembered introducing my mother to Roy Acuff backstage at the Grand Ole Opry in 1991. Identifying herself as a lifelong fan, she told the most popular country musician of her generation that she'd met the love of her life at his concert in the Buchanan High School gymnasium, obliging everyone present, myself included, to imagine this had taken place only a night or two before. The courtly superstar paid rapt attention and then said his most treasured memory from that evening was of two young lovebirds whose faces shone from the audience with the light of love everlasting. The meeting lasted no more than three minutes, but I wish it could've gone on forever. My mother floated out of Mr. Acuff's dressing room, an eighteen-year-old girl again. "Why, Rodney, he was just like I always knew he'd be," she said, as dreamily as any girl of her era would've, had she chanced to meet her favorite matinee idol. "And didn't his hair remind you of your daddy's?"

Acknowledgments

I'd like to express my deepest gratitude to Gary Fisketjon for his invaluable help in bringing these pages to life, and to my songwriting partner, Mary Karr, for her towering spirit and kind heart. I'd also like to thank Amanda Urban, Maria Massey, Joanne Gardner, Steuart Smith, Guy and Susanna Clark, Chely Wright, Cecelia Tichi, Mickey Raphael, Kimmie Rhodes, Rosanne Cash, and Dustin Tittle for their personal and professional resources. And I boastfully acknowledge the love and support of Claudia Church, which I strive to return in kind.

A Note About the Author

Rodney Crowell was born in Houston, Texas, in 1950. A Grammy-winning singer and songwriter, he now lives with his wife, the singer Claudia Church, in Nashville.

A Note on the Type

This book was set in Galliard, a typeface drawn by Matthew Carter
for the Mergenthaler Linotype company in 1978.

Composed by North Market Street Graphics
Lancaster, Pennsylvania

Printed and bound by Berryville Graphics
Berryville, Virginia

Designed by Wesley Gott